CAMBRIDGE

Official Cambridge Exam Preparation

PREPARE

STUDENT'S BOOK

A2

LEVEL 3

Joanna Kosta
Melanie Williams

Second Edition

Cambridge University Press
www.cambridge.org/elt

Cambridge Assessment English
www.cambridgeenglish.org

Information on this title: www.cambridge.org/9781108433297

First published 2015
Second Edition 2019

20 19 18 17 16 15 14 13 12 11 10 9 8 7 6 5 4

Printed in Malaysia by Vivar Printing

A catalogue record for this publication is available from the British Library

ISBN 978-1-108-43329-7 Student's Book
ISBN 978-1-108-38060-7 Student's Book and Online Workbook
ISBN 978-1-108-38094-2 Workbook with Audio Download
ISBN 978-1-108-38595-4 Teacher's Book with Downloadable Resource Pack
(Class Audio, Video, Photocopiable Worksheets)

CONTENTS

LISTENING	SPEAKING	WRITING	VIDEO
A conversation about the Duke of Edinburgh's Award	Talking about yourself ✓ Speaking Part 1		
A conversation about animals ✓ Listening Part 5		An article about an animal	
			▶ Glacier National Park
A conversation with a hotel receptionist	A conversation at a tourist information centre		
Five short conversations ✓ Listening Part 1		A description of a home	▶ Homes
✓ Listening Part 1	✓ Speaking Part 1	✓ Writing Part 7	
An interview about homeschooling	Describing your perfect school		▶ School subjects
Asking people about their favourite things A conversation about people's belongings ✓ Listening Part 5		Adjective order	
			▶ High school in the US
A conversation about an adventure holiday A talk about an adventure holiday ✓ Listening Part 2	Talking about an adventure holiday		▶ Adventures!
An interview about homes of the future Five short conversations ✓ Listening Part 4		*too, also, as well*	▶ Time capsule
✓ Listening Part 4	✓ Speaking Part 2		
A conversation about eSports and mind sports	Talking about eSports		▶ Games
Young app developers talk about their work		An email ✓ Writing Part 6	
			▶ Football

Key to symbols:

ə Pronunciation ✓ *A2 Key for Schools* exam task ▶ Video

WELCOME TO PREPARE

LEARN ABOUT THE FEATURES IN YOUR NEW STUDENT'S BOOK!

PRONUNCIATION
Practise and improve your pronunciation

ABOUT YOU
At the start of the unit, talk about you and your life

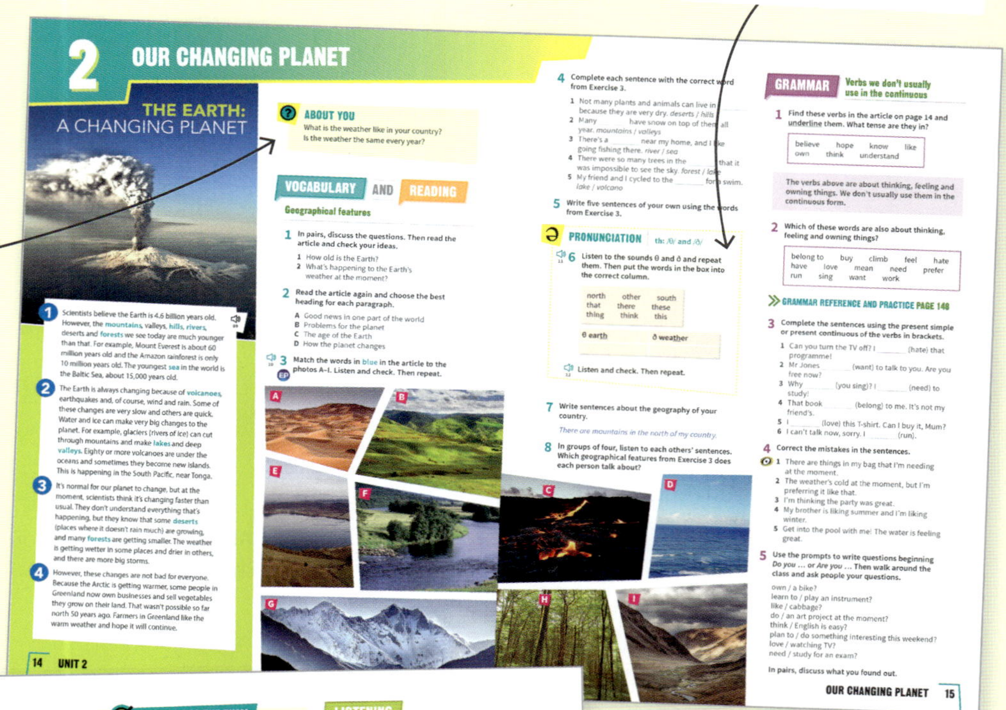

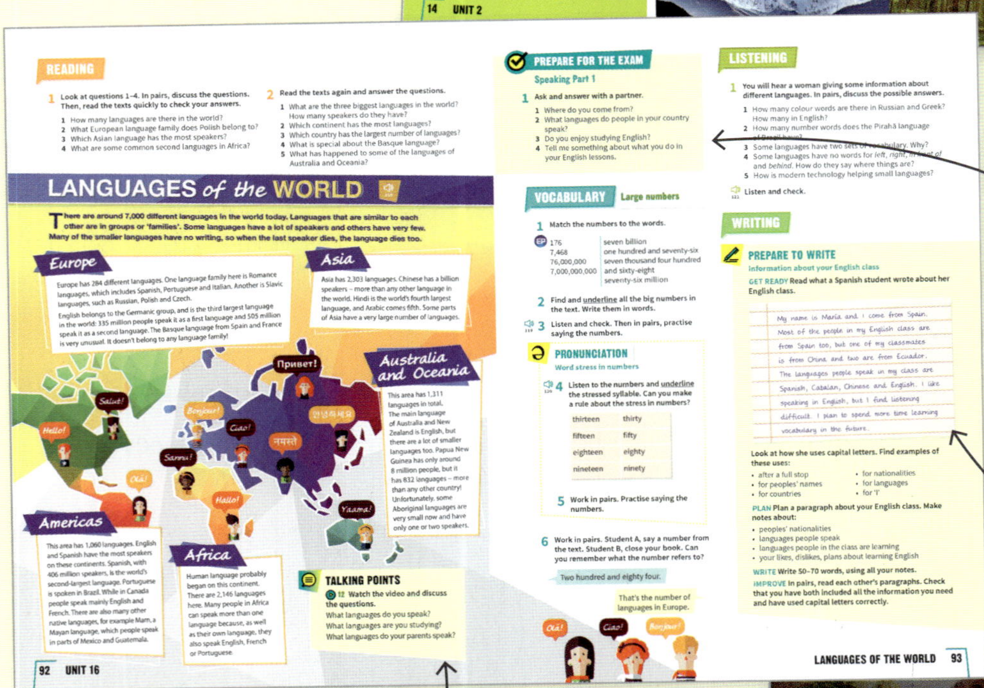

PREPARE FOR THE EXAM
Easy to find exam tasks to get you ready for the exam

PREPARE TO WRITE
Prepare, plan and check your writing

TALKING POINTS
Say what you think about the topic in the text

VIDEO
Watch interviews with teenagers like you

LIFE SKILLS

Develop important skills that you can use in your daily life

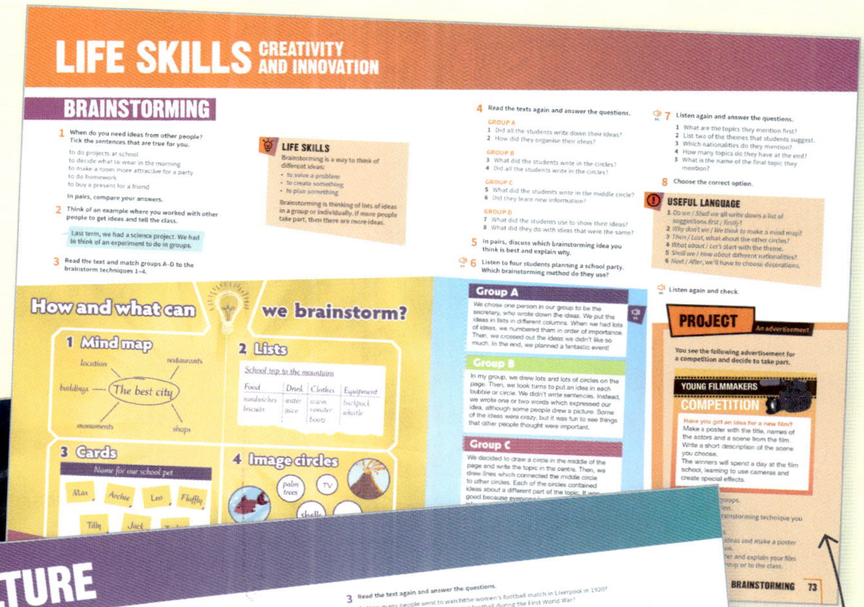

VIDEO

Watch interesting documentaries about the culture topics

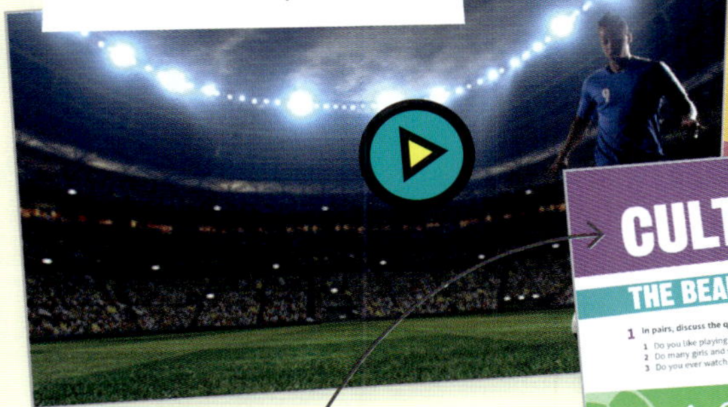

CULTURE

Learn about the culture of English-speaking countries and the wider world

PROJECT

Work together to create something fun and expand your learning

PREPARE FOR THE EXAM

Read useful tips, learn exam techniques, then try a practice exam task

REVIEW

Check your progress

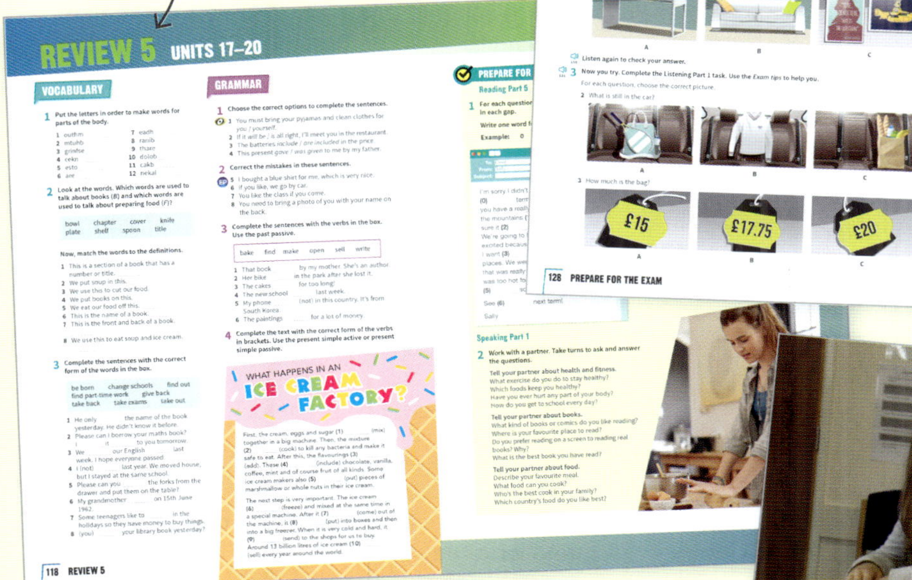

VIDEO

Watch teenagers doing speaking tasks in an exam situation.

1 IT'S A CHALLENGE!

The Duke of Edinburgh's Award

This is a great way to have fun, make new friends and learn new things. The award has four parts: 01

- **VOLUNTEERING** – Give your time to make a difference to people's lives.
- **FITNESS** – Do some exercise and get fitter.
- **SKILLS** – Learn something new – or get better at something you like.
- **EXPEDITION** – Go camping and hiking in the countryside.

If you complete everything, you get a certificate.

Write an email to Mr Jones, The Duke of Edinburgh's Award leader at our school. Describe yourself and say why you want to do the award.

ABOUT YOU

Do you have any awards or prizes?
If yes, what did you win them for?
If no, do you know about any awards or prizes for young people in your country?

VOCABULARY AND READING

Adjectives of personality

1 **Read the poster and look at the photos. Then answer the questions in pairs.**

1. What is The Duke of Edinburgh's Award?
2. What kind of activities do students do for the award?
3. Can you do an award like this at your school?
4. If not, would you like to do one?

2 **Read the students' emails on page 11 and answer the questions with *Daniel* or *Grace*.**

1. Who plays two instruments?
2. Who is happy with a piece of work they're doing?
3. Who is preparing a surprise for another person?
4. Who is teaching another person how to do something?

3 EP **Check the meaning of the words in the emails on page 11. Then use them to complete the sentences.**

1. My brother's very ________. He lies in bed until midday and never does any work.
2. My grandpa's 70, but he's still really ________. He cycles everywhere and plays tennis.
3. Sonia is very ________. She always thinks of other people and is good to them.
4. Everyone likes Toby. He's the most ________ boy in the school.
5. Our teacher is so ________. She always makes us laugh.
6. When I speak to adults, I try to be ________.
7. Sara is very ________. She smiles a lot and she's easy to talk to.
8. Most people in my class talk a lot, but Fred is ________ and doesn't say much.
9. I wasn't sure how to do my project, but the teacher was very ________. She told me about some great websites.
10. Suchitra is very ________. She can paint and draw, and she writes excellent stories.

02 **Listen and check. Then repeat.**

4 **Write sentences about your partner using the adjectives in Exercise 3. Give the sentences to your teacher to read out for the class to try and guess who they are about.**

To: Mr Jones
From: Daniel
Subject: The Duke of Edinburgh's Award

I'd love to do The Duke of Edinburgh's Award. I'm a **friendly** person and I'm **popular** at school. I'm **funny** – I often make people laugh, but I work hard and I'm **polite** to the teachers.

Music is important to me. I'm good at the guitar and I'm learning to play the keyboard. I'm a very **active** person – I play hockey and go swimming every week. I'm also teaching my brother to swim.

To: Mr Jones
From: Grace
Subject: The Duke of Edinburgh's Award

I hope I can do this award. I'm a **quiet** person – I don't talk much, but I'm very **creative**. Art is my favourite subject. At the moment, I'm doing a big painting, and it's going well.

I like to be busy – I'm not a **lazy** person. I'm also **helpful**. My neighbour's quite old, and I often go shopping with her. She always tells me I'm **kind**. It's her birthday soon. My mum and I are planning a party for her, but she doesn't know about it!

GRAMMAR Present simple and present continuous

1 Complete the table with examples of the present simple and present continuous from the two emails.

Present simple	Present continuous
I often make people laugh	*I'm learning to play the keyboard*

2 Look at the examples in Exercise 1 and complete the rules.

1 We use the present ________ to talk about things happening now, around now and at the moment.
2 We use the present ________ to talk about things that are always true or happen regularly.

» GRAMMAR REFERENCE AND PRACTICE PAGE 147

3 Choose the correct form of the verb.

1 I *watch / am watching* Spartak Moscow play football every week.
2 What *do you usually eat / are you usually eating* for dinner?
3 Sorry, I can't talk now, I'm busy. I*'m practising / practise* the piano.
4 We learned about rivers last term, and now we *learn / are learning* about forests.
5 I'm quite lazy – I *don't always do / 'm not always doing* my homework.
6 My dad *is teaching / teaches* me how to play tennis at the moment.

4 Correct the mistakes in the sentences.

1 It rains a lot at the moment.
2 In my free time, I'm usually going to the cinema.
3 I sell my English book. Would you like to buy it?
4 Right now, I watch basketball.
5 I'm usually wearing a jacket, even when it's hot.
6 We are swimming and sunbathing every day.

5 Work with a partner. Look at the photos on page 10. Say what the people are doing. Then say how often / when you do the activities in the photos.

She's playing the guitar.

I never play the guitar, but I sometimes play the piano.

6 Imagine you are writing an email like Grace's and Daniel's. Make notes. Think of some:

- adjectives to describe yourself
- sports and hobbies you usually do
- things you are learning / planning / doing now.

Now write your email.

EAST PARK HIGH SCHOOL

REGISTER TO DO THE DUKE OF EDINBURGH'S AWARD

03

HOME | NEWS | ACTIVITIES | PHOTOS | MESSAGES | SEARCH:

YOUR LEADER: MR JONES

Today, you are going to start using The Duke of Edinburgh's Award part of our school website. This has all your details on it, and it shows the activities you are doing. You can also get news and messages from Mr Jones here.

What you need to do:

- Fill in the online form with all your details.
- Choose your activities. You have to discuss and agree these with Mr Jones first.

Here are some ideas, but there are lots more on the DofE website:

Volunteering – helping older people, picking up rubbish or working with animals

Fitness – dance, sport or exercise classes

Skills – playing an instrument, studying a language, learning chess or improving your drawing skills

- You have to do each activity you choose for at least an hour a week for three months. Take lots of photos, and write about what you are doing. Put all this information on the website. When you finish, you can use it to print a book about your time doing the award. This costs about £20.

PERSONAL DETAILS

FIRST NAME:	Grace
SURNAME:	Hopkins
AGE:	14
FIRST LANGUAGE:	English

CONTACT DETAILS

EMAIL ADDRESS:	g.hopkins@topnet.com
ADDRESS:	44 Meadow Avenue, London N24 6BG
HOME TELEPHONE:	020 7946 0945
MOBILE:	0770 900 573
ACTIVITIES:	

READING

1 **Read the web page quickly. Who is it for?**

2 **Read the information on the website. Are the sentences right (✓) or wrong (✗)?**

1. Mr Jones is going to put news and messages on the website.
2. Mr Jones is going to fill in the students' forms.
3. Students need to talk to Mr Jones before they choose their activities.
4. If students don't like the ideas, they can choose others.
5. Students have to spend several hours a week doing each activity.
6. Students can put information about their activities on the website.
7. Every student gets a free book about their time doing the award.

TALKING POINTS

Which parts of the award do you think are most useful? Why?

Which look most fun? Why?

Why is it a good idea to do awards like this?

VOCABULARY Personal details

1 **Read Grace's details. Match questions 1–7 to the words and phrases on the form above.**

EP

1. What's your family name?
2. How old are you?
3. Where do you live?
4. What do you speak at home?
5. What numbers can we call you on?
6. What's your email address?
7. What's your first name?

04 **Listen and check. Then repeat.**

05 **2** **Listen to Grace's contact details. Then repeat them.**

1. g.hopkins@topnet.com
2. 44 Meadow Avenue, London N24 6BG
3. 020 7946 0945
4. 0770 900 573

PRONUNCIATION | The alphabet

3 Practise saying the letters of the alphabet.

A B C D E F G H I
J K L M N O P Q R
S T U V W X Y Z

4 Decide which letter has a different sound in each group.

1 H J U
2 E M P
3 Z L Y
4 K P V
5 W X U
6 C O G

06 Listen and check.

5 In pairs, ask and answer questions using the contact details for Sam and Jo.

What's your email address?

My email address is sam.brown@coolmail.com

How do you spell that?

Sam
sam.brown@coolmail.com
289 Sandy Lane, Oxford O22 3PG
Tel 01865 995478
Mob 06968 133 254

Jo
jo.marsh@melly.co.uk
72 Hale Street, Manchester M4 8QT
Mob 07473 964 443

LISTENING

07 **1** Listen to the conversation. What are Grace and Daniel talking about? Who is Finn?

07 **2** Listen again. Complete the table with the activities the friends choose.

	Grace	Daniel	Finn
Skill			
Fitness			

08 Listen to the end of the conversation again. Complete Finn's contact details.

1 Address: ....
2 Phone number: ....
3 Email address: ....@facemail.com

SPEAKING

PREPARE FOR THE EXAM

Speaking Part 1

1 In pairs, ask and answer questions to complete the form for each other. Spell your surnames.

FIRST NAME: ....
SURNAME: ....
AGE: ....
ADDRESS: ....
EMAIL ADDRESS: ....
PHONE NUMBER: ....

2 In pairs, ask and answer the questions.

School:
How much homework do you get?
What's your favourite subject?
Tell me something about your school.

Free time:
What do you do in your free time?
Who do you spend your free time with?
Tell me something about what you did last weekend.

» PREPARE FOR THE EXAM PAGE 133

2 OUR CHANGING PLANET

THE EARTH: A CHANGING PLANET

09

1 Scientists believe the Earth is 4.6 billion years old. However, the **mountains**, valleys, **hills**, **rivers**, **deserts** and **forests** we see today are much younger than that. For example, Mount Everest is about 60 million years old and the Amazon rainforest is only 10 million years old. The youngest **sea** in the world is the Baltic Sea, at about 15,000 years old.

2 The Earth is always changing because of **volcanoes**, earthquakes and, of course, wind and rain. Some of these changes are very slow and others are quick. Water and ice can make very big changes to the planet. For example, glaciers (rivers of ice) can cut through mountains and make **lakes** and deep **valleys**. Eighty or more volcanoes are under the oceans and sometimes they become new islands. This is happening in the South Pacific, near Tonga.

3 It's normal for our planet to change, but at the moment, scientists think it's changing faster than usual. They don't understand everything that's happening, but they know that some **deserts** (places where it doesn't rain much) are growing, and many forests are getting smaller. The weather is getting wetter in some places and drier in others, and there are more big storms.

4 However, these changes are not bad for everyone. Because the Arctic is getting warmer, some people in Greenland now own businesses and sell vegetables they grow on their land. That wasn't possible so far north 50 years ago. Farmers in Greenland like the warm weather and hope it will continue.

ABOUT YOU

What is the weather like in your country?
Is the weather the same every year?

VOCABULARY AND READING

Geographical features

1 In pairs, discuss the questions. Then read the article and check your ideas.

1 How old is the Earth?
2 What's happening to the Earth's weather at the moment?

2 Read the article again and choose the best heading for each paragraph.

A Good news in one part of the world
B Problems for the planet
C The age of the planet
D How the planet changes

10 EP

3 Match the words in blue in the article to the photos A–I. Listen and check. Then repeat.

A

B

E

F

G

4 **Complete each sentence with the correct word from Exercise 3.**

1 Not many plants and animals can live in ______ because they are very dry. *deserts / hills*
2 Many ______ have snow on top of them all year. *mountains / valleys*
3 There's a ______ near my home, and I like going fishing there. *river / sea*
4 There were so many trees in the ______ that it was impossible to see the sky. *forest / lake*
5 My friend and I cycled to the ______ for a swim. *lake / volcano*

5 **Write five sentences of your own using the words from Exercise 3.**

PRONUNCIATION th: /θ/ and /ð/

11 **6** **Listen to the sounds θ and ð and repeat them. Then put the words in the box into the correct column.**

north	other	south
that	there	these
thing	think	this

θ ear**th**	ð wea**th**er

12 **Listen and check. Then repeat.**

7 **Write sentences about the geography of your country.**

There are mountains in the north of my country.

8 **In groups of four, listen to each others' sentences. Which geographical features from Exercise 3 does each person talk about?**

GRAMMAR Verbs we don't usually use in the continuous

1 **Find these verbs in the article on page 14 and <u>underline</u> them. What tense are they in?**

believe	hope	know	like
own	think	understand	

The verbs above are about thinking, feeling and owning things. We don't usually use them in the continuous form.

2 **Which of these words are also about thinking, feeling and owning things?**

belong to	buy	climb	feel	hate
have	love	mean	need	prefer
run	sing	want	work	

» GRAMMAR REFERENCE AND PRACTICE PAGE 148

3 **Complete the sentences using the present simple or present continuous of the verbs in brackets.**

1 Can you turn the TV off? I ______ (hate) that programme!
2 Mr Jones ______ (want) to talk to you. Are you free now?
3 Why ______ (you sing)? I ______ (need) to study!
4 That book ______ (belong) to me. It's not my friend's.
5 I ______ (love) this T-shirt. Can I buy it, Mum?
6 I can't talk now, sorry. I ______ (run).

4 **Correct the mistakes in the sentences.**

1 There are things in my bag that I'm needing at the moment.
2 The weather's cold at the moment, but I'm preferring it like that.
3 I'm thinking the party was great.
4 My brother is liking summer and I'm liking winter.
5 Get into the pool with me! The water is feeling great.

5 **Use the prompts to write questions beginning *Do you* … or *Are you* … Then walk around the class and ask people your questions.**

own / a bike?
learn to / play an instrument?
like / cabbage?
do / an art project at the moment?
think / English is easy?
plan to / do something interesting this weekend?
love / watching TV?
need / study for an exam?

In pairs, discuss what you found out.

READING

1 Look at the picture below. In pairs, write down three things you know about pandas. Read the article once to check your ideas.

2 Are these sentences right (✓) or wrong (✗)?

1 The writer helped to look after giant pandas on her trip.
2 It's possible to find wild pandas in several countries.
3 Pandas only eat bamboo.
4 Baby pandas are very light when they are born.
5 Pandas start eating bamboo at the age of 18 months.
6 Scientists know exactly how many wild pandas there are.
7 It's possible to see a panda in Mexico.

Learning about the GIANT PANDA

13

When I planned my trip to China, one of things I really wanted to do was to work at the Dujiangyan Panda Base in Chengdu. I spent seven days there, looking after the pandas, giving them food and cleaning their enclosures.

While I was there, I learned a lot about pandas. Wild pandas live in bamboo forests, high in the mountains of central China. In the past, they also lived in other parts of China and in Myanmar and Vietnam, but they don't any more. They spend about 12 hours a day eating bamboo, but they sometimes eat other plants or small animals. At Dujiangyan, we also gave them fruit, like apples, and special panda cakes made of rice, eggs and flour and other things.

Adult giant pandas weigh between 75 and 135 kilograms. Females usually only have one baby panda, or cub, at a time. The cubs only weigh about 85 grams when they are born! The little cub drinks milk for about four months and then begins to eat bamboo. Young pandas stay with their mothers for around 18 months.

Scientists think there are now between 1,500 and 2,000 pandas in the wild. This is a low number, but it's double what it was in the 1970s. The reason the number is going up is because of all the work scientists are doing at places like the Dujiangyan Panda Base in Chengdu. There are also about 325 pandas in zoos in a number of different countries, including the United States, Mexico, Japan and Germany.

VOCABULARY Animals

14 EP

1 Match the words in the box to the photos A–J. Listen and check. Then repeat.

dolphin elephant giraffe monkey parrot penguin polar bear snake tiger whale

2 Answer the questions about the animals in Exercise 1.

1 Where do the animals come from?
2 Where do they live (sea, mountains, forest)?
3 Which are dangerous?
4 Look at each photo carefully. Are the animals in a zoo or are they wild?
5 How many other animals can you name in English?

TALKING POINTS

What are your five favourite animals?
Why do you like them?
How often do you go to zoos?
Do you like them?

LISTENING

PREPARE FOR THE EXAM

Listening Part 5

1 (audio 15) **You will hear Gina talking to her uncle about some photos of animals. Where did he take each photo? For each question, choose the correct answer.**

Photographs	**Countries**
0 lion *D*	**A** Argentina
1 monkey	**B** England
2 snake	**C** India
3 penguin	**D** Kenya
4 dolphin	**E** Mexico
5 elephant	**F** New Zealand
	G Scotland
	H South Africa

2 (audio 15) **Listen again and check.**

» PREPARE FOR THE EXAM PAGE 132

3 **Work in pairs. Look at the photos of the two animals below. Use the prompts 1–9 to write questions about these animals.**

1 What kind of animal / it?
2 Where / from?
3 Where / live?
4 What / eat?
5 How much / weigh?
6 How many / left in the wild?
7 What / babies / called?
8 How many babies / female have?
9 How long / baby stay with / mother?

» **Student A, go to page 136. You have information about the kakapo there.**

» **Student B, go to page 138. You have information about the sand cat there.**

Kakapo

WRITING

PREPARE TO WRITE

An article about an animal

GET READY **Underline the prepositions *between*, *about*, *around* and *including* in the article about pandas on page 16. Think about their meaning. Which two have the same meaning in the article?**

Complete the sentences with *between*, *about*, *around* or *including*.

1 This competition is for anyone ________ the ages of 10 and 14.
2 There are ________ 40,000 African lions left in the wild.
3 All my friends, ________ Tariq, are interested in animals.
4 The zoo is closed ________ January and March.
5 I've got lots of pets, ________ a rabbit and two cats.

PLAN **Plan your article about an animal. Choose one of the animals in Vocabulary Exercise 1 or a different one. Write three paragraphs. Make notes for what to include in each paragraph.**

Paragraph 1	the kind of animal it is / where it lives / what it eats
Paragraph 2	what it weighs / information about its babies
Paragraph 3	how many are left in the wild / in zoos

WRITE **Write your article. Try to include the prepositions from *Get Ready*.**

IMPROVE **In pairs, compare your articles. Can you improve them?**

Sand cat

CULTURE

NATIONAL PARKS

FACT FILE National Parks

Most countries have beautiful natural places. These places can be mountains, valleys, deserts, beaches, etc. You can see different animals and plants there. People look after them so everyone can enjoy them.

1 Discuss the questions in pairs.

1 What is a national park?
2 Have you ever been to one?
3 Can you name a national park in your country?
4 What can you see there?

2 Where is Yellowstone National Park? What do you know about it? Read the text and check your ideas.

3 Match the texts 1–5 with the photos A–E.

Yellowstone National Park

1 Yellowstone is one of the oldest national parks in the world. It is in the USA in the states of Wyoming, Montana and Idaho. It is also a biosphere reserve – a special national park with interesting and unusual plants, animals and landscapes. In Yellowstone, men and women called *park rangers* look after the animals and plants.

2 Yellowstone is on the site of a very big, ancient supervolcano. The volcano is 640,000 years old and its landscape is amazing. There are large forests and some trees are over 200 years old. The Yellowstone River gives the park its name, but there are many other rivers. The Yellowstone River is in a deep valley called the Grand Canyon of Yellowstone.

3 Over 3 million people visit the park every year and they come to see the hundreds of geysers. These are hot-water fountains that come up out of the ground. Visitors also enjoy the beautiful lakes, where they can swim, fish or go canoeing.

4 There are 67 types of animals in the park, not including birds or water creatures. There are sheep, bison and bears. You don't often see bears because they stay in the forests and mountains, but bison often walk down the roads in the park!

5 Yellowstone is usually cold and dry, but there are sometimes forest fires, so you have to be careful when you have a picnic there. In winter, it is very cold. In summer, it is warm during the day, but at night it can be below 0° C. People need warm clothes when they are camping in the park.

A

B

C

4 **Are these sentences right (✓) or wrong (✗)?**

1. Yellowstone is part of one state in the USA.
2. Park rangers protect the animals and plants in Yellowstone.
3. Yellowstone has a famous glacier.
4. The park contains very old plants.
5. The geysers in the park are popular with tourists.
6. You can't go in the water in the park.
7. People regularly see bison in the park.
8. The temperature can be very different on summer days and nights.

5 **Find words in the text that match the definitions.**

1. different from others (paragraph 1)
2. keep safe (paragraph 1)
3. very old (paragraph 2)
4. fantastic (paragraph 2)
5. travel in a small type of boat (paragraph 3)
6. animals in general (paragraph 4)
7. a meal outside (paragraph 5)

6 **What can you see on a walk in Yellowstone Park? Make a list. Then, listen and check your ideas.**

17 **7** **Listen and complete the information about two guided walks in Yellowstone Park.**

	Mount Washburn	Mystic Falls
Leave hotel at	10 am	[4] .... am
Transport	bus	bus
Lunch	sandwiches, [1] .... and cold drinks	hamburgers and chicken
Things to take	a light jacket and a camera	a [5] ....
Landscape you see	the Grand Canyon of Yellowstone and the Teton Mountains	In Biscuit Basin there are geysers and hot-water pools and a [6] .... in Mystic Falls.
Animals you see	[2] .... and maybe foxes	bison
Arrive back at	4 pm	[7] .... pm
After trip activity	a [3] .... about geography	a meeting to share photos

TALKING POINTS

Which walk would you prefer to go on? Explain why.

PROJECT

Description of a national park

Research a national park in your country. Use the internet or books to find out

- where it is
- what the landscape is like
- what animals and plants there are
- what the climate is like
- why it is a national park

Present your information to the class. Use pictures and photos to make the presentation more interesting.

3 ON HOLIDAY

F

A

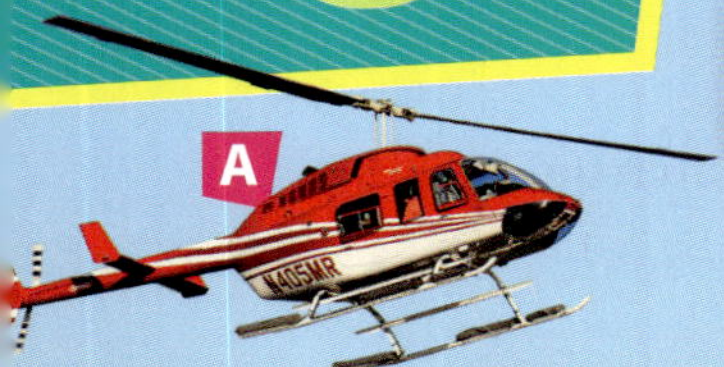

B

C

D

E

FIRST HOLIDAYS WITH FRIENDS

19

Most of us can't wait to go on holiday without our parents. We can choose where to go, what to do and who to go with. But are first holidays with friends always great? Read about Sophie, Fred and Chris. Where did they go? Did they have a good time?

Last summer, after we finished our exams, I invited my friend Paula to go on holiday to Greece with me. We got a flight to Athens and then we went by ship to the island of Milos. We were really tired when we got there, but we both wanted a swim, so we went to the beach. You can guess! We lay down and closed our eyes and when we woke up TWO hours later, we were really hot and thirsty – and red! Never again! **Sophie, 16**

My first holiday was a weekend in London. Jim, Simon and I travelled by tram from my house to the bus station. When we arrived there, I put my hand in my pocket but my wallet wasn't there! Where was it? I think I lost it on the tram. Jim and Simon each lent me money for the coach. We stayed at Jim's aunt's house in London and we had a fantastic weekend. **Fred, 13**

My first holiday was with my friend Tom at a campsite in a forest near our town. We didn't want my parents to drive us there, so we went by bus and then on foot. It was a long walk to the forest and it was raining! I put the tent up quickly because I knew how to do it, but all our things were wet. Then the sun came out the next day. We dried everything and had a great time! **Chris, 12**

G

H

I

J

K

ABOUT YOU

Where do you like going on holiday?
How often do you go on holiday?
Do you always go on holiday to the same place?
How do you usually get there?

VOCABULARY AND READING

Holidays: Ways of travelling

1 **Match the words in the box to photos A–K.**

EP

by bike	by boat	by coach	on foot
by helicopter	by motorbike	by plane	
by scooter	by ship	by tram	
by underground			

18 **Listen and check. Then repeat.**

2 **Decide whether each type of transport from Exercise 1 moves in the air, on land or in the water.**

3 **Read the article quickly and find out where Sophie, Fred and Chris went on holiday. How did each of them get there?**

4 **Read the article again and answer the questions.**

1. What does the article mean by 'first holidays'?
2. What did Sophie and Paula do when they arrived on the island?
3. What happened while they were sleeping?
4. What did Fred lose?
5. How did he pay for the coach?
6. What was the weather like when Chris and Tom were putting up the tent?

PRONUNCIATION Silent letters

5 **In pairs, read the words aloud. Which are the silent letters?**

climb	flight	guess	half
island	knew	two	where

20 **Listen and check. Then repeat.**

PREPARE FOR THE EXAM

Speaking Part 2

6 **Look at the photos A–K on page 20. Discuss the questions with your partner.**

1 Do you like these different ways of travelling? Why? / Why not?
2 Do you think riding a bike is difficult? Why? / Why not?
3 Do you think going in a boat or a ship is enjoyable? Why? / Why not?
4 Now tell your partner which of these ways of travelling you like best.
5 How do you like to travel when it's very hot?
6 Do you prefer going on holiday to the sea or in the mountains?

» PREPARE FOR THE EXAM PAGE 134

GRAMMAR Past simple

1 **Underline the past simple forms in the sentences.**

1 Where did they go?
2 Where was it?
3 Did they have a good time?
4 We closed our eyes.
5 Jim, Simon and I travelled by tram to the bus station.
6 My wallet wasn't there.
7 My first holiday was with my friend Tom.
8 We didn't want my parents to drive us, so we went by bus and then on foot.
9 We dried everything.

Now answer these questions.

1 Which past simple verbs are regular?
2 Which past simple verbs are irregular?
3 Which verb never has *did* in questions and negatives?

2 **Underline all the examples of the past simple in the article.**

3 **Complete the sentences using the past simple of the verb in brackets.**

1 .... (you / go) on holiday with your family last year?
2 They .... (not travel) by boat to the island because the weather .... (be) bad.
3 We .... (want) to visit the museum, but we .... (not have) time.
4 .... (the plane / arrive) on time?
5 The holiday .... (not be) great, but I .... (enjoy) the afternoons on the beach.
6 .... (you / be) in the mountains for the whole holiday?

4 **Read questions a and b and complete the answers. Then answer questions 1–4.**

a Who did Sophie invite to go on holiday with her? She invited .... to go on holiday with her.
b Who lost his wallet? .... lost his wallet.

1 Which past simple question uses *did* + infinitive, **a** or **b**?
2 What is the verb form in the other question?
3 Is question **a** asking for information about the subject or object?
4 Is question **b** asking for information about the subject or object?

5 **Choose a or b for each question.**

1 Who did the boy see?
a His mother saw him.
b He saw his mother.

2 Who saw the boy?
a His mother saw him.
b He saw his mother.

» GRAMMAR REFERENCE AND PRACTICE PAGE 149

6 **Complete the sentences using the past simple of the verbs in brackets.**

1 What .... (you / eat) when you were on holiday in Italy?
2 Who .... (take) you to the airport?
3 Where .... (you / go camping) last summer?
4 Who .... (book) the flights, your mum or your dad?
5 Who .... (you / go) on holiday with last summer?
6 Who .... (buy) you your new bike? Was it your parents?

7 **Correct the mistakes in the sentences.**

1 I maked two new friends on my holiday.
2 Sorry we couldn't meet yesterday. I go shopping and then cycling with my mum.
3 It was a rainy day on Saturday, so I spended the day at home.
4 I watch TV and played on the computer yesterday evening.
5 It was a pity you lefted the party early last Friday.

8 **In pairs, ask and answer the questions.**

1 Where did you go on your last holiday?
2 Who did you go with?
3 How did you get there?
4 What did you do there?
5 What was the best thing you did? Why?

READING

1 Look at the photos of Moscow. Do you know any of these places? Read the text quickly and find out who visited which place.

Red Square

The Kremlin

Old Arbat

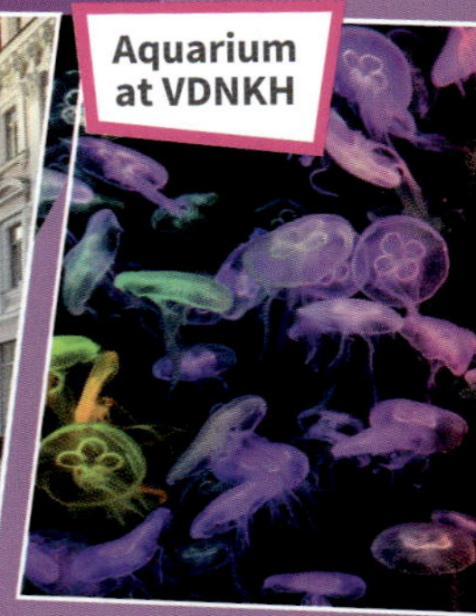
Aquarium at VDNKH

Moscow Metro

Yuri Kuklachev Cat Theatre

TEEN TRAVEL TIPS ▶ MOSCOW

21

MONIQUE

Moscow is great for sightseeing! I took photos everywhere I went. The only problem was that I don't speak Russian, so it was hard to get a taxi, and I hate walking. My advice is to take some Russian lessons before you go. I went to the aquarium on my first day. I enjoyed it, but there were a lot of tourists. I preferred the quieter streets with little shops selling postcards and presents. After I got gifts for my friends, I didn't have much money left!

CARLA

The underground, or metro, is a great way to travel around, but too crowded for me. My favourite place was Red Square. The buildings are amazing. But don't spend all your time taking photos – I didn't. I bought postcards from the little shops. You don't need Russian. Everyone speaks English. Oh, and I loved the street food and ate lots of it, but it wasn't cheap! The aquarium is fantastic. If you only go to one place, go there.

OLIVIA

My favourite place was Old Arbat, one of the oldest streets in Moscow. I wanted to get presents for my mum and dad, but all the shops had the same presents, so I didn't buy much. I mostly ate street food because it didn't cost much, and it was delicious. I went to the metro to look at the amazing stations, but I didn't travel on it. I went everywhere on foot. You see so much that way.

PREPARE FOR THE EXAM

Reading Part 2

2 For each question, choose the correct answer. Write *M* for Monique, *C* for Carla or *O* for Olivia.

1 Who thinks walking is the best way to travel around Moscow?
2 Who found the street food in Moscow expensive?
3 Who says it's important not to miss the aquarium?
4 Who spent a lot of money on presents?
5 Which person enjoyed visiting the metro?
6 Who says you should learn some Russian before going?
7 Who said it was better to buy postcards than to take photos?

» PREPARE FOR THE EXAM PAGE 122

TALKING POINTS

In pairs, look at the photos of the six places in Moscow in Exercise 1. Discuss which ones you think look more interesting to visit.

VOCABULARY Holiday vocabulary

1 EP Match the words in the box to the things in the photo A–E. There are three words for A. There are two words for D.

guest guidebook luggage map receptionist suitcase tourist visitor

22 Listen and check. Then repeat.

2 Now complete the sentences with the words from the box in Exercise 1.

1 You can find the names of streets on a .... of the city.
2 Millions of .... visit Moscow every year.
3 It's always a good idea to buy a .... to help you plan activities for your holiday.
4 I've only got one small .... for all my clothes. I hope I can get everything in it.
5 We stayed in a really small hotel in Moscow. It only had room for eight ....
6 We put all our .... in the back of the taxi. We didn't want to have the bags on the seats.
7 When we arrived at the hotel, the .... gave us our room key.
8 The Space Museum in Moscow has lots of .... every year.

3 In pairs, ask and answer the questions.

1 How much luggage do you take with you on holiday?
2 Who packs your suitcase?
3 What do you put in your suitcase when you go on summer holidays?
4 Do you or your parents usually buy a guidebook when you go on holiday?
5 Do you use maps? When was the last time you used a map?
6 Do many tourists come to visit your town? What do they like to see?
7 What does a receptionist do?
8 Did you stay in a hotel on your last holiday? Did you like it?

LISTENING

1 Look at the photo in Vocabulary Exercise 1. In pairs, discuss the questions.

1 What can you see?
2 Who are the people?
3 What are they doing?

23 **2** Listen to the conversation between John, a student on holiday in Moscow with his parents, and the hotel receptionist and check your ideas.

Why is John speaking to the receptionist?

23 **3** Listen again. Are the sentences right (✓) or wrong (✗)?

1 John is an only child.
2 John wants to look around the city in the afternoon.
3 The tourist information centre is a long way from the hotel.
4 The receptionist hasn't got an underground map.
5 John thinks taxis are faster than the underground.
6 John forgot his bag.
7 The guest before John had several suitcases.
8 There is a lift in the hotel.

SPEAKING

24 **1** John phones the tourist information centre for some more information. Listen to his conversation. What are John and his family going to do that day?

24 **2** Listen again and repeat the phrases from the conversation.

John: Can you give me some information about the space museum, please?
Clerk: Yes, certainly. The museum's near the centre, and you can book online. You'll really enjoy it.
John: That's perfect. Thanks.
Clerk: It's the best way to learn about the history of our country.
John: That's a really good idea. Oh, by the way, have you got any information about the Kremlin?
Clerk: Yes, of course. It's all on our website. Have a good day.

3 In pairs, choose a city you both know. What four places would tourists like to visit in this city? Role-play a conversation at a tourist information centre. Use phrases from Exercise 2 to help you.

4 Make questions. Then in pairs, ask and answer them using the information below.

1 address?
2 open every day?
3 what time / close?
4 how much / drinks?
5 web address?

4 MY PLACE

ABOUT YOU

02 **Watch the video and discuss the questions.**

Where do you live? Who do you live with?
How many bedrooms are there in your home?
Do you share a bedroom?
What's the most interesting thing about your room?
Would you like to live in an unusual house?

VOCABULARY AND READING

Homes

1 **Match the words in the box to A–K in the picture.**

EP

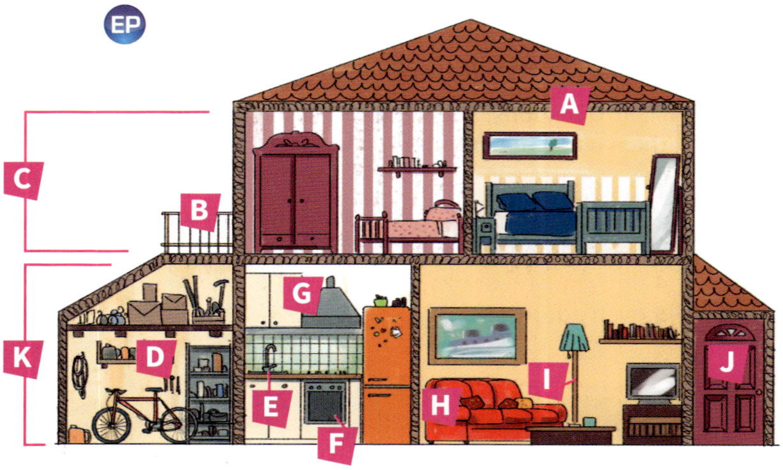

balcony	ceiling	cooker	cupboard
entrance	first floor	garage	
ground floor	lamp	sink	sofa

25 **Listen and check. Then repeat.**

2 **Describe your home to your partner using words from Exercise 1.**

3 **Read the article about Paula and Gary's homes and look at the photos. Which photo, A or B, shows where Paula and Gary live now?**

A New HOME

26

A

Paula and Gary lived in a modern house. It had a living room and a kitchen on the ground floor and on the first floor two bedrooms, one with a balcony and a bathroom. Next to the house they had a garage for their car, and they even had a small garden with a little gate painted green. It sounds perfect!

But Paula and Gary weren't happy. They both wanted to live somewhere more interesting, so they started to look for a new home. They were looking at homes on the internet one day, when Tim, Gary's dad, had an idea. Tim had his own lorry business and he was selling one of his lorries. Why didn't Paula and Gary buy it and make it into their new home? Gary and Paula thought this was a brilliant idea and bought it that same day.

It was a busy year: Gary was building everything for their new home, while Paula was working. He built cupboards around the cooker and the sink and he even built the shower. They bought a small sofa because there wasn't enough space for a big one.

Finally, six months ago, Gary finished the work on the lorry and they moved in. Gary and Paula love their new home! Paula thinks the best thing is the entrance made of wood and glass and Gary loves the high ceiling because he's tall.

There's no place like home!

B

4 **Read the text again. Answer the questions.**

1 How many floors did Paula and Gary's old house have? What was on each floor?
2 Why did Gary and Paula want to leave their old home?
3 What did Gary and Paula buy from Tim?
4 Who built the things for the new home?
5 When did Gary and Paula move into their new home?
6 What do Paula and Gary like most about their new home?

ə PRONUNCIATION /iː/ and /ɪ/

27 **5** **Listen to the two words. Which has an /iː/ sound and which has an /ɪ/ sound?**

s<u>i</u>nk   c<u>ei</u>ling

6 **In pairs, match the words to the sounds in Exercise 5.**

eat	feet	fit	he'll
he's	hill	his	it
leave	live	seat	sit

28 **Listen and check. Then repeat.**

GRAMMAR Past continuous and past simple

1 **Look at the example sentences from the text. Find and <u>underline</u> all the verbs in the sentences. Which verbs are past simple and which verbs are past continuous?**

a Gary was building everything for their new home, while Paula was working.
b They were looking at homes on the internet one day, when Tim, Gary's dad, had an idea.
c Finally, Gary finished the work on the lorry and they moved in.

2 **Match i–iii to sentences a–c in Exercise 1.**

i One action follows the other.
ii The actions are happening at the same time.
iii One action interrupts the other.

3 **Choose the correct words to complete the sentence.**

To form the past continuous, we use the *present* / *past* simple of the verb *be* and the *present* / *past* participle.

» GRAMMAR REFERENCE AND PRACTICE PAGE 150

4 **Complete the sentences using the past simple or the past continuous. Sometimes more than one answer is possible.**

1 While my brother was painting his bedroom, my sister .... (help) our mum in the garden.
2 We .... (live) in an apartment for a year and then we moved to a house.
3 My dad .... (cook) dinner in the kitchen when I arrived home from school.
4 I did my homework and we .... (eat) dinner in the kitchen.
5 When Mum phoned me, I .... (leave) my classroom with my friends.
6 While my parents .... (watch) TV, I was playing computer games with my friends.

5 **Correct the mistakes in the sentences.**

1 I felt very nervous while we watched the match.
2 We waited at a bus stop when we first met.
3 We were amazed when we were finding so much money.
4 While I cleaning the kitchen, I saw the broken window.
5 It is snowing when we went outside.
6 I was leaving the house just after you called me.

PREPARE FOR THE EXAM

Writing Part 7

6 **Look at the three pictures. Write the story shown in the pictures using the past simple and past continuous. Write 35 words or more.**

» PREPARE FOR THE EXAM PAGE 127

7 **In pairs, take turns to describe what you did yesterday.**

Use the past simple and past continuous with *when* and *while*.

While I was having breakfast …

When I got to school …

READING

1 Look at the photos of the unusual homes. What do you think they are like inside?

2 Read the article and match the photos A–D to paragraphs 1–4.

STRANGE HOUSES

29

Most of us live in an apartment or in a house. Our homes often look similar to our neighbours' from the outside, but on the inside they can be very different. Most of us like our homes to be cosy and comfortable, but we have very different ideas about what that means. Some people like to have bright colours and lots of furniture, others prefer a cool, modern-looking home.

However, some houses look very unusual from the outside. Have a look at these four photos.

1 Do you like flying? Then, this attractive house is for you. It's in Lebanon and is the shape of a plane. It's got small windows, so it's not very light inside, but in a warm country, small windows keep a house cool in summer.

2 This very unusual house is in Mexico. It looks like part of the rock – and it is! The walls and the roof of the house are part of a very big rock. The family made the house more than 30 years ago. We can't see inside, but it looks quite dark, cool and peaceful.

3 In 1968, a group of swimmers first had the idea to build this tiny house on a rock in the middle of the River Drina in Serbia. It's not only small but, as you can see, it's also not easy to get there. In winter it can be quite cold, so people use it mostly in summer.

4 A Japanese company designed this football-shaped house in 2006. It's got 32 sides and four legs and can sit on top of water. It's very small but has big windows, so there is lots of light. What a great place to live!

3 Read the article again and answer the questions.

1. What does the house in Lebanon look like?
2. Why are small windows important in a warm country?
3. What is the Mexican house made of?
4. How old is the house?
5. What can you find in the middle of the River Drina?
6. When do most people use the house? Why?
7. What does the Japanese house look like?
8. Why is it very bright inside?

TALKING POINTS

Which of these houses would you like to live in? Why?

Which of these houses would you not like to live in? Why?

Do you know about any other unusual homes? Tell your partner about them.

VOCABULARY Adjectives to describe homes

1 EP Find these words in the article and complete the table.

attractive bright cold comfortable
cool cosy dark light peaceful
tiny unusual warm

30 **Listen and check. Then repeat.**

Opinion	Size	Temperature	Sound	Light

2 In pairs, tell your partner about your home. Use the words in the box to help you.

3 In pairs, choose one of the unusual places in the article and decide how you can make it into a comfortable and cosy home. Present your unusual home to the class.

LISTENING

PREPARE FOR THE EXAM

Listening Part 1

1 For each question, choose the correct answer.

31

1 What is the number of Maria's house?

2 Which is Jason's house?

3 What time is Jenny going to leave school today?

4 What colour does Ben want to paint his bedroom?

5 What is Sarah going to do this afternoon?

» PREPARE FOR THE EXAM PAGE 128

WRITING

PREPARE TO WRITE

A description of a home

GET READY Read Fernanda's description of her home. Which city does she live in? How many rooms does her family's apartment have?

To:
From:
Reply Forward

Hi, I'm Fernanda. I live with my family in an apartment in São Paulo, Brazil. It's on the ninth floor of a big block near the city centre. It's got a kitchen, a living room, a bathroom and two bedrooms. I share one of the bedrooms with my sister, Luiza. She's 15. I'd like my own bedroom, but it's OK sharing with Luiza. We like the same things and we enjoy talking at night.

We use pronouns instead of nouns, so we don't have to repeat nouns. Which nouns do the underlined pronouns in Fernanda's description replace? Now replace the underlined nouns in this paragraph with pronouns.

David lives with his family in a small house in York. The house is quite new and the house has two bedrooms. David shares his bedroom with his baby sister, Mia. Mia is two and a half. David's mum, Helen, is a doctor and his dad, Francisco, is a nurse. Helen and Francisco both work at the local hospital.

PLAN Think about your home. Where is it? What kind of home is it? Who lives there? How many rooms has it got? Do you have your own room, or do you share a bedroom? Make notes.

WRITE Write a description of your home. Use pronouns for some of the nouns.

IMPROVE Read your description and look for mistakes. Check that you included all the information from your plan and that you have used some pronouns.

LIFE SKILLS CRITICAL THINKING

ACCEPTING OTHER PEOPLE'S OPINIONS

LIFE SKILLS

Other people's ideas
- can help us learn
- can be fun
- make life interesting

We should listen to other people and enjoy learning new things when we discuss opinions.

1 Make sentences that are true for you.

I	always often sometimes never	agree with my parents. agree with my best friends. agree with my teachers. change my opinion. like new ideas.

In pairs, compare your sentences. Did you have the same ideas?

2 Explain why each sentence is true for you.

I sometimes agree with my parents because they know more than me, but other times they are too strict.

3 Look at the words in the box. In pairs, discuss the questions.

films food holidays homework music sports

1 Do you talk to your friends or family about these topics?
2 Do you always have the same opinions?

4 Do the quiz and choose the two best options. Then in pairs, compare your answers.

How important is it to listen?

We talk to other people and give our opinions every day. Maybe you talk about what to do after school with your friends, or about plans for the weekend with your family. It's important to give your opinions, but it is also important to listen to other people's opinions and think about the best option. How good are you at listening? Do the quiz.

1 When you listen to someone, do you …
a look at him/her and smile?
b say, 'That's interesting' or 'That's a good idea'?
c interrupt and give your own opinion as soon as possible?

2 When someone has an idea, do you …
a always agree with him/her and think his/her ideas are good?
b ask questions about the idea to get more information?
c always disagree with him/her and often think he/she is wrong?

3 When you have a different opinion to someone else, do you …
a ignore him/her by not listening and turning your head away?
b think about his/her opinion before you say you don't like it?
c explain your opinion and ideas?

4 How can a group of people agree when they have different opinions?
They can …
a explain their reasons for their opinions.
b exchange ideas with each other by talking and listening.
c not work together.

5 Is it good to change your opinion when you listen to other people's ideas?
a Sometimes. I respect other people and know I am sometimes wrong.
b Never. I'm always right and I don't like to change.
c Maybe. If I have a good reason.

5 **Match the questions 1–5 in Exercise 4 to the advice a–e.**

a It's important to have your own opinions. Don't always agree immediately.
b Sometimes you can change your opinion because you listen and decide another idea is better.
c You should be polite to other people and listen carefully when they are speaking.
d It's best to talk to other people when there is a problem and think of ideas that make everyone happy.
e It is important to listen to other people's opinions and decide if the ideas are good or bad. Don't get angry or stop listening. Maybe they are really good ideas!

6 **Match the highlighted words in the quiz to the definitions.**

1 not pay attention to ....
2 have the same opinion as ....
3 speak when another person is speaking ....
4 be polite to ....
5 give and receive ....

33 7 **Listen to David and Jenny discussing what to do for their friend Martha's birthday. Do they agree in the end?**

33 8 **Listen again and answer the questions.**

1 Why doesn't David like the idea of a surprise party?
2 Why does Jenny think the cinema could be a good idea?
3 What's the weather going to be like on Saturday?
4 Who will pay for the food and drink?
5 Who will send the invitations?
6 What does Jenny want to give Martha?

33 9 **Listen again and complete the sentences with the phrases in the *Useful language* box.**

USEFUL LANGUAGE

great idea	I'm sure	Yes, but
I'm not sure	Maybe, but	

Jenny: We did it last year and it was fun.
David: **(1)** .... why not do something different?
Jenny: We could go to the cinema.
David: **(2)** .... the cinema is expensive.
Jenny: You're right. Do you like the idea of a picnic in a park?
David: Yes, I do. That's a **(3)** ....
David: Do you think she wants to go to the park in the centre for her birthday?
Jenny: **(4)** .... that's the best place.
David: Do you think Martha likes orange or lemon?
Jenny: **(5)** .... What do you think is best?

10 **Are the statements true (T) or false (F) for you? In pairs, compare your answers and explain your opinion. Be polite!**

I think …
1 football is more interesting than basketball.
2 pizza is better than pasta.
3 cats are nicer than dogs.
4 maths is easier than history.

PROJECT
Planning an exchange visit

A group of students from another country are coming to visit your school. Your teacher wants you to plan some activities for the day. Prepare a timetable for the day.

- Work in small groups.
- Read the situation.
- Individually, think of an activity you could do with the students and think of a reason why it is a good idea.
- Write your ideas in your notebook.
- In your group, decide what activities to do and prepare a timetable for the day. Use the *Useful language* from Exercise 9 to discuss the best options.
- Make a welcome poster for the visiting students to see when they arrive. Include pictures and photos to make it attractive.
- Present your poster to another group or to the class.

REVIEW 1 UNITS 1–4

VOCABULARY

1 **Write the missing letters to complete the word for each set.**

0 dolphin penguin giraffe
a *n i m a l s*
1 receptionist luggage tourist
h _ _ _ _ _ _ _
2 land hill sea
E _ _ _ _
3 tram underground scooter
t _ _ _ _ _ _ _ _ _
4 balcony ceiling cupboard
h _ _ _ _
5 address age surname
i _ _ _ _ _ _ _ _ _ _ _ _

2 **Complete the sentences with the correct words.**

1 I don't want to go in the car to the beach. Walking is good for us, so let's go ________.
2 My parents packed our ________ for our skiing holiday last night.
3 Have you got a ________ of the city? I want to see where the museum is.
4 We've got a ________ in our apartment block, but I don't use it. I always use the stairs.
5 Do you ever come to school ________ bike?
6 ________ are large white animals and they live in the cold Arctic.
7 ________ are birds with brightly coloured feathers. Some of them can talk.
8 ________ are birds too, but they can't fly. They spend a lot of time swimming in the ocean.

3 **Read the descriptions of some nature words. Write the missing letters to complete the words.**

0 This place is water, but has land all around it.
l a k e
1 This place is very dry. It's hot in the day and often cold at night.
_ _ _ _ r _
2 This place has lots of trees.
_ _ r _ _ _
3 This place is all water and it moves all the time.
_ i _ _ _
4 This place is low and is often between two mountains.
_ _ _ l _ _
5 This place is a kind of mountain, but it has a hole in the top.
v _ _ _ _ _ _ _

GRAMMAR

1 **Choose the correct options to complete the sentences.**

1 I like to watch swimming competitions because *I'm swimming / I swim* too.
2 Of course everyone *wants / want* to have more friends.
3 The weather was really hot, but I still *have / had* a great time there.
4 In my town, *there is / there are* a lot of shopping centres and sports centres.

Correct the mistakes in the sentences.

5 I visited Thao Cam Vien zoo, but I didn't liked it.
6 Every day we doing different tests or exams at school.
7 Do you liked the competition?
8 I can't go shopping today because I working.

2 **Complete the sentences. Use the present simple or present continuous.**

0 I *really like* (really like) my new bedroom. I *am painting* (paint) it blue.
1 I ________ (think) that's Olivia over there. What ________ (she / do)?
2 Sorry, I ________ (not know) where the station is. I ________ (come) from another town.
3 That aeroplane ________ (fly) very low. I ________ (hope) everything's OK.
4 My aunt ________ (travel) a lot, but she ________ (not travel) at the moment.
5 I'm sorry, I ________ (not understand). Can you say it again, please?

3 **Complete the text about Gabby using the past simple and past continuous.**

Gabby wants to do dance for the fitness part of a competition. Last month, she **(0)** *bought* (buy) a dance DVD, so she **(1)** ________ (can) learn at home.

But it was quite difficult because while she **(2)** ________ (watch) the DVD, she **(3)** ________ (also practise) the dance steps. When her mum **(4)** ________ (come) home, she **(5)** ________ (say) to Gabby, 'Why don't you join a dance class? It's a much better way to learn.' 'That's a good idea,' **(6)** ________ (answer) Gabby.

PREPARE FOR THE EXAM

Listening Part 1

1 **For each question, choose the correct picture.**

34

1 What day does Antonio play football?

2 How much is a family ticket to the zoo today?

3 What time does the girl's coach arrive?

4 What is the number of Rosa's house?

5 What did Marco buy for his bedroom?

Speaking Part 1

3 **Work in pairs. Make questions and then ask and answer with your partner. Take turns to speak.**

1 Name?
2 Age?
3 Live?
4 Country?

4 **Take turns to ask and answer the questions in the table.**

Now let's talk about your home.	Now let's talk about your school.
5 When did your family move into this home?	5 When do you arrive at school in the mornings?
6 How many rooms has your home got? What are they?	6 Which languages do you learn at school?
7 What colour is the furniture in the living room?	7 How many students are there in your class?
8 Which is your favourite room?	8 What's your favourite subject?
9 Tell me something about your bedroom.	9 Tell me something about your classroom

Writing Part 7

2 **Look at the three pictures. Write the story shown in the pictures. Write 35 words or more.**

5 SCHOOL

ABOUT YOU

03 **Watch the video and discuss the questions.**

How many different subjects do you study?

How much homework do you usually get each day?

VOCABULARY AND READING

School subjects

1 **Match the school subjects in the box to the pictures A–L.**

EP

biology	chemistry	
design and technology		drama
foreign languages		geography
history	ICT	maths
PE	physics	science

35 **Listen and check. Then repeat.**

2 **Read the article about schools in Finland and choose the best title.**

A Starting young
B New ways of learning
C Time for homework

3 **Read the article again and answer the questions.**

1 At what age do Finnish students go to school?
2 How long are they at school every day?
3 Do students have any homework?
4 Do subject words appear on all school timetables?
5 How do some experts think our brains work?
6 In Finland, do students
   a complete a project at the same time as they learn school subjects, or
   b study school subjects and then complete a project?
7 What subjects do students learn when they do the project on Pompeii?

4 **In pairs, ask and answer the questions.**

1 Which are your favourite subjects?
2 Which subjects don't you enjoy as much?
3 Which subjects are you best at?

A
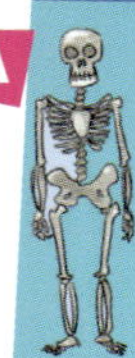

B
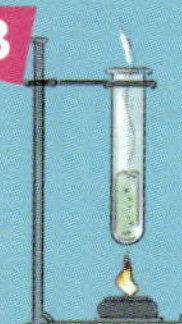

C

D
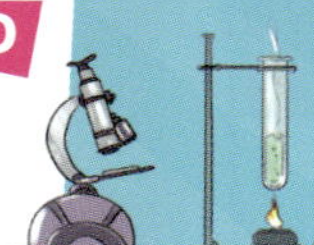

E

F

G

H

I

J

K
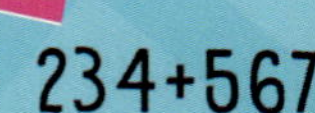

L
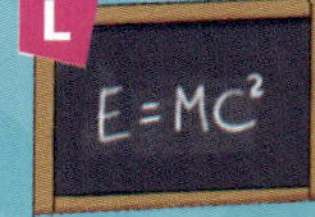

36

In international tests of maths, science and reading, students in Finland do well. This is good news! But when you look more carefully at the schools, it's not easy to explain. Finnish students don't start school until they are seven years old. The school day is short, about five hours, and there are only three or four classes a day. Students don't have much homework and there are no exams. So, why don't they do badly in tests? Perhaps something else can explain it.

There is another unusual feature of schools in Finland. For most of us, the school timetable is a list of subjects, for example ICT, history, foreign languages, geography, with one lesson following another. But some experts believe our brains work in a different way. They say our brains don't divide our learning into subjects. Our brains learn better when they get new information in context. This is why some Finnish schools don't teach subjects separately. Instead, they give students a project, such as 'the weather', and then bring school subjects into the project.

So how do some experts believe we learn most easily? Here's an example of a project with a class of 12-year-olds. Students watch a video re-enactment of the end of the city of Pompeii. Then on their laptops they compare ancient Italy under the Romans with modern Finland. Groups look at different parts of the topic and then share their ideas. They also use 3D printers to make a tiny Roman building. Later, they use the pieces of the building for a game. This project includes history, ICT, and design and technology.

ə PRONUNCIATION | Word patterns

37 **5** **Listen and look at the word patterns in the table. Then put the words in the box into the correct column.**

Oo	Ooo	oOoo
topic	*audience*	*communicate*

biology chemistry classroom favourite geography
history languages science technology

38 **Listen and check. Then repeat.**

GRAMMAR Comparative and superlative adverbs

1 **Look at the adverbs in the sentences. Decide which ones are simple adverbs, comparative adverbs or superlative adverbs.**

1 In international tests of maths, science and reading, students in Finland do **well**.
2 When you look **more carefully** at the schools, it's not easy to explain.
3 So, why don't they do **badly** in tests?
4 Do students learn **better** when the school day is shorter?
5 When there is no exam, do students study **hard**?
6 Do students learn **more efficiently** when they study subjects or when they study a topic?
7 So, how do some experts believe we learn **the most easily**?

2 **Look at the comparative and superlative adverbs and in Exercise 1 again and answer the question.**

Which word do we often use before superlative adverbs?

3 **Complete the table.**

Adjective	Simple adverb	Comparative adverb	Superlative adverb
bad	1	*worse*	*the worst*
2	3	4	*the best*
5	6	7	*the most carefully*
8	*efficiently*	9	10 ....
easy	11	12	13 ....
14	15	*harder*	16 ....

» GRAMMAR REFERENCE AND PRACTICE PAGE 151

4 **Write the correct form of the adverb for the adjective in brackets.**

1 Laura often makes mistakes because she always does her homework very .... (quick).
2 Hans speaks .... (fast) in our class.
3 You speak English much .... (good) than me.
4 Please can you speak .... (slow)? I didn't understand you before.
5 None of us did well in the exam, but I did .... (bad)!
6 I think I work .... (hard) in English lessons than I do in science.

5 **Correct the mistakes in the sentences.**

1 You speak English really good.
2 I made friends much easier at my new school.
3 Drama classes helped me speak clearer and better.
4 Catch this bus and you can get more quickly home.
5 My brother likes best the music class.

6 » **Work with a partner. Go to page 136.**

READING

1 **Read Clarissa's blog quickly. Where is she studying now, at home or at school?**

Clarissa's blog

39

31 July 2018

A few years ago, I wasn't very happy at school and I wasn't doing well in tests. So, when I was eight, Mum and Dad decided to teach me at home.

Homeschooling – great, I thought! I could stay in bed all day! Well, it wasn't quite like that! My parents found out what I needed to learn. Sometimes I had lessons, but most of the time I studied things I liked and found interesting. That's how homeschooling works best.

My favourite hobby was playing computer games, so, with Dad's help, I began to write my own computer programs. But I liked making models too, and for that I needed … maths! At school, maths was boring, but now it was useful for making my models. I made a model boat and I needed to understand science and maths to do that – oh, and design and technology too!

So were there any bad things about homeschooling? Not really. I missed my friends, but I saw them at weekends and we talked about school! They told me about their week at school, and I told them about mine. Mine always seemed more fun to me. Some weeks I studied more than they did. Other weeks I didn't study much at all. And I never had homework!

I'm 15 now, and I'm back at school because I need to take exams. I don't mind. It's nice to study with my friends again.

PREPARE FOR THE EXAM

Reading Part 3

2 **Read Clarissa's blog again. For each question, choose the correct answer.**

1 Why did Clarissa's parents teach her at home?
- **A** Her parents didn't like her school.
- **B** She was too old for her school.
- **C** She was having problems at school.

2 What does Clarissa say about homeschooling in the second paragraph?
- **A** She only learned what her parents told her to.
- **B** She chose what she wanted to learn.
- **C** She studied in bed a lot of the time.

3 Clarissa preferred doing maths at home because
- **A** her dad was able to explain it to her.
- **B** it helped her do things she enjoyed.
- **C** she had more time to spend on it.

4 What was the difference between Clarissa's and her friends' school experiences?
- **A** Clarissa didn't have to do any homework.
- **B** Clarissa always had more work to do than they did.
- **C** Her friends enjoyed themselves more.

5 What does Clarissa say about homeschooling in her blog?
- **A** It's important to have daily lessons.
- **B** It's hard to find time to see friends.
- **C** Learning doesn't always have to come from books.

» PREPARE FOR THE EXAM PAGE 123

TALKING POINTS

What do you like about going to school?
What are the good things about homeschooling?
What are the bad things about it?
Would you like to study at home? Why? / Why not?

VOCABULARY *take*

1 **What does *take* mean in this sentence?**

I'm 15 now, and I'm back at school because I need to take exams.

2 **Now look at the mind map. Match the meanings of *take* a–g to these words.**

EP

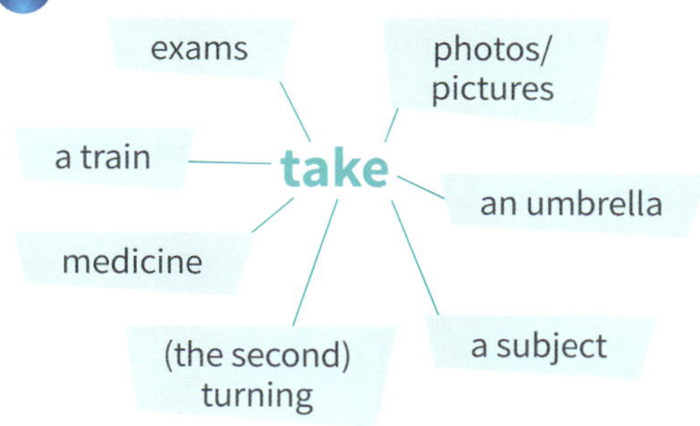

a carry
b make
c do
d study
e go along
f use
g catch

40 **Listen and check. Then repeat.**

3 **Write an example sentence for each meaning of *take*.**

4 **Complete the questions with the correct form of the words from Exercise 2 and then answer them.**

1 When did you last take an ________ out with you in the rain?
2 Which ________ do I need take to get to the park from here? The one on the left or the one on the right?
3 What extra ________ would you like to take at school ?
4 Have you taken any ________ today with your new camera? How many?
5 When was the first time you took a ________ to go somewhere? Were you on holiday?
6 Do you usually take ________ when you are ill?
7 How do you feel when you take an ________ at the end of the school year?

5 **In pairs, compare your answers.**

LISTENING

41 **1** **Listen to the *What's New* section on a morning radio show. A boy called Ethan is talking about his experience of schooling. What phrase does Ethan use for the education he had on the trip?**

41 **2** **Listen again. Are the sentences right (✓) or wrong (✗)?**

1 There are four people in Ethan's family.
2 Ethan's mum left her job because she wanted to see the world.
3 Ruth and Ethan were homeschooled before they went travelling.
4 Ethan's parents didn't tell anyone else about their plans.
5 Ruth and Ethan's parents helped with the 'world schooling'.
6 Ruth and Ethan do a lot of different things when they are travelling.
7 Ethan's parents wanted him to go back to school.
8 Ethan says he works harder at school than he did when he was world schooled.

3 **In pairs, discuss the questions.**

1 Would you like to be 'world schooled'?
2 Would your parents be good teachers?
3 Which parts of the world would you like to visit?
4 What would you miss about your school?

SPEAKING

1 **In pairs, or a small group, use the questions to describe your perfect school. Make notes about what you discuss.**

1 Where is the school?
2 What lessons do you have?
3 How many students are there?
4 Who are the teachers?
5 Do you have homework?
6 How many lessons do you have in a day/week?
7 How long are the school days/holidays?
8 Do you wear a uniform?
9 What's the food like?
10 Do you sleep there?
11 What makes your school better than other schools?

2 **Now tell the rest of the class about your perfect school. Take turns in your group to speak.**

6 FAVOURITE THINGS

ABOUT YOU

Do you have a favourite thing? What is it?
Where did you get it?
Why is it special?
What do you like about it?

VOCABULARY AND LISTENING

Materials

1 **Look at the photos below. Match the materials in the box to the photos A–J.**

EP

cotton	glass	gold	leather
metal	paper	plastic	silver
wood	wool		

42 **Listen and check. Then repeat.**

2 **What are the things in the photos made of? Talk about the photos with your partner.**

The headphones are made of plastic.

3 **Look at the examples. Which word is a noun and which is an adjective?**

The box is made of wood. It's a wooden box.

4 **Work with your partner. Use the materials as adjectives to describe and find the things in the photo.**

They're cotton T-shirts. Photo B

5 **In pairs, look around the classroom and at what people are wearing. Find as many things as you can that are made from the materials in Exercise 1. Say what they are.**

43 **6** **Cam is doing a project for school. He asks three people in the street about their favourite things. Listen to the recording. Which thing was a present?**

43 **7** **Listen again and complete the table.**

	Speaker 1	Speaker 2	Speaker 3
What is the thing?			
Who does it belong to?			
What is it made of?			

A

B

C

D

E

F

G

H

I
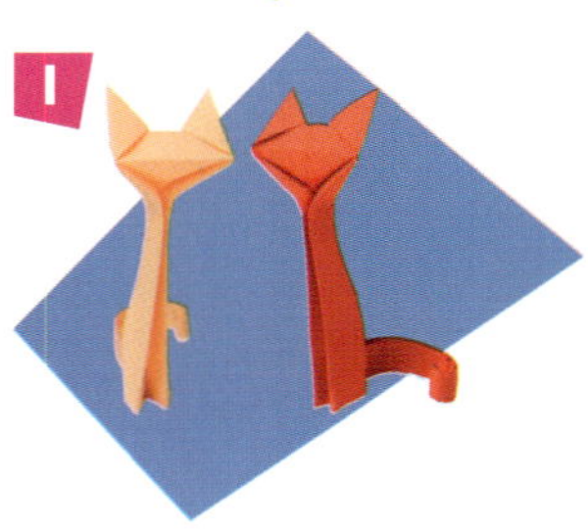

J

GRAMMAR Possession

1 **Look at the pictures. Match sentences 1 and 2 to pictures A and B.**

1 It's my brother's dog.
2 It's my brothers' dog.

2 **Look at sentences 1 and 2 in Exercise 1. Which sentence has *'s* and which sentence has *s'*? Why?**

3 **Complete the sentences. Use the word in brackets in the singular or plural and *'s* or *s'*.**

1 That's my ______ (sister) car. My dad bought them one to share last year.
2 I don't have a computer, but I use my ______ (brother) when I need to. I lend him my camera when he needs it because he hasn't got a good one.
3 My little sister loves going to the ______ (child) disco. It's specially for little kids and there are games and activities.
4 Don't put any cake on those plates! I use them for the ______ (dog) food. They don't like the bowls from the pet shop.

4 **Look at the words in purple in the two examples from the listening. Underline the determiners and circle the pronouns.**

1 They're not mine. They're my sister's.
2 Oh and what are theirs? Your dad's for example.

5 **Now complete the table.**

Determiners	Pronouns
my	*mine*
your	
his	
her	
our	
their	

» GRAMMAR REFERENCE AND PRACTICE PAGE 152

6 **Look at the pictures and decide who the football player is. Match sentences 1 and 2 to pictures A and B.**

1 He's a friend of theirs.
2 He's a friend of hers.

7 **Complete the sentences with the correct word.**

1 That's not Robert's book, it's Paula's. Robert lost ______ yesterday.
2 My parents had a holiday on a boat last summer. I think it belonged to a friend of ______.
3 A cat plays in our garden sometimes, but it's not ______. We've got a dog.
4 You can't use my brother's football. But you can borrow ______ if you like. I got it for my birthday.
5 Are you looking for your hat? I saw Paul's in the garden, but I don't know where ______ is.
6 Sally is so good at art. That picture is ______.

8 **Correct the mistakes in the sentences.**

1 You can read your favourite book's there.
2 My friends name's Ben.
3 The bus stop is just five minutes walk from my house.
4 Bring your computer because my is broken.
5 My bedroom is bigger than their.

ə PRONUNCIATION Weak forms: *a* and *of*

44 **9** **Listen and repeat.**

She's a friend of mine.
He's a friend of hers.
They're friends of ours.
Is he a friend of yours?

10 **Think of three things that are special and belong to different people in your family. In pairs, tell each other about them. Use the questions to help you.**

1 What are they? What are they made of?
2 Who do they belong to?
3 Where did they come from?
4 Why are they special?
5 What else can you say about them?

READING

1 In pairs, tell your partner about a special present someone gave you. What was it?

2 Anja and Pete wrote about special memories in their online school magazine. Look at objects A–F. What present did Anja get? What present did Pete get?

HILL CREST ACADEMY

Special Memories

ANJA, AGE 13

My special memory is from when I was three years old. We were staying with my grandparents at their house in the country. They lived in an old wooden house. I remember the house was always cold and it was near a forest. When it was time for bed, Grandma took me upstairs to read me a story. On my bed there was a lovely wool blanket. It was really colourful. I remember touching it and it was so, so soft. 'It's yours. I made it for you,' my grandma said. I still have the blanket on my bed at home. It looks really small there, but I remember when I was younger it seemed so big!

PETE, AGE 14

My special memory isn't from very long ago. I was opening presents on my 13th birthday. My older brother gave me a large box. It was very hard. What could it be? I opened it and felt inside. I'm blind, so I needed to touch everything because I can't see. It was smooth and round. I remember thinking 'It's a leather football' and feeling upset. I can't play football because I can't see the ball. I picked it up. It felt quite heavy, and it made a noise. My brother told me it was a special football for blind people. There are little metal balls inside that make a noise when someone kicks or throws it. Perfect! Now I play football all the time.

3 Read the article again and answer the questions.

1. What was Anja's grandparents' house like?
2. When did Anja first see the blanket?
3. What was it like?
4. Why do you think Anja remembers it as big when in fact it's quite small?
5. Who was Pete's present from?
6. What did it feel like?
7. Why did he feel sad when he first felt the present?
8. What happened when he took it out of the box and why?

TALKING POINTS

Anja's memory is from when she was three years old. What's your earliest memory?

Pete's memory is of his special football. What other special things can help someone like Pete?

VOCABULARY Adjectives for describing objects

1 Match the words in the box to photos A–F.

EP

colourful	hard	heavy	large
little	lovely	old	pretty
round	small	smooth	soft

Listen and check.

2 In pairs, describe the objects in the photos. Use the adjectives from Exercise 1 and others you know.

3 Take turns to describe something in the classroom to your partner for them to guess what it is. Use the words from Exercise 1 to help you.

It's large, smooth and colourful. It's made of paper and it's on the wall.

A map?

Yes.

LISTENING

PREPARE FOR THE EXAM

Listening Part 5

1 (47) **For each question, choose the correct answer. You will hear Carmen talking to Murat about some things she has found in her grandparents' house. Who does each thing belong to?**

Things		People
0 clock	*E*	**A** aunt
1 computer	☐	**B** brother
2 hat	☐	**C** cousin
3 toy bear	☐	**D** father
4 painting	☐	**E** grandfather
5 jacket	☐	**F** grandmother
		G mother
		H uncle

2 (47) **Listen again and check your answers.**

WRITING

PREPARE TO WRITE

Adjective order

GET READY

THE CITY MUSEUM

Have you got a favourite thing or something from the past you want to tell us about? Send us an email. Describe the object and say why it's special for you and attach a photo if you have one.

Email: citymuseumfavobs@museum.uk

To: citymuseumfavobs@museum.uk
From: Ben
Reply Forward

I've got a beautiful, old, silver ring. It was my uncle's. I keep it in a small, red, wooden box as it's very special. He gave it to me when I was ten. I never wear it, but I like to look at it.

From
Ben

Read the notice from the museum and then read Ben's email reply. What's his favourite thing?

Put the adjectives from the email in the correct column in the table.

Adjective order						
Opinion (pretty)	Size (big)	Physical quality (hard)	Shape (square)	Age (new)	Colour (blue)	Material (gold)

Find three more examples of pairs of adjectives in the texts on page 38 and add them to the table.

PLAN **You are going to write to the museum about something special. Use these questions to plan your email.**

What is it? Where/who did it come from? What does it look like?

Plan your email to the museum.

What groups of adjectives can you use to describe your object? What order do they go in?

WRITE **Write an email to the museum. Use Ben's email to help you. Write about 35 words.**
Draw a picture of the object.

IMPROVE **In pairs, read each other's email. Check for mistakes with adjectives. Rewrite your emails.**

CULTURE

SECONDARY SCHOOL IN THE UK

1 **Discuss the questions with your partner.**

1. Do you like going to school?
2. Why? / Why not?
3. At what age do people start secondary school in your country?

2 **Work with a partner. What do you know about secondary schools in the UK? Discuss your ideas. Read the web page. Were any of your ideas mentioned?**

48

The secondary school system in the UK

From the age of 11 to 16, children go to secondary school. Most take children of all abilities and are called comprehensive schools. But there are also grammar schools, where children take an exam to enter, especially in Northern Ireland. In Scotland, secondary schools are called high schools or academies. When they are 14, all children choose the subjects they want to study at GCSE (or National 5 exams in Scotland). These are national exams you take at 16. Everyone has to do English and maths. Students also choose four or more additional subjects from a list. This includes subjects like languages and sciences but also photography and drama.

The school year

The school year goes from September to July in England and Wales, August to June in Scotland and September to June in Northern Ireland. There are three terms and short holidays in the middle of each term. The Christmas and Easter holidays are usually two weeks, and the summer holiday is six weeks, or two months in Northern Ireland.

The school day

The school day at secondary schools goes from about 8.45 am to 3.30 pm. There's a break in the morning and another for lunch. Most British school students have to wear a uniform. Each school has its own colours for the uniforms.

Sixth form / S5 and S6

When students are 17 and 18, they take more exams. In Scotland, these exams are called Highers in the first year and Advanced Highers in the second year. In the rest of the UK, students go into the sixth form to study four subjects at AS level in their first year and three of these at A level in the second year. You need to pass these high-level exams to go to university.

3 **Read the web page again and complete the table.**

Types of public secondary schools in the UK

1 .... schools – These schools take children of all abilities.
2 .... schools – Children need to pass an exam to get in these schools.
3 .... schools or academies – These are secondary schools in Scotland.

Secondary school	England and Wales	Northern Ireland	Scotland
National exams at age 16	GCSEs	4	National 5 exams
National exams at age 17	AS levels	AS levels	5 ....
National exams at age 18	6	A levels	Advanced Highers
School year starts	September	7	August
School year finishes	8	June	June

TALKING POINTS

In groups, compare the UK secondary school system with your own.

4 Read the information on the Woodedge Secondary School website. Is this school similar to your school? Answer the questions.

Parents | Teachers | Students

Woodedge

Secondary School

49

Welcome to the Woodedge School website. We are a comprehensive school for girls and boys aged 11–18. Our children come from many different cultures and backgrounds. We are a popular school and children who come here do very well in their exams. As well as excellent teaching, we offer many interesting after-school clubs, including sports, drama and dance.

School Diary

Important dates for November

Friday 13th: **Charity Day** Can everyone please bring £1.00. This is a non-uniform day. Wear your own clothes, but no hats, please, and don't colour your hair. There will be things for sale, so bring in some extra money. All the money we make will go to the charity Save the Children.

Friday 20th: **Autumn concert** Tickets £3.00 on sale now – maximum four per student.

Tuesday 24th: **Years 7–10 Girls' indoor football competition** Sports Hall – trainers only, please.

Monday 30th: **Year 11 school trip to the National Theatre**

1 At what age do students leave Woodedge School?
2 Why do students need to bring money to school on 13th November?
3 Do students have to wear their school uniform on 13th November?
4 How many tickets can each student buy for the concert?
5 What must students wear for the football competition?
6 Where are Year 11 students going on 30th November?

50 **5** Listen to Aleesha talking about Woodedge School. Answer the questions.

1 How many pupils are there at Woodedge?
2 What is Aleesha's cultural background?
3 What time does school finish?
4 What do students learn about in PDT?
5 What kind of food can you get at lunchtime?
6 How does Aleesha pay for her lunch?
7 What after-school clubs is she doing this term?
8 What is she making for Charity Day?

6 Compare Woodedge School with your own. Talk to your partner about these things.

- after-school clubs
- how long the day is
- mix of cultures
- number of students
- school concerts
- special days (like Charity Day)
- school lunches
- school trips

PROJECT

A school web page

Design a web page for your school. Include this information:

- a description of the school
- photos of your friends and the building
- a newsletter with school events for one month

Present your web page to the class.

04 NOW WATCH THE CULTURE VIDEO

7 ADVENTURE HOLIDAYS

ABOUT YOU

05 **Watch the video and discuss the questions.**
What adventure holiday would you like to go on?
How would you like to get/travel there?
Who would you like to travel with?

VOCABULARY AND LISTENING

Holiday activities

1 **What activities can you do on adventure holidays? Match the words in the box to photos A–J.**

EP

camping	diving	hiking	horse riding
kite surfing	mountain biking	paddle boarding	
sailing	waterskiing	zip wiring	

51 **Listen and check. Then repeat.**

52 **2** **Listen to Tara and her friend Dan talking about their adventure holiday. Which activities from Exercise 1 do they not mention?**

52 **3** **Listen again. Complete the table with Tara's and Dan's holiday activities.**

Monday	Tuesday	Wednesday	Thursday	Friday

4 **Complete the sentences with the verbs in the box.**

EP

get back   get lost   getting on
getting to   getting up

1 Tara's .... the airport by car.
2 Tara and Dan have to .... from the mountains to the activity centre alone.
3 Tara and Dan are .... a bus at 5 am in the morning.
4 Tara and Dan are .... early on Monday morning.
5 Dan hopes he doesn't .... in the mountains.

5 **In pairs, ask and answer the questions.**

1 What time do you get up in the morning?
2 When was the last time you got lost?
3 How do you get to school?
4 How did you get back home from your last holiday?
5 When did you last get on a train?

PREPARE FOR THE EXAM

Speaking Part 2

6 **Work with a partner. Talk together about the adventure activities in Exercise 1. Do you like these activities? Say why or why not.**

7 **In pairs, ask and answer the questions.**

Do you think:
- going sailing is dangerous?
- going camping is boring?
- going kite surfing is difficult?
- going paddle boarding is amazing?
- going horse riding is exciting?
- going mountain biking is hard?

8 **In pairs, ask and answer the questions.**

1 Which of these adventure activities do you like best? Why?
2 Do you like doing activities on the water? Why?
3 Is it better to do adventure activities when the weather is rainy or cold? Why? / Why not?
4 Do you prefer doing activities on your own or with other people? Why?

GRAMMAR Present continuous for future

1 **Look at the examples. Then choose the correct words to complete the sentences below.**

We're getting on a bus at five o'clock in the morning!
I'm not taking my keyboard with me next week.
When are we going mountain biking and paddle boarding?

1 We can use the present continuous to talk about *now* / *the future* / *now and the future*.
2 The three example sentences are about *now* / *the future*.
3 We *usually* / *never* use a time word with the present continuous for the future.

>> GRAMMAR REFERENCE AND PRACTICE PAGE 153

2 **Look at Bella's diary for this weekend. Write her plans using the present continuous and mention the day and time for each activity. Is there anything she isn't doing?**

She isn't cleaning her room at 2 pm on Sunday.

3 **Correct the mistakes in the sentences.**

1 Taylor Swift sings at the football stadium next Saturday.
2 We meet at 3 pm tomorrow, at the bus station.
3 I'm very excited that you come to visit next summer.
4 Do you bring any money with you this evening?
5 I don't visit my grandparents next weekend.

PRONUNCIATION

Sentence stress: present continuous

4 **Look at the sentences. Decide which words in each sentence are stressed and underline them.**

1 We're going kite surfing next week.
2 Are you going mountain biking in the summer?
3 They aren't buying a paddle board this weekend.
4 He's going camping next month.
5 Is she coming horse riding with us this evening?
6 He isn't going hiking during the holidays.

53 **Listen and check. Then repeat.**

5 **In pairs, take turns to read out your sentences from Exercise 2.**

6 **In pairs, write a list of all the activities you'd like to do on an adventure week. Where would you like to go? Now plan your week. Choose at least one activity for each day.**

7 **Work with another pair. Use the present continuous to ask and answer questions about each other's adventure weeks.**

What are you doing on Tuesday?

On Tuesday, we're …

Choose the best activities from your group to make a perfect week. Tell the class.

This is our perfect adventure week on the Black Sea. On Monday morning, we're learning how to waterski and then in the afternoon we're …

READING

1 **Look at the photo on the leaflet and answer the questions.**

1 What kind of place are the students going to on their adventure weekend?
2 What activities do you think people can do here?

2 **Read the leaflet from the school quickly and check your answers to the two questions in Exercise 1.**

3 **Read the leaflet again and answer the questions.**

1 What can the weather be like in the Brecon Beacons?
2 Where can parents find information on what students should bring?
3 Why should students not take too much in their bags?
4 What's the reason for the length of the walk?
5 How many nights are students spending in their tents?
6 How are they getting to Wales?

VOCABULARY Things to take on an adventure holiday

EP **1** **Match the words from the kit list to photos A–L.**

55 **Listen and check. Then repeat.**

2 **Read the kit list again. Which of the things on the list do the students need for:**

wet weather?	eating and drinking?
sunny weather?	sleeping?
cold weather?	keeping clean?
having fun?	not getting lost?

TALKING POINTS

Do you like the idea of an adventure weekend with the school? Why / why not?
Do you like hiking? Why / why not?
Do you like camping? Why / why not?
What else would you like to do on an adventure weekend?

Brecon Beacons adventure weekend

54

Students are going to the Brecon Beacons in Wales for our adventure weekend in May this year. The Brecon Beacons are mountains and the weather there can be sunny one minute and raining or foggy and cold the next. Please make sure that your son or daughter brings the right clothes. See the kit list below.

It's important students don't bring too many clothes because each group is going to carry everything they need for camping and cooking.

There are lots of different walks in the mountains. We know that some students don't walk very much, so our walk over the two days is only 25 km long.

- Students spend Saturday and Sunday hiking.
- Students camp for one night, on Saturday.
- Students sleep in tents in groups of three or four.

We are travelling to the Brecon Beacons by bus. The bus leaves from the school on Saturday at 6 am and returns on Sunday at 8 pm.

Please contact Mr Jones at the school if you have any questions or would like more information.

KIT LIST

CLOTHES
- **walking boots**
- **waterproof trousers** and **jacket**
- walking socks
- underwear
- T-shirts
- pyjamas
- sweaters
- **trainers** (for the evening)
- walking trousers (not jeans!)

KIT FOR EACH GROUP
- **tent**
- **map** and **compass**
- food

OTHER KIT
- **backpack**
- towel
- **sleeping bag**
- **torch**
- **wash bag**
- **first-aid kit**
- plate, bowl, mug, knife, fork, spoon
- water bottle

YOU MAY ALSO WANT:
- warm hat or sun hat
- gloves
- **sun cream**
- sunglasses
- playing cards
- **snacks**

A

B

C
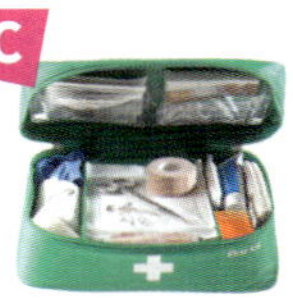
D

E

F

G

H

I

J

K

L

LISTENING

1 Work in pairs. How do you say these dates?

17th August
21st November
3rd February

Write down four other dates. In pairs, say them for your partner to write down.

2 Read the information sheet about the adventure holiday. What kind of information are you going to listen for?

PREPARE FOR THE EXAM

Listening Part 2

3 (56) For each question, write the correct answer in the gap. Write one word or a number or a date or a time.

You will hear a teacher telling students about an adventure holiday.

Exciting New
Adventure Holiday

Name: *Across the Water*

Start date: (1) ....

Number of student places: (2) ....

Place: Close to a (3) ....

Cost: (4) £ ....

For more information, phone:
(5) ....

» PREPARE FOR THE EXAM PAGE 129

SPEAKING

1 Laura is on an adventure holiday with her parents. Read the conversation and answer the questions.

1 What are Laura and her dad going to do on Saturday morning and Saturday afternoon?
2 What's Laura's dad going to do on Sunday morning?
3 What's Laura going to do on Sunday morning?

Dad: Let's go waterskiing on Saturday morning, Laura.
Laura: I'm not that interested in waterskiing, Dad. How about mountain biking?
Dad: I'd prefer to go kayaking or something like that.
Laura: Kayaking! That's a great idea!
Dad: What shall we do in the afternoon? Would you like to go horse riding?
Laura: I'd love to. Where is it?
Dad: It's near the beach. It's a shame about the waterskiing. I wanted to do that. Never mind.
Laura: Why don't you go on Sunday morning with Mum, and I can sleep late?
Dad: Good idea. So, on Saturday we're going kayaking in the morning and …
Laura: … we're going horse riding in the afternoon!

2 Look at the words in the conversation.

Which phrases are used:
a to make suggestions
b to agree
c to disagree
d to express regret

3 (57) Listen to the conversation. Then practise it in pairs.

4 Read the programme for an adventure weekend. Circle the activities you want to do.

GOLDEN SANDS BEACH
Come and join us this weekend!

SATURDAY	SUNDAY
MORNING surfing OR waterskiing	MORNING zip wiring OR mountain biking
AFTERNOON climbing OR hiking	AFTERNOON tennis OR beach volleyball
EVENING barbecue OR night walk and picnic in the forest	**Write your name on the list or speak to John.**

5 In pairs, talk about your weekend choices. Use Exercise 1 to help you.

Make suggestions, agree and disagree, depending on what you are planning for the weekend.
Can you get your partner to change their mind?

8 LIFE IN THE FUTURE

Homes of the future

ABOUT YOU

In pairs, look at the words. Imagine it's the year 2040. Describe what these things are like.

books cars computers homes
planes smartphones televisions

VOCABULARY AND LISTENING

Furniture and household appliances

1 **Match the definitions 1–12 to the words in the box.**

EP

air conditioning barbecue
bin bookcase drawer
fridge heating lights roof
seat stairs washing machine

1 This keeps your food cold.
2 This makes your clothes clean.
3 This keeps you cool.
4 This is a place for things you like to read.
5 This keeps the rain out of your home.
6 This is for cooking food outside.
7 These take you from one floor to another.
8 You put clothes and small things in it.
9 These make it easier to see when it's dark.
10 This is for sitting on.
11 This keeps your home warm.
12 You put things you don't want in this.

58 **Listen and check. Then repeat.**

2 **In pairs, answer the questions about the words in Exercise 1.**

1 Which things need electricity to work?
2 Which things are furniture?
3 Where in a home do you usually find each thing?

3 **Look at these actions. Write *H* (using my hands) or *T* (using technology) next to each one. In pairs, compare your answers. Discuss the technology you use for actions you marked *T*.**

open your front door turn off the TV
turn on the computer lock the car
turn on the lights close the windows
close the garage door

59 **4** **Listen to a radio interview about homes of the future. What furniture do they talk about?**

59 **5** **Listen again. Number the information in the order you hear it.**

☐ **a** changing the temperature, music and lights in different rooms
☐ **b** changes to the outside of buildings
☐ **c** having a computer as part of a table
☐ **d** homes of the future looking different from homes of today
☐ **e** using smartphones to turn washing machines on and off

6 **In pairs, discuss which things in your house you would like to control using your hands and which you would like to control without touching anything.**

GRAMMAR Future with *will*

1 **Look at these examples from the interview.**

I think they'll (will) be very different from today's homes.
You won't (will not) have to use your hands to do it.
Will it work for the heating and the lights too?

2 **Choose the correct words to complete the rules.**

1. We use **will** when we think something is going to happen *now* / *in the future*.
2. We *often use* / *don't use* 'think' before **will**.
3. After **will**, we use the infinitive *without* / *with* 'to'.
4. We *use* / *do not use* third person 's' with **will**.
5. To make a negative, we put 'not' *before* / *after* **will**.
6. To make a question with **will**, we *use* / *don't use* the auxiliary 'do'.

» GRAMMAR REFERENCE AND PRACTICE PAGE 154

3 **Complete the sentences with the correct form of *will*.**

1. My phone isn't working very well. It .... (not be) possible to text you later.
2. I think my sister .... (arrive) late because she missed her train.
3. People .... (use) different new technology, not only their smartphones.
4. .... (people / live) on the moon in the future? I don't think so, do you?

Future with *may* and *might*

4 **Look at these examples from the interview.**

Seats, bookcases and things like that might not look very different.
But you may have a table or drawer with a computer inside it.
Might our homes look different on the outside, too?

5 **Choose the correct words to complete the rules**

1. We use ***may***, ***might*** when we think something is *possible* / *definitely going to happen* in the future.
2. We *often use* / *don't use* 'think' before ***may***, ***might***.
3. After ***may*** and ***might***, we use the infinitive *without 'to'* / *with 'to'*.
4. We *use* / *do not use* third person 's' with ***may*** and ***might***.
5. To make a negative, we put 'not' *before* / *after* ***may*** and ***might***.
6. To make a question with ***may***, ***might***, we *use* / *don't use* the auxiliary 'do'.

» GRAMMAR REFERENCE AND PRACTICE PAGE 154

6 **Put the words in brackets in the correct order to complete the sentences.**

1. Next summer, ... (do / I / may) an online course on ICT. I'm not sure yet.
2. How .... (help / might / technology) ill people in their homes?
3. We .... (be able / not / may) to see you tomorrow. We're very busy.
4. I .... (not / might / want) robots in my house.

7 **Correct the mistakes in the sentences.**

1. A few other friends come to my house later.
2. I met a new friend, and I think you can like her.
3. It don't rain this evening. The weather app on my phone says sunshine all day.
4. I'm not sure, but the book will be on your kitchen table.
5. I meet you in the skatepark later. I've got nothing else to do today.

ə PRONUNCIATION *will* and *won't*

60 **8** **Listen and repeat.**

Houses will be smaller.
I'll live in a big house.
People won't use door keys.
I won't walk anywhere.

9 **Work with a partner. Use *will*, *won't*, *may*, *may not*, *might*, *might not* to talk about your ideas from *About you* at the beginning of this unit.**

10 **Read the sentences. Do you think these things will happen in the future? When?**

1. People will live under the sea.
2. During the summer, there might not be any ice at the North Pole.
3. Space travel will get cheaper and might even cost the same as a plane ticket.
4. People may travel to Mars and live there.
5. There will be cars without drivers.
6. People might be able to communicate with technology by just thinking.
7. Most people will live to be 100 and their bodies won't get old.

11 **In groups of three, discuss your answers. Use *will*, *won't*, *may*, *may not*, *might*, *might not*.**

I think people might live under the sea in the future. What do you think?

WHAT WILL YOU PUT IN YOUR TIME CAPSULE?

61

A ....

There is a little bag on the moon with a time capsule inside it. The capsule is tiny, about the size of a small **(1)** .... At the top, it says: 'Goodwill messages from around the world brought to the moon by the astronauts of Apollo 11.' The Apollo 11 Astronauts **(2)** .... it there in 1969. There are 73 messages from **(3)** .... countries written on the time capsule in very small letters. Each one is smaller than a human hair. The messages are to anyone who **(4)** .... the time capsule in the future. Who will that be? Who **(5)** .... where those people will come from? They might come from Earth, but they might be from **(6)** .... else in the solar system.

B ....

Harold Davisson had a shop in Seward, Nebraska in the USA. He thought it was important for his children and grandchildren to touch and see real things, not just to read about them in books. So he decided to build the biggest time capsule in the world. He put more than 5,000 real objects inside, including clothes and even a new car and buried it on 4th July 1975 in front of his shop. Then he heard there was another time capsule bigger than his, so he put a second time capsule on top of the first one. His grandchildren will open them both on 4th July 2025. They know some of the things they will find, but they might find things Harold didn't tell them about!

READING

1 **Look at the photos of the time capsules. What do you think a time capsule is? Do you think time capsules are a good idea? Why / Why not?**

2 **Read both texts quickly. Choose the best title for each text.**

1 Two are better than one   2 Out of this world

PREPARE FOR THE EXAM

Reading Part 4

3 **Read text A. For each question, choose the correct answer for each gap.**

	A	B	C
1	A money	B coin	C pence
2	A arrived	B travelled	C left
3	A usual	B different	C available
4	A finds	B looks	C learns
5	A understands	B thinks	C knows
6	A everywhere	B nowhere	C somewhere

» PREPARE FOR THE EXAM PAGE 124

4 **Read the texts again and answer the questions.**

Which time capsule, A or B

1 is older?
2 is under the ground?
3 might people open first?
4 is smaller?
5 is for someone's family?
6 has something for people to read?

5 **Discuss with your partner. Which time capsule do you think will be the most interesting for the people who will open it? Why?**

TALKING POINTS

06 Watch the video and ask and answer the questions in groups.

What will you put in your time capsule to show people in the future what life is like today?

What eight things will you put in your group time capsule? Say why.

VOCABULARY Words with two meanings

1 **Some English words have two meanings. Read the sentences. What are the two meanings of *letter*?**

EP

There are 73 messages written on the time capsule in tiny letters.
Some people wrote letters to people in the future and put them inside their time capsules.

2 **Each word in the box has two meanings. What are they?**

book	kind	picture	ring	watch

3 » Go to page 136.

LISTENING

1 **Read the five questions and the possible answers. In which questions will you hear one person speaking, and in which questions will you hear two people speaking?**

PREPARE FOR THE EXAM

Listening Part 4

2 **For each question, choose the correct answer.**

62

1 You will hear two friends talking about technology. What do they think they will use in the future?
A smartphones
B smart watches
C smart glasses

2 You will hear a teacher talking about an activity students are doing in class. What does she say?
A They will finish the project in groups.
B They will complete the project at home.
C They will write the project on a computer.

3 You will hear a boy talking about his shopping trip. What did he buy?
A something to wear
B something to read
C something to eat

4 You will hear a daughter talking to her father about a new computer he is buying for her. What does she like best about the computer?
A the software
B the colour
C the size

5 You will hear a boy talking to his mother about the weather for his holiday. What will the weather be like tomorrow?
A It'll be wet.
B It'll be cloudy.
C It'll be sunny.

» PREPARE FOR THE EXAM PAGE 131

WRITING

PREPARE TO WRITE

too, also, as well

GET READY **More than 50 years ago, some children buried a time capsule in their town. In a few years, people in the town will open it. Read one of the letters in it. How many predictions does Liliana make? How many of them are true now or will be true in a few years?**

Hello,

I'm writing this in 1965. Here are my predictions for 2025. There will be cities under the sea and there might be cities on Mars, too. There may not be any teachers because robots will teach the students. Most doctors will be robots as well. Also, I think there will be cars that drive themselves.

Are my predictions true?

Liliana

Look at the words in blue.

We use *too*, *as well* and *also* to add more information to our writing.

Choose the correct options to complete the sentences.

1 ***Too*** comes at *the beginning / the middle / the end* of a sentence.
2 ***As well*** comes at *the beginning / the middle / the end* of a sentence.
3 At the beginning of a sentence, ***also*** *has / doesn't have* a comma (,) after it.

PLAN **You are going to write a letter for a time capsule for your own town. Plan your ideas. What do you think the world will be like in 50 years?**

WRITE **Write your letter. Use Liliana's letter to help you and all your ideas.**

Write about 60 words. Use *also, too* and *as well* to join your ideas.

IMPROVE **In pairs, read each other's letters. Check for mistakes and try to make your letters better.**

LIFE SKILLS COMMUNICATION

HAVING A GOOD CONVERSATION

LIFE SKILLS

To have good conversation, you should remember that:

- when only one person talks and the other listens, it is not a conversation!
- some people are quiet, some people like talking more.
- a good conversation includes everyone.

Good conversations

Imagine you have to spend an hour with a student you don't know from another class. Maybe you're going to take a test, or you're waiting to see the head teacher. For some people, it's a difficult situation because you don't know the person very well. For other people, it's easy to start a conversation and say, for example, *How are you?* or *Are you nervous?*

Talking to an older person can be even more difficult. For example, your parents' friends or aunts, uncles or grandparents. Sometimes they ask all the questions and you only answer! The best way to manage this is to think of questions to ask the other person. People like to talk about their experiences and to give an opinion about things.

Group conversations are also difficult to manage sometimes, but there are some easy ways to make sure everyone speaks, including yourself! If you are a person who can talk easily, then think about the others in the group. If you notice one person is not speaking, then ask them a question. A simple *And you?* or *Why?* Or show interest – *Really?*

When you are in a group and everyone is talking at the same time, it is sometimes hard to interrupt, especially if you think this is not a polite thing to do. When you want to give your own opinion politely, you can use *Excuse me, can I say something?* Then other people know you have something to say.

We can all learn to have good conversations.

64

1 **Are these statements true (*T*) or false (*F*) for you? In pairs, compare your ideas.**

- I talk more than I listen.
- I'm quiet, so I don't want to talk.
- I prefer to talk in pairs than in groups.
- I like to hear different opinions.

63 **2** **Listen to the conversations and answer the questions.**

Conversation 1 Does the conversation include everyone?
Conversation 2 Is the girl, Poppy, polite?
Conversation 3 How does the boy stop his grandmother's questions?

3 **Read the text above and tick (✓) the best sentence.**

The text explains how to …

a speak more clearly.
b improve your conversation skills.
c ask questions.
d make more friends.

4 Read the text again and match the two halves of the sentences.

1 To start a conversation with someone you don't know well
2 To have a good conversation with someone
3 To help quiet people to speak
4 To give your opinion when other people are talking

a you should ask him/her questions as well as answer.
b you should interrupt politely.
c you can ask how they feel.
d you can ask them a question.

5 Complete the sentences with a verb from the box. Find the verb in the text to check your answers.

answer	ask	give
make	show	speak

1 You should always .... in English in the class.
2 I couldn't .... a question in the test because it was very difficult.
3 I wanted to .... interest in his life, so I asked him about his hometown.
4 Please .... sure you bring a calculator to class tomorrow.
5 Can I .... a question? What time does the bus leave?
6 At the end of the video, you should .... your opinion.

6 Do you prefer to listen or to speak? Tell your partner about a time when you preferred to listen and a time when you wanted to speak.

65 7 In Newton school, the students are working on a time capsule project. Each group has to choose a country and an object from that country to include in the capsule. Listen to the conversation. Which country and which object does the group choose?

65 8 Listen again and answer the questions.

1 Which country is good at football?
2 Why isn't a football a good object to choose?
3 What did the children study about Russia last term?
4 What object do they think about for Italy?
5 How many other dolls are there in Laura's Russian doll?

65 9 Listen again and tick the expressions you hear.

USEFUL LANGUAGE

Helping others to speak	Interrupting politely
Do we all agree?	Excuse me
What about you?	Can I say something?
Come on!	Pardon?
Why?	

10 Complete the conversation with some of the phrases from the *Useful language* box.

Ali: I think we should choose a small country. **(1)** ...., Jamie?
Jamie: I'm not sure. Maybe a big country is better.
Ali: **(2)** ....?
Jamie: Because people in the future will know more about a big country.
Lily: **(3)** ....? I think it's better to choose a country with interesting history.
Ali: Sorry, Lily. We didn't ask your opinion.
Lily: Thanks, Ali. Then we can choose an object from its history.
Jamie: Good idea.

PROJECT *A time capsule*

You are going to make a time capsule that you will open in two years' time.

- Work in small groups.
- In your group discuss these questions:
  - What will you make the time capsule with: a box, a bag, a tin?
  - How will you decorate it? Will you write anything on it?
  - Where will you keep it? Remember, in two years you are going to open it.
  - What will you put in it?

Draw your time capsule and present it to the rest of the class.

REVIEW 2 UNITS 5–8

VOCABULARY

1 Use the correct form of *get*, *go* or *take* to complete the sentences.

1 At our school, we ______ exams at the end of every term.
2 Last summer, we ______ paddle boarding when we were on holiday. It was amazing!
3 I ______ back from school at about 5.30 every day.
4 My friends ______ sailing this afternoon at the activity centre.
5 Our flight was at 6.00 in the morning, so we ______ up at 3.00.
6 ______ the third turning on the left after the supermarket. That's the quickest way to my house.
7 My friends ______ lost in the mountains, but another hiker found them.
8 Next year, we can ______ another language and another science subject.
9 I think I prefer ______ kite surfing to waterskiing.

2 Put the words in the correct column.

air conditioning bookcase compass cotton first-aid kit fridge gold heating leather map metal plastic roof silver sleeping bag stairs tent torch

Materials	Home	Adventure

3 Match the school subjects in the box to the pictures 1–10.

biology chemistry drama foreign languages geography history ICT maths PE physics

1 ______

2 ______

3 ______
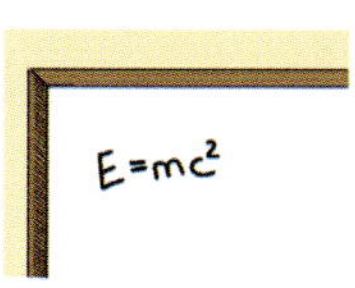

4 ______
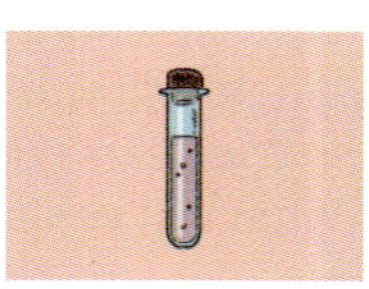
5 ______
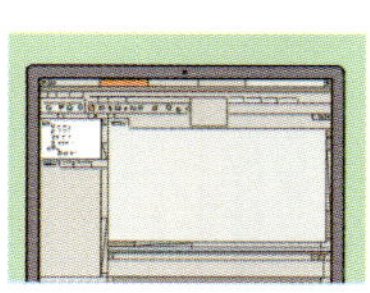
6 ______

7 ______
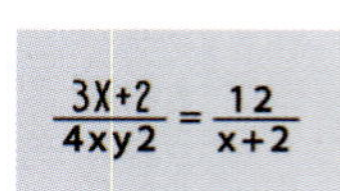

8 ______

9 ______
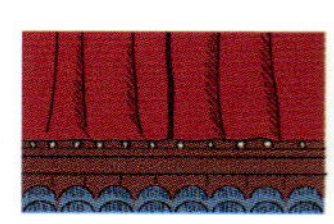
10 ______

GRAMMAR

1 Choose the correct words to complete the sentences.

1 She is very *good* / *well* at climbing.
2 You have to bring a pencil and an *art's* / *art* book.
3 We *meet* / *are meeting* at 5 pm tomorrow.
4 How was *you* / *your* dinner yesterday?

Correct the mistakes in these sentences.

5 I went to the beach and swam with parents, then we flew a kite.
6 I want to be a friend of him because he is funny.
7 I going to Mexico to visit Manuela, a friend.
8 We are meeting at the park at two o'clock because before that I going to the dentist's.

2 Put the words in brackets in the correct order to make sentences.

1 ______ (will / brother / study / My) drama when he's older.
2 ______ (It / not / might / snow) tomorrow.
3 ______ (may / We / not / get) lost if we follow the path.
4 ______ (visit / you / Will) your grandparents at the weekend?
5 What time ______ (will / get / they) back?
6 ______ (I / take / may / not) my camera on the school trip.
7 ______ (might / People / share) cars in the future.
8 What ______ (we / will / learn) in today's English lesson?

3 Complete the sentences with the correct adverb form of the adjective in brackets.

1 Please write your name ______ (clear) on the exam paper.
2 Our team didn't win on Saturday. I played ______ (bad) of all!
3 You have to speak ______ (loud) than that. No one can hear you.
4 Usain Bolt ran ______ (fast) of all the runners in the 2016 Olympic Games.
5 Our new television works ______ (good).
6 My dad had an accident last year. Now he drives ______ (careful) than before.
7 My baby brother smiles ______ (happy) of all the babies I know.
8 Fred usually gets up ______ (early) than his twin brother.

PREPARE FOR THE EXAM

Reading Part 4

1 **For each question, choose the correct answer.**

Bill Gates

Bill Gates was born on 28th October 1955. He **(1)** ________ reading as a child and did very well in maths and science at school. He went to Harvard University to study law in 1973, but he **(2)** ________ more time on computers than in the classroom. In 1975, he left university without **(3)** ________ his studies and started Microsoft with his friend Paul Allen. Microsoft grew quickly to **(4)** ________ one of the biggest companies in the world and soon Bill Gates was one of the world's richest men. In 1994, he married Melinda French in Hawaii. Six years **(5)** ________, he and his wife started the Bill and Melinda Gates Foundation because they wanted to do good things with their money. This company **(6)** ________ people all over the world with health and education.

	A	B	C
1	**A** wanted	**B** enjoyed	**C** hoped
2	**A** spent	**B** made	**C** took
3	**A** closing	**B** finishing	**C** testing
4	**A** go	**B** happen	**C** become
5	**A** later	**B** soon	**C** next
6	**A** sees	**B** gives	**C** helps

Speaking Part 2

2 **Work with a partner. You are going to talk about the six homes in the pictures. Discuss these questions with your partner. Take turns to speak.**

Section 1

1 Do you like these different homes? Why / Why not?

2 Do you think
- sleeping in a tent is comfortable?
- staying on a mountain is dangerous?
- living near water is unusual?
- making a home from a bus is difficult?
- sleeping in a tree house is fun?

Section 2

3 Which is better? A small home or a large home? Why?

4 Which is better? A home on land or on the water? Why?

5 Which is better? A home you can move or a home that stays in one place? Why?

Listening Part 4

67

3 **For each question, choose the correct answer.**

1 You will hear a teacher talking to students about a school trip. What do they need to bring?
A some snacks
B a torch
C their walking boots

2 You will hear a girl talking about her history homework. What does she say about it?
A She didn't understand it.
B She didn't finish it.
C She didn't have her book.

3 You will hear a woman talking to her son. What is she most unhappy about?
A He didn't eat his breakfast.
B He missed the bus.
C He got up late.

4 You will hear two friends talking about a visit to the sports centre. What did they do there?
A They had a snack.
B They played tennis.
C They went swimming.

5 You will hear a man talking to his daughter. What's the weather like at the moment?
A It's raining.
B It's windy.
C It's sunny.

9 SPORTS, GAMES AND ACTIVITIES

ABOUT YOU

How many sports can you name?
Which ones do you do at your school?
Do you play video games?
Which are your favourites?

VOCABULARY AND READING

Sports and activities

1 Match the words in the box to photos A–O.

EP

badminton	board game		
card game	climbing	cricket	
dance class	diving	fishing	
fitness class	golf	karate	puzzle
skateboarding	skiing	video game	

68 Listen and check. Then repeat.

2 Look at the photos in Exercise 1 again. In pairs, decide which activities need special equipment or a sports kit.

3 Write about your favourite sport or activity, using the ideas below.

number of players
sports kit special equipment
how you play who wins

4 Read Max's message and the climbing club rules. Answer the questions.

1 What sort of club is Cool Zone?
2 What does Max want his friend to do?
3 Can you climb? If not, would you like to learn?
4 What sports clubs are there in your school or local area? Do you belong to any of them?

I belong to Cool Zone climbing club now! You don't have to be a member to climb there, but it's cheaper if you are. Why don't you become a member too? It's really easy to join. I just had to fill in a form and agree to the club rules. I didn't have to bring a photo – they took one of me there and made my membership card. Max

COOL ZONE
Climbing Centre Rules

69

1. You must show your membership card every time you come.
2. You must not lend your membership card to anyone else.
3. You do not have to bring your own climbing shoes.
4. You must not talk to people when they are climbing.
5. You must not take photos or record videos.
6. If you are under 12, you must climb with an adult.
7. You must climb with a partner if you are a beginner.
8. You do not have to book if you come on a weekday.
9. You must not stand under people when they are climbing.
10. If you have an accident, you must tell a member of staff.

GRAMMAR *must, mustn't, have to, don't have to*

1 Underline the examples of *must*, *must not*, *have to* and *don't have to* in the club rules on page 54. Match sentences 1–4 to meanings a–c. Use one of the meanings twice.

1 You must do this.
2 You have to do this.
3 You mustn't (must not) do this.
4 You don't have to do this.

a Do not do this.
b It's not necessary to do this.
c It's necessary to do this.

2 Underline the main verb after *must* and *have to*. Is it the infinitive with *to* or without *to*?

The past of *must* and *have to* is *had to*.
I had to fill in a form.

The past of *don't have to* is *didn't have to*.
I didn't have to bring in a photo.

» GRAMMAR REFERENCE AND PRACTICE PAGE 155

3 Read the climbing club rules again and answer the questions.

1 Is it OK for your friend to use your membership card?
2 Can you chat to your friends while climbing?
3 Can you take photos in the club?
4 Is it OK to climb alone if you are 14?
5 Is it necessary to book if you go on a Monday?
6 Can you stand under people when they are climbing?

4 Read the dance class rules. Rewrite them using *must*, *mustn't* and *don't have to*.

1 Don't chew gum or bring food into the class.
2 Don't talk while the teacher is talking.
3 Special clothes are not necessary.
4 Put your phone on silent during the lesson.
5 Don't leave a class before the end.
6 Don't wear street shoes inside the dance studio.
7 It's not necessary to call if you need to miss a class.
8 Take off all jewellery before class.

5 Last week, there was a swimming competition. Write sentences about what people had to do and what they didn't have to do.

0 Cost: £5 to enter the competition.
They had to pay £5 to enter the competition.
1 Arrive at the pool at 8.30 am.
2 Wear a swimming hat.
3 You can wear goggles if you want, but it's not necessary.
4 Bring sandwiches for lunch.
5 Last race at 6 pm. Not necessary to stay until 6 pm.

6 Think of eight things you had to / didn't have to do last week. Then ask and answer with a partner.

I had to clean my room.

I had to finish my geography project.

Did you have to … ?

Yes, I did.

7 Correct the mistakes in the sentences.

1 The skatepark is free – we haven't to pay anything.
2 You must to bring your pencil case to the next lesson.
3 We mustn't bring food to the party – Jake's mum is making everything.
4 When I was younger, I must live far away from my grandparents.
5 Dad says I mustn't help him on Saturday, so I can come to your house!

PRONUNCIATION *must and mustn't*

70 **8** Listen and repeat.

You must listen carefully. /məs/
You mustn't speak now. /mʌsnt/

71 **9** For each sentence, put a (✓) if you hear *must* and a (✗) if you hear *mustn't*.

1 .... 2 .... 3 ....
4 .... 5 .... 6 ....
7 ....

71 Listen again and repeat.

10 » Work with a partner. Go to page 137.

READING

1 Look at the photos. What do you think is happening? Who do you think the people in the photos are? Read the article quickly to check your ideas.

72

Playing a good video game is an exciting experience. Games are full of light, sound, action and surprises, and this makes them fun to watch as well as to play. Because of this, more and more people are taking part in eSports. This is the short name for electronic sports – playing video games against other people in competitions. There are huge tournaments all over the world, where big crowds watch matches on giant screens, and millions more watch online.

Just like many normal sports, eSports players usually play in teams, and have fans who follow them through every competition. Prizes for important eSports competitions are very large, and eSports champions can earn more than £1 million a year. That makes it sound like a great job, but in fact it's not easy to be a winner. Players have to practise for up to 14 hours a day, so they don't get much rest. The games they play change often and there are always new things to learn.

ESports stars are not well known in the way that some football stars are. However, some top eSports players now work for real football teams. For example, Koen Weijland, a professional player of the football video game FIFA, is part of Ajax, a famous Dutch football team. As a little boy he wanted to be a footballer and was a big fan of Ajax, so for him this is like a dream come true. And who knows, maybe one day, eSports stars like him will be as famous as today's top footballers.

PREPARE FOR THE EXAM

Reading Part 3

2 For each question, choose the correct answer.

1 What does the writer say about eSports in the first paragraph?
 - **A** They are more fun to watch than to play.
 - **B** They are becoming more popular.
 - **C** Most people don't understand them.

2 What is hard for top eSports players?
 - **A** They don't have a lot of free time.
 - **B** They don't make much money.
 - **C** They get bored of playing video games.

3 What is the writer doing in the third paragraph?
 - **A** explaining why eSports stars are not famous
 - **B** showing how eSports and normal sports can come together
 - **C** describing the daily life of an eSports star

4 What is a 'dream come true' for Koen Weijland?
 - **A** meeting some famous footballers
 - **B** winning a video game competition
 - **C** working for his favourite football team

5 What is the best title for this article?
 - **A** Are eSports a good thing?
 - **B** The history of eSports
 - **C** What are eSports?

3 In small groups, ask and answer the questions.

1 Do you play video games? If yes, which ones?
2 Would you like to watch an eSports competition? Why / Why not?
3 Do you know any eSports stars?
4 Do you think eSports is a good name for these competitions? Why / Why not?

VOCABULARY Sports vocabulary; Suffix -*er*

1 **Find these words in the article, then match them to the definitions.**

EP

1 take part
2 tournament
3 fan
4 prize
5 champion
6 professional

a This person or team comes first in a competition.
b This person loves a sports star or team.
c This describes a person who earns money for something most people do as a hobby.
d This is a competition that includes several matches or games.
e You sometimes get this if you do well in a competition.
f This means to join other people in an activity.

2 **Find these words in the text: *winner*, *player*, *footballer*. What do they mean?**

We can add -*er* to some verbs and nouns to make a person. If the spelling is vowel + consonant + vowel, you must double the last letter before adding -*er*.
win – winner
If the word already ends in *e*, add -*r*

3 **Make people from these words.**

EP

clean climb dance dive golf photograph run sing ski swim teach work

4 **Make some sentences using at least one word from Exercise 1 and at least one word from Exercise 3. In pairs, compare your sentences.**

There were lots of photographers at the sports tournament.

LISTENING

73 **1** **You will hear a girl called Lily talking to her dad about eSports and mind sports. Which of these words do you think you will hear? Listen once and tick the ones you hear.**

board games body brain card games chess competition equipment football medal prize Olympics tournament video games

73 **2** **Read the sentences, then listen again. Decide if each sentence is right (✓) or wrong (✗).**

1 Lily explains to Dad what eSports are.
2 Dad thinks it's a good idea to have mind sports in the Olympics.
3 Lily says fitness is the most important thing for sportspeople.
4 Dad agrees that thinking is important in sport.
5 Lily says some chess competitions are more famous than the Olympics.
6 Dad and Lily both think that Olympic medals are special.
7 Dad and Lily both think that chess will be in the Olympics one day.

TALKING POINTS

07 **Watch the video and ask and answer the questions.**

What board games do you have at home?
How often do you play board games?
Do you like playing chess? Are you good at it?
Do you think that games like chess should be in the Olympics? Why? / Why not?

SPEAKING

1 **In small groups, talk about the sentences. Say if you agree with them or if you don't and say why. Use the phrases in the box to help you.**

1 eSports are not sports because you don't have to be fit to do them.
2 It's a good idea to have eSports in the Olympics.
3 Thinking and using your brain is important in every sport.
4 Mind sports will be in the Olympics in ten years' time.

I think / I don't think …
I agree / I don't agree …
I suppose so …
I see!
That's true.
I'm not sure.
Maybe

10 USEFUL WEBSITES

VOCABULARY AND READING

Relationships

? ABOUT YOU

Do your friends or family ever have problems? What kind?

What do you do when you have a problem? Who do you talk to? Do you often try to find advice online?

1 Read the problems on the website. In pairs, discuss the problems and think of some advice for each person.

TEEN TROUBLES

Got a problem and not sure who to ask for advice? Write to us and we will help! When you see this 🔊, click to hear some advice from Dr Mandy, our top teen expert! 🔊 74

I go to dance lessons with some close friends of mine. The teacher moved me to a higher-level group, but she says my friends have to stay in the lower level. I'm worried about moving to a new class without them. I'll really miss seeing them! What should I do? 🔊

Andrea, 13

I am homeschooled and I don't spend much time with people my age. I am friends with some of my neighbours, and I have old friends from primary school, but they often forget to invite me when they go out. I have penfriends as well, but it's not the same as seeing people. 🔊

Ben, 15

My best friend won't stop copying me! I love wearing bright clothes and looking different from everyone else. But last month my friend started buying all the same things as me. Now we look exactly the same as each other! 🔊

Katy, 14

🔊 75 **2** Listen to Dr Mandy giving three pieces of advice to the teenagers. Write the correct name beside each number.

1 .... 2 .... 3 ....

🔊 75 **3** Listen again and make notes about the advice for each person. Was any of the advice the same as yours?

4 Match the people 1–10 to the descriptions a–j.

EP

1 guest	a You live near this person.
2 old friend	b This person is a visitor in your home.
3 neighbour	c You have this person's details in your phone or online.
4 close friend	d This person belongs to a group or club.
5 member	e You like this person very much and you know each other well.
6 contact	f You met this person a long time ago.
7 best friend	g This person is part of your family.
8 classmate	h This is your one special friend.
9 penfriend	i You study with this person.
10 relative	j You don't meet this person, but you write to them.

🔊 76 Listen and check. Then repeat.

5 In pairs, ask and answer the questions. Then write three more questions.

1 How many contacts do you have online?
2 Are you friendly with your neighbours?
3 How many of your relatives live near you?
4 Who do you miss when you go away on holiday?

6 With a different partner, ask and answer your new questions together.

PRONUNCIATION *gh*

7 Listen to the words and repeat them. Then put them into the correct column.

bright caught daughter
enough flight neighbour
right straight thought

/aɪ/	/eɪ/	/ʌf/	/ɔː/
night	eight	rough	bought

Listen and check. Then repeat.

GRAMMAR Verb patterns: gerunds and infinitives

1 Look at the example sentences. Then complete the rules about verb patterns.

I'm worried about moving to a new class.
You'll get better at dancing.
Thank you for writing to the website.

Try to talk to her about how you feel.
If you decide to do this, you can give her advice.
They often forget to invite me when they go out.

My best friend won't stop copying me.
I'll really miss seeing them.

1 We use the **gerund** (*-ing* form) after prepositions: *about* , ________ , ________ (also *by*, *of*, *with*, etc.)
2 We use the **infinitive** + *to* after some verbs: *try* , ________ , ________ (also *choose*, *learn*, *hope*, *plan*, *need*, *want*)
3 We can use the **gerund** after some verbs: *stop* , ________ (also *finish*, *don't mind*)
4 We can use either the **gerund** or the **infinitive** after these verbs: *start*, *begin*, *enjoy*, *like*, *love*, *prefer*.

2 Look at three more examples. What form do we use when the verb is the subject of a sentence?

Studying alone isn't easy.
Leaving your friends behind is difficult.
Waiting for them to contact you first isn't always a good idea.

GRAMMAR REFERENCE AND PRACTICE PAGE 156

3 Choose the correct form of the verb. In one sentence, both forms are possible.

1 My friend decided *buy* / *to buy* a new pair of sunglasses.
2 *Wait*/ *Waiting* for people makes me angry.
3 I helped the teacher by *carry* / *carrying* her books.
4 One day, I hope *to be* / *being* a doctor.
5 *Swim* / *Swimming* in the sea on a hot day is lovely.
6 I don't mind *to sit* / *sitting* by the window.
7 I think *to run* / *running* is the best kind of exercise.
8 Everyone loves *to get* / *getting* presents!
9 I'm thinking of *get* / *getting* a new poster for my room.
10 *Saving* / *Save* a bit of pocket money every week is a really good idea.

4 Correct the mistakes in the sentences.

1 I hope see you very soon, and I hope that you like my mobile phone.
2 I want write about my life.
3 I like play computer games best.
4 You can get to my house taking the number 6 bus.
5 I think it's better to finish study before we go out.
6 Would you mind come with me to the shops?

5 Complete each sentence with a verb from the box in the gerund or infinitive.

chat	come	eat	go	improve
pass	play	spend	watch	make

1 We need ________ a cake, but we don't know how to do it.
2 ________ chocolate isn't very good for you.
3 I need ________ the marks I get in maths. Mine are terrible.
4 ________ TV late at night makes you tired the next day.
5 I'm angry with my neighbour for ________ his music really late at night.
6 ________ my exam is very important to me.
7 Jack didn't want ________ to my party.
8 ________ with friends is really good fun.
9 My best friend spends all her free time ________ to the shops with the new girl in our class.
10 ________ a lot of time indoors is quite boring.

6 In groups of three, each person writes a few sentences about a problem. Listen to each other's problems and give advice. Who has the most interesting problem? Who gives the best advice?

READING

1 Tick (✓) the things you use websites and apps for.

- playing games ☐
- watching videos ☐
- chatting to friends ☐
- finding information ☐
- doing schoolwork ☐
- reading articles ☐
- listening to music ☐
- sharing photos, stories, etc. ☐

2 What are your three favourite websites or apps? In pairs, compare your answers.

3 Read what the people say. Which of the activities in Exercise 1 do they want to do?

1 I'm working on a project about the human body at the moment and I'm interested in learning about animals. I like having fun online too.

2 I'm hoping to become a writer one day. I'd like to put my stories online and discuss ideas with people my age.

3 I like to know what is happening in the world. I'm also interested in music and would like to learn more about my favourite stars.

4 I'm interested in nature and wildlife and want to learn about ways to help the planet. I like making short films and want to share them with others.

4 Read about six websites and decide which is best for each person. In pairs, compare your answers.

79

SIX GREAT WEBSITES FOR TEENAGERS

A EcoCentral

This **site** is all about looking after the Earth. There are facts about different animals as well as information about forests, deserts and oceans. You can **upload** your own videos onto the site for everyone to see.

B TeenPress

This is one of the best sites on **the web** for teenagers who love writing. You can share your work with others, and there is a **message board** where you can chat about things that are important to you.

C ChannelTwenty

On this site, you can watch a daily news programme and **search** for information about big news stories. There are also videos on different subjects, articles about famous bands, games and competitions. The app is free and works on all kinds of smartphones.

D ScienceZone

There's lots of information on this site about maths, chemistry and biology. You can 'visit' some of the world's most famous museums and watch wildlife via webcams. There are also some very cool games, such as *Save the Planet*.

E Tune-in

There are millions of songs on this site for you to **download** or listen to online. You can **save** your favourite songs in your own list. If you're in a band, you can **record** your music and upload it. The website is large, but the **menu** is easy to use. The app that goes with it is excellent.

F Inside-the-cover

Finding out about your favourite writers is easy on this site. There are lots of interesting articles and information about the latest books. You can read **blogs** by well-known writers and **post** questions and messages to them. There are **links** to other sites too.

VOCABULARY Internet nouns and verbs

1 EP **Look at the words in the texts on page 60. Find six nouns and six verbs.**

Match the nouns to definitions 1–6.

1 This is all the pages online that you can visit.
2 You can write things here for others to read and reply to.
3 If you click on these, they take you to another website.
4 This is another way of saying 'website'.
5 These are online diaries.
6 You look at this list to choose which part of a website to visit.

Use the verbs to complete the sentences.

7 You can .... a short voice message and then share it with friends.
8 You can .... for information online by typing a word into a box.
9 You can .... a message or question on the internet for others to read.
10 You can .... a file from your computer onto a website.
11 You can .... a file from the internet to your computer.
12 You can .... a document or other file on your computer so you don't lose it.

80 **Listen and check. Then repeat.**

PREPARE FOR THE EXAM

Reading Part 4

2 **For each question, choose the correct answer.**

Catherine Cook

Catherine Cook was only 15 when she started myYearbook.com. She had the idea of creating a new **(1)** .... to help people find friends. She also had lots of great ideas about how to make myYearbook.com different from everything else on the **(2)** ....

myYearbook.com is now called MeetMe.com. When you join, you fill in a form and **(3)** .... a photo of yourself to the site. After that, you can start **(4)** .... for friends to add. It's not difficult to explore the site and **(5)** .... people. You can play games, post **(6)** .... , do quizzes and more. It's available on the web and as an app.

	A	B	C
1	website	computer	file
2	information	link	internet
3	record	upload	copy
4	searching	finding	missing
5	talk	contact	speak
6	screens	menus	messages

LISTENING

81 **1** **Listen to three young app developers talking about their work. Match each speaker to what the app they made helps you do.**

Speaker 1 — **a** use your time well
Speaker 2 — **b** learn things
Speaker 3 — **c** play games

81 **2** **Listen again and complete the table.**

	Speaker		
	1	2	3
How old was each person when they wrote their first app?			
How much is it?			
How many people download it per week?			
What can you do on the app?			

WRITING

PREPARE TO WRITE

Writing Part 6 An email

GET READY **Count how many times these phrases are used to start sentences in the texts in Reading Exercise 4. Then find three other ways of starting sentences in the texts.**

1 There is / There are …
2 You can …
3 This …

PLAN **You are going to reply to this email from your penfriend.**

To:
From: Sal
Reply Forward

Tell me about your favourite website or app. What's it called? What can you do on it? Why do you like it?

Make notes to help you answer each question.

WRITE **Write your email. Use the descriptions of the websites in Reading Exercise 4 to help you. Try to begin each sentence with a different phrase.**

Begin *Dear Sal*, and end with your name.

IMPROVE **In pairs, read each other's emails. Check that you both included all the information from your plan and that you started each sentence with a different phrase.**

» PREPARE FOR THE EXAM PAGE 126

CULTURE

THE BEAUTIFUL GAME

1 **Discuss the questions with your partner.**

1. Do you like playing or watching football?
2. Do many girls and women play football in your country?
3. Do you ever watch girls or women playing football on TV or live?

2 **What can you see in the photos? Read the text and check your ideas. Match the photos A–D to the paragraphs 1–4.**

A SPORT FOR ALL?

82

1 In 1920, there was a match between two women's football teams at Everton's football ground in Liverpool. Around 53,000 people went to watch it! Just a few years earlier, during the First World War, many men were fighting abroad. This meant there were no football players and no important games. People loved the sport and wanted to watch it, so women started to play. Some of the best players, such as Lily Parr, are still famous today. She became famous when she was only 14 and scored 43 goals in one season.

2 A year later, in 1921, the Football Association (FA) decided to stop women's football because they thought it was not a sport that women should play for payment. Fifty years later, in 1971, women could finally play football as a profession and not just as a hobby. However, it wasn't until 1993 that the English FA recognised international women's football. After that, women could play in competitions with other countries.

3 Nowadays, nearly three million girls and women play football in the UK, and there are 100,000 registered players who can play official tournaments. There are only about 200 professional players, and many have to do other work to earn enough money, but you can often see women's football on television. They sometimes play in really famous places, such as Wembley Stadium in London.

4 In schools, girls and boys play football in the playground – there are teams with both boy and girl players. Recently, all-girl teams are playing against all-boy teams. So football is really a sport for everyone!

A

B

C

3 Read the text again and answer the questions.

1 How many people went to watch the women's football match in Liverpool in 1920?
2 Why did many women start playing football during the First World War?
3 Why did women stop playing football after 1921?
4 When did the Football Association in England allow women to play in international competitions?
5 Do professional women players receive a lot of money nowadays?
6 Do boys and girls always play in separate football teams?

4 Match the highlighted words in the text to the definitions.

1 three words for a place or places where people can play football
2 two words for football competitions
3 one word that means 'job'

TALKING POINTS

Are some sports in your country only for girls or only for boys? Which ones are played only by girls or only by boys?

5 Look at the table about different types of football. In pairs, try to complete the gaps.

	When people first played it	Number of players	Indoors or outdoors	Where people play it most
Table football	1	Usually two or four	Indoors	Europe and the USA
Futsal	1930	ten (five in each team)	2	South America and 3 ....
FIFA video game	4	Maximum 8	5	All over the world
Football for the blind	1920s	6	Both indoors and outdoors	7 ....

83 Listen and check. Complete the information you didn't know.

D

PROJECT *The history of a sport*

Find out about the history of a sport in your country. Make a poster to present the information to the class. Use pictures and photos to make the poster more interesting. Include information about:

- when and where it started
- who plays the sport: only men, only women or both
- some famous teams or players
- what competitions there are for this sport

Present your poster to the class.

08 NOW WATCH THE CULTURE VIDEO

11 CITY LIVING

ABOUT YOU

What are the three biggest cities in your country?
What are they famous for?
What's good or bad about living in cities?

VOCABULARY AND LISTENING

Places in a city

1 **Think about what can you do at the places in the box. Write five questions. Then test your partner.**

café church hospital library
museum park police station
post office restaurant shop
sports centre theatre train station
university

Where do you go to buy a stamp?

A post office. What do you use a bridge for?

2 **Match the words in the box to photos A–L.**

EP

art gallery cathedral embassy
fountain mosque old town palace
shopping area skyscraper stadium
statue temple

84 **Listen and check.**

3 **In pairs, talk about the city where you live, or your capital city. What things from Exercises 1 and 2 does it have? What are their names?**

4 **What countries are these cities in? Which are capital cities? What are they famous for?**

Beijing Cairo London Madrid
Mexico City Mumbai New Delhi
New York Paris Rio de Janeiro
Rome San Francisco Tokyo

85 **5** **Listen to the quiz. Match the questions to the names of the cities.**

Question 1	Mumbai
Question 2	Tokyo
Question 3	Rio de Janeiro
Question 4	Paris
Question 5	New York
Question 6	Beijing

85 **6** **Read the sentences and write the name of the city. Then listen again and check.**

1 It's the largest city in the world.
2 Every year, there's a big carnival here.
3 Lots of films are made here.
4 The city has a lot of bridges.
5 The Olympic Games were in this city in 2016.
6 It has a statue that's known around the world.
7 It's the second-biggest city in China.
8 Its most famous cathedral is on an island.

GRAMMAR Determiners

1 **Read the sentences in Exercise 6 on page 64 again and underline all the examples of *a/an* and *the*. Choose the correct word to complete the rules.**

We use ***the*** / ***a/an*** to introduce something for the first time.
We use ***the*** / ***a/an*** to talk about something already mentioned; with superlatives; if there is only one in the world; in front of *first*, *second*, etc.

2 **Complete the email with *the* or *a/an*.**

To: Camilla
From: Rosa
Reply Forward

I'm having **(1)** _______ great holiday in Rome with my family! Today we visited **(2)** _______ Colosseum, and we went to **(3)** _______ fantastic museum called MAXXI. Afterwards, my brother and I each had **(4)** _______ ice cream in **(5)** _______ city centre. We both said it was **(6)** _______ best ice cream in **(7)** _______ world! Tomorrow, we're going to see **(8)** _______ Trevi Fountain and also **(9)** _______ palace – but I can't remember which one. Rome is **(10)** _______ really wonderful city!

ə PRONUNCIATION *the*

86 **3** **Listen and repeat. When do we say /ðiː/ and when do we say /ðə/?**

/ðiː/ the	/ðə/ the
the oldest	the youngest
the east	the north
the Atlantic Ocean	the Pacific Ocean
the Olympic Games	the World Cup

4 **Put the words into the correct column in the table.**

the apple	the Arctic
the dog	the Earth
the Indian Ocean	the North Sea
the orange	the River Nile
the Statue of Liberty	the umbrella

87 **Listen and check. Then repeat.**

5 **Read the examples below and underline all the examples of *all*, *both*, *other* and *another*. Choose the correct word to complete the rules.**

All the questions are about cities.
Are you all ready?
The city has both beaches and museums.
Central Park and Times Square are both popular.
There are many other great places to visit.
The other famous thing here is the statue of Jesus.
There's another beautiful church in the city.

We use ***all*** / ***both*** to talk about two things.
We use ***all*** / ***both*** to talk about a total number of things.
Another / ***Other*** means 'one more'.

» GRAMMAR REFERENCE AND PRACTICE PAGE 157

6 **Complete the text about Australian cities with *all*, *both*, *other* and *another*. Use each word twice.**

Australian cities have a lot to offer visitors to the country. **(1)** _______ visitors to Australia should go to Sydney. It's the largest and oldest city in the country, and **(2)** _______ the Opera House and Harbour Bridge are important world-famous monuments. **(3)** _______ popular cities are Perth, Brisbane and Cairns.

Cairns is in Queensland, in the northeast of Australia. From this city, you can enjoy **(4)** _______ the rainforest and the ocean, including the Great Barrier Reef. **(5)** _______ thing you can do in Cairns is learn **(6)** _______ about the culture of the Aboriginal people of Australia.

Melbourne is **(7)** _______ great Australian city. It has excellent museums and also a modern arts centre. Phillip Island is not far from Melbourne, and you can see koalas, penguins, kangaroos and many **(8)** _______ animals here.

7 **Correct the mistakes in the sentences.**

1 It's a biggest museum in my town.
2 It's not boring like others computer games.
3 The T-shirts cost both £15.
4 This phone has very good screen and camera.
5 I went to park and I played football with my friends.
6 We went on holiday to the Edinburgh.

8 **In pairs, write a city quiz.**

- Choose three cities.
- Write some notes about each one.
- Describe the cities to another pair of students.
- Can they guess your cities? Can you guess theirs?

READING

1 Look at the signs, notices and messages. For 1–4, where would you see them? For 5 and 6, where is the writer? Match each sign to a place in the box.

at school	in a shop	by a river
at a train station	in a café	on a website

1

2

3

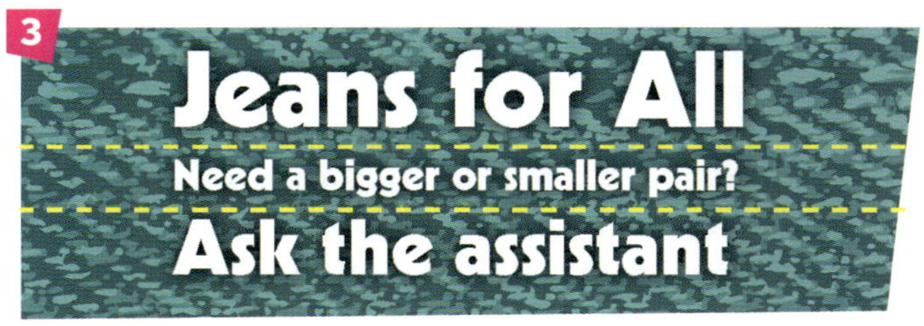

4

5

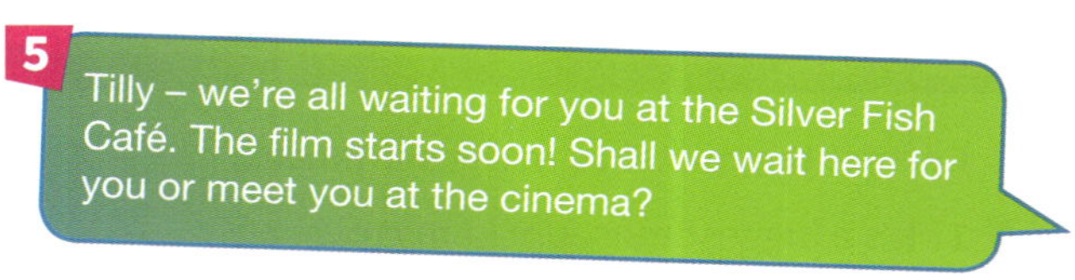

6

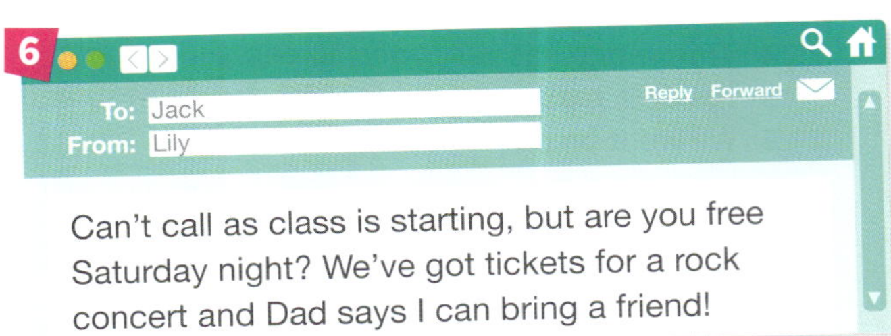

PREPARE FOR THE EXAM

Reading Part 1

2 **For questions 1–6, choose the correct answer. In pairs, compare your answers and say why you chose the answer you did.**

1 **A** Children cannot come here without an adult.
B It's not possible to see the animals all year.
C Summer prices are lower than winter ones.

2 **A** There's one trip in the morning and another in the afternoon.
B Go online to get more information about the boat trips.
C One of the boat trips is longer than the other.

3 **A** Some of these jeans aren't available in all sizes.
B The assistant can tell you which size looks best.
C Staff here can help you find the right size.

4 **A** You can leave your suitcases here.
B You must arrive early to leave your bag.
C If you have two bags, you get a discount on the smaller one.

5 What must Tilly do now?
A Go to the cinema as quickly as possible.
B Let her friends know what to do next.
C Stay where she is until her friends arrive.

6 Why did Lily write this message?
A to give Jack some bad news about the concert on Saturday
B to tell Jack to get a ticket for the concert
C to invite Jack to a concert

» PREPARE FOR THE EXAM PAGE 120

TALKING POINTS

09 Watch the video and ask and answer the questions.

What's your favourite city?
Why do you like it there?
Is there anything you don't like about it?
What places in your city do you go to regularly and why?

VOCABULARY Uncountable nouns

1 EP **Complete the table. Match the uncountable nouns in the box to the countable nouns in the table.**

electricity food ~~furniture~~
homework information
jewellery luggage money
news staff traffic wildlife

Countable	Uncountable
1 desk	*furniture*
2 project	
3 article	
4 car	
5 coin	
6 meal	
7 battery	
8 details	
9 animals	
10 shop assistant	
11 suitcase	
12 necklace	

2 Complete the sentences with the countable or uncountable form of the words in the table in Exercise 1.

1 I haven't got much ________ in my room – just a bed and a chair.
2 I've got two science ________ to finish this weekend!
3 There's an interesting ________ about Rihanna in this magazine.
4 There's too much ________ on the streets in my town.
5 Have you got a 50p ________? I need it for the drinks machine.
6 Mum prepared a lot of ________ for our picnic.
7 Dad says my new radio doesn't use much ________.
8 You can find all the ________ you need about the competition on the website.
9 The number of ________ in Africa is going down.
10 I couldn't find a member of ________ to help me.
11 I took a really small ________ when I went on holiday.
12 My sister gave me a lovely piece of ________ for my birthday.

3 » **Work with a partner.** **Go to page 137.**

LISTENING

1 Read the six conversations. Which conversations do pictures A and B show?

A

B

1 **A:** Hi. Can I help you?
B: (1) ________ go bowling this afternoon.
A: Ah, **(2)** ________ we're closing in ten minutes. Come back tomorrow morning.
B: Oh, OK. Thanks.

2 **A:** Excuse me. **(3)** ________ open the door for me?
B: (4) ________. There you are.
A: Thanks!

3 **A: (5)** ________ leave my guitar here while I go round the museum?
B: (6) ________. You need to put it in the cloakroom. It's over there, next to the shop.
A: Thank you.

4 **A:** Excuse me. **(7)** ________ open the window? It's really hot in here.
B: (8) ________. I'm hot too!

5 **A:** Excuse me. **(9)** ________ the way to the skatepark?
B: (10) ________. Walk along this road for about 100 metres, then turn left. You'll see the park on your right.
A: Great! Thanks very much.

6 **A:** Excuse me. **(11)** ________ have a can of lemonade, please?
B: (12) ________. That's £1.50, please.

2 Complete the conversations with the phrases from the box.

Can you tell me Could I
Could you Do you mind if I
I'd like to I'm afraid not
I'm sorry, but Is it OK if I
No problem Of course
Sure That's fine

89 **Listen and check. In pairs, practise the conversations.**

SPEAKING

1 In pairs, write three new conversations. For each conversation choose:

- a different place – shop / café / park / tourist information office, etc.
- a different request – something to eat / drink / a ticket / help / advice / directions, etc.

2 Role-play your conversations for the class for them to guess where you are.

12 FILMS

ABOUT YOU

How often do you go to the cinema?
What's your favourite film? Who is in it? What is it about? Why do you like it?

VOCABULARY AND READING

Types of film

1 **Match the types of film in the box to the pictures A–I.**

EP

action film	adventure film	animated film
comedy	drama	horror film
musical	science-fiction film	thriller

90 **Listen and check.**

2 **In groups, answer the questions.**

1 Name an example of each type of movie in Exercise 1.
2 Which is your favourite type of film?
3 What's the worst film you've ever seen? Why didn't you like it?

3 **Read the blog about the 'tricks' movie companies use to make their films into hits. Match the 'tricks' a–e to paragraphs 1–5.**

a Make a movie that might win a prize.
b Make a film that has a story or characters that the audience knows and likes.
c Advertise the movie well.
d Use actors who are really famous.
e Make a film which people will write or talk about.

4 **Read the blog again. Are the sentences right (✓) or wrong (✗)?**

1 Great acting is the most important aspect of a good film.
2 It costs film companies a lot of money to use famous actors.
3 People only use reviews in papers to decide which film to watch.
4 The job of a famous actor includes telling the public how good the film is.
5 Awards can make more people go to see a movie.

5 **In pairs, look at the points in Exercise 3 again and discuss what is most important to you when choosing a film to see.**

WHAT MAKES A MOVIE A HIT?

91

We all know a good film when we see it. It has a great story, excellent photography and wonderful acting. But what makes a good movie into a big hit? This is a question that filmmakers are always asking themselves! Of course, there is no perfect answer. However, movie companies have a few tricks which help make their films become as successful as possible.

1 ....

Some stars have fans who will go and see any movie they are in. Unfortunately, not all movies that have big stars in them are successful, and using famous actors can be expensive!

2 ....

There are lots of movies which come from books, comics, computer games or TV shows. Just think of Harry Potter, Wonder Woman, X-Men, Star Wars, etc. People already love these, so they can't wait to see the film.

3 ....

People often check to see what newspapers or websites are saying about a film before they go and see it. Also, people who love a movie will tell their friends how good it is.

4 ....

This is really important. As well as posters and trailers, most big films will now have a website that gives extra information about the film. Also, when a new film comes out, the stars of the movie usually travel around the world and give interviews to get people interested in the film.

5 ....

Awards like the Oscars and the Golden Globes let people know which films are good to watch. A movie that gets an award often becomes much more popular than before.

GRAMMAR Relative pronouns *who, which, that*

1 **Find and underline the examples of *who*, *which* and *that* in the blog post.**

Choose two words to complete each sentence.

1 We use *who* / *that* / *which* when we talk about people.
2 We use *who* / *that* / *which* when we talk about things.

» GRAMMAR REFERENCE AND PRACTICE PAGE 158

2 **Choose the correct answer for each sentence. Write *A* (*who/that*) or *B* (*which/that*).**

1 I like films ________ make me laugh.
2 I have a friend ________ watches two movies a day during the holidays.
3 There's a cinema near my home ________ is over 100 years old.
4 I know a person ________ knows Jaden Smith.
5 I can't remember the name of the film ________ was on TV last night.
6 There are quite a lot of actors ________ can speak two or more languages.

3 **Choose the correct words to complete the text.**

Cinemas of the future?

In the past, people **(1)** *who* / *which* wanted to see a film had to go to the cinema. That's not true any more, and these days many cinemas can't find enough customers **(2)** *which* / *that* are happy to pay their high ticket prices. That's why some cinemas are starting to try different ideas. There are cinemas **(3)** *which* / *who* have giant beds instead of seats, and one in Malaysia **(4)** *who* / *that* has bean bags. Others have sofas, dining tables or even hot tubs! Some cinemas even show '4D' films. These are 3D films with special effects **(5)** *who* / *that* happen in the cinema at the same time as in the film. These can be rain, wind, smoke and smells. The seats also move around, so you really feel like you are in the movie!

4 **Match the two halves of the sentences and join them with *who* or *which*.**

1 IMAX cinemas are popular with people
2 The cinemas have special seats
3 It's not possible for children
4 You need to wear special glasses
5 Some IMAX cinemas have screens
6 There's a 3-D film called *Bugs*!

a ________ let you see in 3D.
b ________ shows you the world of rainforest insects.
c ________ move, and sometimes you feel wind or water during the film.
d ________ are under 13 to go in alone.
e ________ are as tall as four double-decker buses – about 16 metres.
f ________ like 3-D films.

5 **Correct the mistakes in the sentences.**

1 My favourite colour is blue, so I bought a mobile phone who was blue.
2 There are two windows don't close very well.
3 He told me about something interesting happened in the film.
4 I want to sell a TV who is two years old.
5 It's a music concert it's going to be in São Paulo.
6 There are some great books can help you learn English.

PRONUNCIATION Spelling and syllables

6 (92) **Listen and repeat the words. How many letters does each word have? How many syllables?**

action adventure because
children chocolate cinema
dictionary different horror
interesting medicine
photography sometimes where
which while who

action – 6 letters, 2 syllables

7 » **Work in small groups. Go to page 137.**

Showing today at

STAR CINEMA

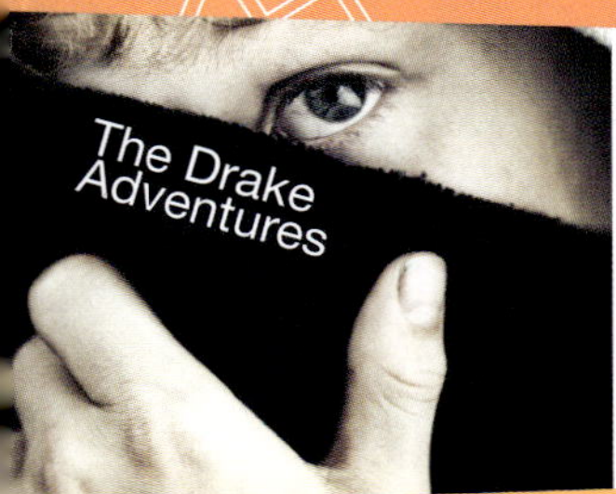

A The Drake Adventures

93

Tom Drake is on holiday with his family, visiting various European cities. He doesn't enjoy sightseeing or museums, so he is really bored and can't wait to go home. But things change when the family visits a castle, where Tom sees two men steal a painting. He is in big trouble when the men come after him. Things get really exciting when Tom finds out who the men are and what their real reason for stealing the painting is.

B Body Swap

Hannah and her brother Chris were good friends when they were little, but now they hate each other. Everyone thinks Hannah is really cool, but no one wants to be Chris's friend, and she says she won't help him. Then, one morning, they wake up in each other's bodies. They have to learn to understand each other better, or they'll stay this way forever. This film will make you laugh till you cry!

C Game, Set and Match

Carly James is a brilliant young tennis player, but has lots of problems in her life. She's not close to her parents because they're often away on business, and she doesn't find schoolwork easy. But while she's preparing for a big competition, she starts working with a new coach. It seems he is the one person who really understands her. He knows that she can be a big star if she listens to him and works hard. Finally, things start to improve for Carly, but can she do well in the competition?

READING

1 **Read about the films on the cinema web page. What type of film do you think each one is?**

PREPARE FOR THE EXAM

Reading Part 2

2 **For each question, choose the correct answer. Write *A* for *The Drake Adventures*, *B* for *Body Swap* or *C* for *Game, Set, Match*.**

1 Which film is about someone who is in danger?
2 Which film is about someone who gets the help she needs?
3 Which film is about someone who isn't very popular?
4 Which film is about someone who might win a prize?
5 Which film is about someone who learns why something happened?
6 Which film is about someone who is happier after meeting someone new?
7 Which film is about someone who doesn't like a family member?

TALKING POINTS

Which of these films would you like to see? Why?
Do you prefer watching films at home or at the cinema? Why?

VOCABULARY Conjunctions

Conjunctions are words that join parts of sentences together.

I enjoy films. I don't like going to the cinema.
*I enjoy films, **but** I don't like going to the cinema.*
I want to go shopping. I haven't got any clothes.
*I want to go shopping **because** I haven't got any clothes.*
I'm having a party on my birthday.
I'm visiting my family on my birthday.
*I'm having a party **and** I'm visiting my family on my birthday.*

EP **These words can also be conjunctions:**

if	or	so	that
when	where	while	

1 Find and <u>underline</u> all the conjunctions on the cinema web page. Study the sentences carefully, then match the two halves of the sentences below.

1 My friends and I go to the cinema if
2 My friend says that
3 I like eating popcorn while
4 We usually sit at the back, where
5 I don't like it when
6 I could have a party for my birthday or
7 The film was very scary, so

a we get the best view of the screen.
b we have enough money and there is a good film on.
c the Harry Potter books are better than the films.
d people talk during the film.
e I'm watching a film in the cinema.
f I didn't stay till the end.
g we could go to the cinema.

2 Complete the sentences so that they are true for you. Then, in groups, compare your answers.

I often listen to music while I'm ....
I'd like to live in a place where ....
In the future, I am sure that ....
I'm happiest when ....
I only get angry if ....
This weekend, I'll .... or
....

LISTENING

PREPARE FOR THE EXAM

Listening Part 3

1 (94) For each question, choose the correct answer. You will hear Finley inviting a friend to the cinema.

1 What day will they go to the cinema?
A Friday
B Saturday
C Sunday

2 What does Ana say about *Body Swap*?
A It's a bit too short.
B It's got famous actors in it.
C It's popular with her friends.

3 What time does the film begin?
A 6.10 B 6.30 C 6.45

4 How much are the tickets?
A £5.00 B £7.50 C £10.00

5 How will they get home?
A They'll get a lift.
B They'll walk.
C They'll get the bus.

2 (94) In pairs, compare your answers. Then listen again to check your answers.

» PREPARE FOR THE EXAM PAGE 130

WRITING

PREPARE TO WRITE

An invitation to the cinema

GET READY Read the invitation to the cinema in the email and answer the questions.

1 Who is Jake inviting?
2 What film does he want to see?
3 When does he want to go?

Look at the **prepositions**. Which preposition do we use with:

a times? b days? c streets?
d places where you do something?
e if you are moving to a place?

To: Leo
From: Jake
Reply Forward

Hi Leo,

Would you like **to** come to the cinema with me and a few friends **on** Saturday? We want to see *Ghostbusters*. It's about a group of women who try to find ghosts **in** New York. It sounds really good! It's on **at** Galaxy Cinema and it starts **at** 6.45 pm. We're meeting **at** the bus stop **on** Friar Road **at** 6 pm. Let me know if you can come!

Jake

PLAN Plan your own invitation to the cinema. Make notes.

- What day are you going?
- Which film are you going to see?
- What's it about?
- What time does it start?
- Which cinema are you going to?
- How are you getting there?

WRITE Write your invitation. Begin with *Hi/ Dear* and your friend's name. End with your name. Use some relative pronouns, conjunctions and prepositions in your invitation. Write 50–80 words.

IMPROVE In pairs, read each other's invitations. Check for mistakes with relative pronouns, prepositions and conjunctions.

LIFE SKILLS CREATIVITY AND INNOVATION

BRAINSTORMING

1 **When do you need ideas from other people? Tick the sentences that are true for you.**

to do projects at school
to decide what to wear in the morning
to make a room more attractive for a party
to do homework
to buy a present for a friend

In pairs, compare your answers.

2 **Think of an example where you worked with other people to get ideas and tell the class.**

Last term, we had a science project. We had to think of an experiment to do in groups.

3 **Read the text and match groups A–D to the brainstorm techniques 1–4.**

LIFE SKILLS

Brainstorming is a way to think of different ideas:

- to solve a problem
- to create something
- to plan something

Brainstorming is thinking of lots of ideas in a group or individually. If more people take part, then there are more ideas.

How and what can we brainstorm?

1 Mind map

The best city
- location
- restaurants
- buildings
- monuments
- shops

2 Lists

School trip to the mountains

Food	Drink	Clothes	Equipment
sandwiches	water	warm sweater	backpack
biscuits	juice	boots	whistle

3 Cards

Name for our school pet

Max, Archie, Leo, Fluffly, Tilly, Jack, Tucker

4 Image circles

palm trees
TV
shells
hamburgers
console

4 **Read the texts again and answer the questions.**

GROUP A

1 Did all the students write down their ideas?
2 How did they organise their ideas?

GROUP B

3 What did the students write in the circles?
4 Did all the students write in the circles?

GROUP C

5 What did the students write in the middle circle?
6 Did they learn new information?

GROUP D

7 What did the students use to show their ideas?
8 What did they do with ideas that were the same?

5 **In pairs, discuss which brainstorming idea you think is best and explain why.**

96 **6** **Listen to four students planning a school party. Which brainstorming method do they use?**

95

Group A

We chose one person in our group to be the secretary, who wrote down the ideas. We put the ideas in lists in different columns. When we had lots of ideas, we numbered them in order of importance. Then, we crossed out the ideas we didn't like so much. In the end, we planned a fantastic event!

Group B

In my group, we drew lots and lots of circles on the page. Then, we took turns to put an idea in each bubble or circle. We didn't write sentences. Instead, we wrote one or two words which expressed our idea, although some people drew a picture. Some of the ideas were crazy, but it was fun to see things that other people thought were important.

Group C

We decided to draw a circle in the middle of the page and write the topic in the centre. Then, we drew lines which connected the middle circle to the other circles. Each of the circles contained ideas about a different part of the topic. It was good because everyone knew different pieces of information, like names or places, so when we finished, we had a lot to write about.

Group D

Each person in the class wrote one idea on a card. Then, we put all the cards on the board at the back of the room. We put the cards that had the same ideas together in groups on the board and then we voted to decide on the best one.

96 **7** **Listen again and answer the questions.**

1 What are the topics they mention first?
2 List two of the themes the students suggest.
3 Which nationalities do they mention?
4 How many topics do they have at the end?
5 What is the name of the final topic they mention?

8 **Choose the correct options.**

USEFUL LANGUAGE

1 *Do we* / *Shall we* all write down a list of suggestions *first* / *firstly*?
2 *Why don't we* / *We think to* make a mind map?
3 *Then* / *Last*, what about the other circles?
4 *What about* / *Let's* start with the theme.
5 *Shall we* / *How about* different nationalities?
6 *Next* / *After*, we'll have to choose decorations.

96 **Listen again and check.**

PROJECT *An advertisement*

You see this advertisement for a competition and decide to take part.

YOUNG FILMMAKERS COMPETITION

Have you got an idea for a new film?
Make a poster with the title, names of the actors and a scene from the film. Write a short description of the scene you choose.
The winners will spend a day at the film school, learning to use cameras and create special effects.

- Work in small groups.
- Read the situation.
- Decide which brainstorming technique you are going to use.
- Brainstorm ideas.
- Choose the best ideas and make a poster for the competition.
- Present your poster and explain your film idea to another group or to the class.

REVIEW 3 UNITS 9–12

VOCABULARY

1 **Match the words 1–8 to a–h to make compound nouns. Use each word once only.**

1	shopping	**a**	class
2	card	**b**	film
3	old	**c**	game
4	fitness	**d**	board
5	art	**e**	assistant
6	action	**f**	area
7	message	**g**	gallery
8	shop	**h**	town

2 **Find the odd word out in each set. Say why it does not fit.**

0 blog link (prize) site
'Prize' is the odd one out. The others are all about the internet.

1 traffic stadium cricket fan
2 horror skier musical adventure
3 embassy mosque temple cathedral
4 guest member statue relative
5 climber diver runner golfer
6 board game puzzle video game badminton
7 skyscraper tournament champion professional

3 **Write the missing letters to complete the word in each sentence.**

1 Ben loves all kinds of sport. He's starting k _ _ _ _ _ _ lessons on Saturday.
2 I was really sad when my mum was in hospital. I m _ _ _ _ _ _ her a lot.
3 Do you have a c _ _ _ _ _ _ _ _ at the school? Then I can phone and ask for that person.
4 I don't want to play cards. Let's do a p _ _ _ _ _ _ instead.
5 My favourite type of film is a c _ _ _ _ _ _ because they always make me laugh.
6 It didn't take a long time to u _ _ _ _ _ _ all the photos to my blog.
7 I found a great new website for teens. You don't have to pay. It's free to j _ _ _.
8 I got my mum a necklace for her birthday as I know she loves j _ _ _ _ _ _ _ _ _ _.

GRAMMAR

1 **Choose the correct words to complete the sentences.**

1 My dad *hadn't* / *didn't have* to work yesterday.
2 I'm happy with your idea about *go* / *going* shopping.
3 I think that I lost it on *the* / *a* sofa in the living room.
4 I bought three shirts *who* / *which* cost £10, £17 and £25.

Correct the mistakes in these sentences.

5 Oh, and we must forget to take our video and camera.
6 I will try call to you on Wednesday.
7 Where can I find an information about the bus times?
8 My favourite meal is pizza. I love it, especially the pizza who my mum cooks!

2 **Put the words in the correct order to make sentences.**

1 lots / I / to / listening / of / kinds / of / enjoy / music / different / .
2 for / contact / Could / to / school / you / try / the / me / ?
3 anyone / speak / exam / mustn't / to / before / Students / the / .
4 I / this / is / than / interesting / think / film / the / one / more / other / .
5 helping / the / I / with / mind / activities / don't / tomorrow / you / sports/ .
6 worried / was / about / another / Frank / dance / joining / class / .
7 caught / bus / outside / hospital / that / Elsa / stops / the / the / .

3 **Complete the sentences with the correct form of the verbs in brackets.**

1 I might stop .... (have) piano lessons next year.
2 My best friend hopes .... (take part) in the cricket match on Saturday.
3 We decided .... (visit) the art gallery first.
4 I forgot .... (do) my maths homework last night.
5 My mum really misses .... (see) my brother now that he's at university in the USA.
6 You need .... (write) your names on this list before we start.
7 I didn't enjoy .... (watch) that horror film last night.

PREPARE FOR THE EXAM

Reading Part 1

1

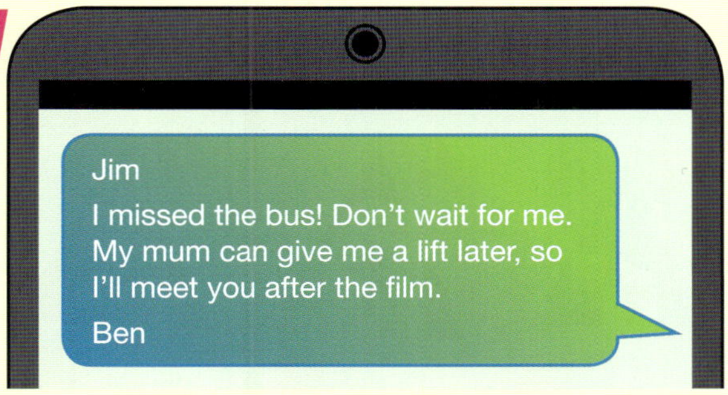

2

3

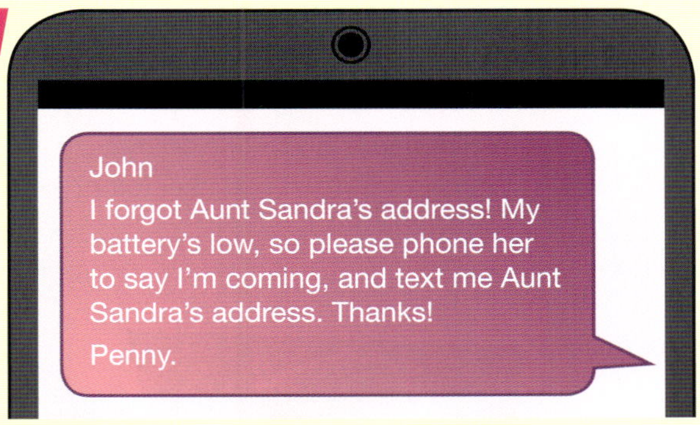

4

5

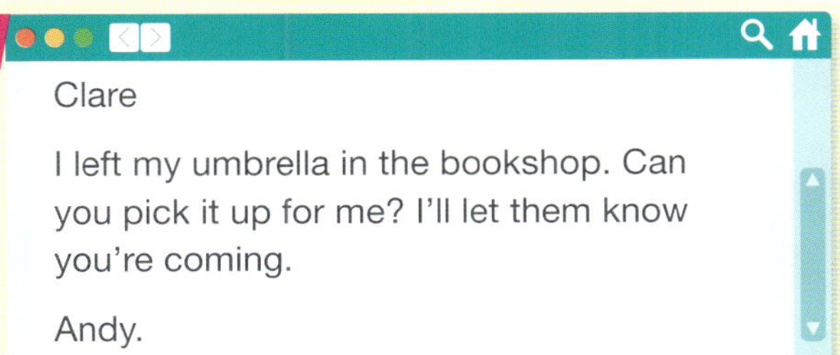

6

1 **For each question, choose the correct answer.**

1 **A** Ben wants Jim to go to the cinema without him.
B Ben will catch the next bus.
C Ben is meeting his mum at the cinema.

2 **A** There is something missing from the skateboard.
B The skateboard is several years old.
C The skateboard is too small for Diana.

3 **A** Penny asks John to send a text to Aunt Sandra.
B Penny wants to call Aunt Sandra.
C Penny needs to get Aunt Sandra's address.

4 **A** All pizzas are free in the evening.
B Two pizzas cost the same as one.
C The cheapest pizzas cost £6.

5 **A** Andy tells Clare that he found her umbrella in the bookshop.
B Andy will contact the bookshop to tell them Clare will collect his umbrella.
C Andy dropped his umbrella and wants Clare to find it for him.

6 **A** There are classes twice a week.
B All classes are full price at the moment.
C The classes are for adults only.

Listening Part 3

2 **For these questions, choose the correct answer.**

97 You will hear Serena talking to her friend Ed about the new sports centre.

1 What does Serena like best about the new sports centre?
A she can take fitness classes.
B she can play racket sports.
C she can go climbing.

2 The sports centre closes
A at the same time every day.
B later on Saturdays and Sundays.
C earlier in the holidays.

3 Serena thinks Ed will like climbing because
A he already knows the teacher.
B he doesn't like team sports.
C he's got a strong body.

4 Ed likes board games because
A they make him think.
B he doesn't have to move around.
C he can't play them at school.

5 Ed can contact the games club
A by text.
B by letter.
C by email.

13 LIFE EXPERIENCES

The Great Outdoors:

10 things to do before you're 16

98

Have you ever climbed a tree or kayaked down a river? No, you haven't? Well, now's the time to do it!

Start with these ten activities. Download the app and tick the activities off as you do them. You can do them in any order and at any time. When you have finished these ten, click on another section, *Animals, People* or *Sport,* and download ten more. Compare your activities with your friends.

› **Off you go! No time to lose.**

ABOUT YOU

List as many outdoors activities that you can think of.

Which ones do you like doing?

Which ones don't you like doing?

VOCABULARY AND READING

Outdoor activities

1 **Match the phrases in the box to the pictures on the website A–J.**

EP

camp under the stars	climb a tree	explore a cave
kayak down a river	look for fossils	pick wild fruit
play in the snow	record birdsong	track wild animals
try rock climbing		

99 **Listen, check and repeat.**

100 **2** **Listen to Juan talking to his friend Susanna about the activities on the website. Which activities would Juan like to do?**

100 **3** **Listen again and complete the table about Susanna. Which activities are new for Susanna and which are not new?**

Activity								
New								
Not new								
When?								
Where?								

4 **Look at the table. In pairs, ask and answer the questions.**

1 Which of the outdoor activities on the website do you like doing or would you like to do? Why?
2 Which ones don't you like doing or wouldn't you like to do? Why?

GRAMMAR Present perfect with *ever* and *never*

1 Read the statements and questions. Then, choose the correct words to complete the rules.

Statements	Questions	Short answers
I've picked wild fruit. I've **never** tracked wild animals.	Have you **ever** kayaked down a river? Have you **ever** climbed a tree?	Yes, I have. No, I haven't.

1 We use ***have*** or ***has*** and the *present / past* participle of the main verb to form the present perfect.
2 We use the **present perfect** to talk about experiences in the *past / present / future.*
3 We *can / can't* use words like *last week* or *ago* with the present perfect.
4 We use *never / ever* in present perfect questions about people's experiences.
5 We use *never / ever* in present perfect statements about people's experiences.

GRAMMAR REFERENCE AND PRACTICE PAGE 159

2 Make sentences and questions in the present perfect.

1 My mum / visit / a safari park.
2 I / never camp / in the winter.
3 you / ever pick / fruit from a tree?
4 Kris / ever climb / a mountain?
5 We / never return / to the amazing campsite in the woods.
6 My little sisters / play / in snow.

3 Correct the mistakes in the sentences.

1 I never try sleeping under the stars before.
2 These are the best apples I ever picked.
3 My mother has never play the piano.
4 And it is in a forest. The best place I never visited.
5 No, I've ever failed an exam.

PRONUNCIATION Past participles

101 **4** Listen to the past participles and decide in which words we say *-ed* as an extra syllable.

Write these verbs as past participles in the correct column.

climb collect end explore
finish hate jump paint
play tidy try want

camped	recorded

102 **Listen and check. Then repeat.**

5 Make questions about the activities on the website on page 76 using the present perfect. Then, in pairs, ask and answer them.

Have you ever played in the snow?

Yes, I have.

Have you ever explored a cave?

No, I haven't.

READING

PREPARE FOR THE EXAM

Reading Part 5

1 **Read the introduction to the quiz. For each question, write the correct answer. Write ONE word for each gap.**

To: Nina
From: Marco

Reply Forward

Hi Nina

Have **(0)** ___a___ look at this quiz. I found it **(1)** ________ the internet and thought you'd like to see it. It's about people's different life experiences, both good **(2)** ________ bad. Don't worry! I did the quiz and there are quite a **(3)** ________ things I haven't done. Some things are more fun **(4)** ________ others – for example who wants to ride a horse? However, I read that it's important to have different kinds of life experiences because they help us learn **(5)** ________ the world. Let **(6)** ________ know what you think.

Marco.

>> PREPARE FOR THE EXAM PAGE 125

2 **Match the questions in the Life Quiz to photos A–L.**

3 **Answer the questions in the Life Quiz. In pairs, compare your answers. Are your answers the same or different?**

A

B

C

D

E

F

G

H

I

J

K

L

103

Life Quiz

1. Have you ever **swum** with sharks?
2. Have you ever **broken** anything valuable?
3. Have you ever **met** a famous person?
4. Have you ever **had** a bad dream?
5. Have you ever **eaten** Korean food?
6. Have you ever **been** in a film?
7. Have you ever **made** fresh pasta?
8. Have you ever **slept** in a tent?
9. Have you ever **grown** vegetables to eat?
10. Have you ever **ridden** a horse?
11. Have you ever **flown** in a plane?
12. Have you ever **sent** a message in a bottle?

TALKING POINTS

10 Watch the video and ask and answer the questions.

What's the most amazing thing you've ever done?

What's the most interesting place you've ever visited?

What's the most unusual thing you've ever done?

Have you swum with dolphins?

Have you ridden a camel?

Have you eaten a frog?

VOCABULARY Past participles

1 **What is the past simple form of each verb in the box?**

EP **Now, match each verb to a past participle in the quiz.**

be break eat fly grow have
make meet ride send sleep swim

2 **In pairs, take turns to name a photo from the Life Quiz and make a true statement about it.**

Picture I

I've ridden a horse. Picture A

I've never slept in a tent. I like sleeping inside.

3 **In groups, ask and answer questions about the most exciting thing each of you has done. Tell the class.**

LISTENING

104 **1** **Listen to the radio show. Jim is talking to Christina Wells, an explorer. Which three parts of the world does she talk about?**

104 **2** **Listen again. Complete the questions about each trip. Then in pairs, answer the questions.**

Trip 1

1 Complete Jim's question to Christina: Have you ever ....?
2 What was she doing in the rainforest?
3 What information did she not want to share with people?

Trip 2

4 Complete Jim's question to Christina: Have you ever ....?
5 How was she travelling to the North Pole?
6 What did she do to help her think more clearly?

Trip 3

7 What is different for Christina about this trip?
8 How will she travel?
9 How long will it take?

SPEAKING

1 **Now, you're going to write your own Life Quiz.**

a In pairs, think of other life experiences you think are important. They can be good or bad.
b In pairs, write six questions beginning *Have you ever …*
c In small groups, read each other's questions and choose eight questions you think are the best.
d Individually, write the eight questions for the Life Quiz on a piece of paper. Make sure there is room to write answers for at least two students.
e Ask your questions to at least two other students in the class. Don't ask students from your group.
f In your original group, discuss the answers students gave you to the eight questions.
g Report back to the class about the results of the Life Quiz. Use the phrases in the box to help you.

We asked … students.
Some of the students we asked have …
Most of the students we asked have …
Most of the students we asked haven't …
None of the students we asked have …
All of the students we asked have …

14 SPENDING MONEY

ABOUT YOU

Do you like shopping? Why? / Why not?
What shops do you go to the most?

VOCABULARY AND READING

Shops

1 Match the shop words in the box to the photos A–L.

EP

bakery	bookshop	butcher's
café	chemist's	clothes shop
department store	market	
newsagent's	shoe shop	
sweet shop	supermarket	

105 **Listen and check. Then repeat.**

2 Where can you buy these things? Choose from the shops in Exercise 1. Sometimes, there is more than one possibility.

apples	bread	burgers
chocolates	dictionary	
magazines	sandwich	socks
sun cream	tea towels	trainers

3 In pairs, think of at least two more things you can buy in each shop.

4 Read the advertisements in a magazine. What kind of shops are they?

5 Where can you …

1 surf the internet?
2 buy something to wash your hands with?
3 buy something for a lower price than usual?
4 have some free food?
5 pick up something you bought online?

6 Read the advertisements again and answer the questions.

1 What is the date of the magazine?
2 When does each shop open?

YORK TIMES

106

21st March

Reading Time

16 Old Road

Are you a reader? Then this is the place for you. Choose something from the shelves. Then relax, have a coffee and read.
Comfortable sofas and free wi-fi.

Doors open ***6th March***

Something Special

52 Main Street

Do you like sweets and chocolates?
Come and choose from the hundreds we have in our shop.
You can even try before you buy!
Opening 20th March.

One Foot After Another

13 River Avenue

We've got everything you need for your feet.
There's something for everyone in our store.
Walking boots on sale.
Our first day is 3rd April.

Shop and Try

www.shopandtry.net

All the latest fashions in clothes.
Order online, collect from our shop in York.
Try your jeans, jumpers and dresses on in store.
Make sure they're right for you!

Open from 24th March

Brown's Chemist's

30 Grove Street

As well as medicines, get soap and make-up here.
Everything you need for baby too.
Free coffee.

Opening 19th March

GRAMMAR Present perfect with *just*, *yet*, *already*

1 **The date of the magazine is 21st March. Which shops are open and which shops will be open soon?**

Reading Time (6th March). It has already opened.
Something Special (20th March). It has just opened.
One Foot After Another (3rd April). It hasn't opened yet.
Has One Foot After Another opened yet? No, it hasn't.

Choose the correct sentence, a or b, for these two shops. Today is 21st March.

Shop and Try opens on 24th March.
Brown's Chemist's opened on 19th March.

a It hasn't opened yet.
b It has just opened.

2 **Study the examples in Exercise 1. Then match 1–4 with a–d to make sentences about the present perfect.**

1 To talk about something which happened a very short time ago,
2 To talk about something which we expect to happen in the future,
3 To talk about something which happened not long ago, or sooner than someone expected,
4 To ask about something which we expect to happen in the future,

a we use the present perfect negative with *yet*.
b we use present perfect questions with *yet*.
c we use the present perfect with *already*.
d we use the present perfect with *just*.

GRAMMAR REFERENCE AND PRACTICE PAGE 160

3 **Look at the things in the picture that Carla has just bought for a camping trip. Then, look at her shopping list. Answer the questions using *yet* and *already*.**

1 Which things has she already bought?
2 Which things hasn't she bought yet?

4 **Write a list of six things you've just done. In pairs, compare your lists.**

I've just opened my book.

5 **Correct the mistakes in the sentences.**

1 You already borrow my book for a week.
2 I've just bought a new smartphone, but I didn't put music on it yet.
3 I just see a football match with my father.
4 I already have bought something to eat.
5 Are you still looking for your keys? If you don't find them yet, I think they are in your bag.

PRONUNCIATION
Intonation: questions and statements

107 **6** **Listen and repeat.**

Has your brother arrived yet?
Yes, he's just arrived.
Has your sister arrived yet?
Yes, she's already arrived.

7 **Make a list of ten things you do every day. In pairs, ask and answer questions about today.**

Have you done your homework yet?

Yes, I've already done my homework.

Have you used the computer yet?

Yes, I've just used the computer.

POCKET MONEY

Did you know? 108

1 Most teenagers receive pocket money every week. But not everyone gets the same amount of money. Have you asked your friends how much they get? You might be surprised. And if you're a girl you'll be amazed to learn that boys often get more than girls of the same age!

2 Teenagers up to the age of about 15 in the UK have about £5 a week in pocket money. But in Italy, France and Spain, the same age group gets about €9, which is a bit more. In the US, pocket money is called 'an allowance'. Most teenagers get an allowance of about $30, which is more than £20 or €25.

3 Quite a lot of teenagers do. They have to do things in the house, like washing-up and cleaning and then they get their pocket money. If they don't do the jobs, they don't get the money. Some teenagers have part-time jobs too, which means they have more than their pocket money to spend each week.

4 You might be surprised at the answer. Teenagers in the UK spend more of their money on food than on clothes. Is that true for you too? Teens do more shopping online than before and online clothes shopping is cheaper. So perhaps this is one reason they don't spend so much on clothes.

5 Some parents do! They only let them buy some things. Other parents want their teens to save all their pocket money and spend it on something big in the future, or not spend it at all.

TALKING POINTS

What was the most surprising thing for you in the article?

READING

1 **In pairs, ask and answer the questions.**

1 What is pocket money?
2 Do you get pocket money?
3 How much do you get a week?
4 Do you spend more of your pocket money on food or clothes?

2 **Read the article quickly. Match the question to the correct paragraph.**

a So what happens in different countries?
b Do teens have to work for their pocket money?
c Do parents tell teens what to spend pocket money on?
d What do teenagers spend their money on?
e Do all teenagers get pocket money?

3 **Answer the questions about the article.**

1 What's the difference between the pocket money girls get and the pocket money boys get?
2 Where do teenagers get more pocket money, the USA, the UK or Italy, France and Spain?
3 What is pocket money called in the USA?
4 What do some teens have to do before they get their pocket money?
5 How do some teenagers add to their pocket money?
6 What do some parents want their children to do with their pocket money?

VOCABULARY Units of measurement and money

1 **Complete the sentences using words from the box.** EP

centimetres dollars and cents euros and cents grams kilograms kilometres litres metres millilitres pounds and pence

1 You buy food in ______ or ______.
2 You buy drink in ______ or ______.
3 You use ______, ______ and ______ to buy things.
4 You find out how far away something is in ______, ______ and ______.

2 **Work with a partner and decide how you say the amounts.**

260 g	€15.34	700 ml	55 cm	2.5 l
37 p	£19.99	6 kg	62 c	$27	1.65 m

109 **Listen and check. Then repeat.**

3 **Complete the descriptions for photos 1–4 with the words in the box.** EP

a pair of a set of a slice of a variety of

1 ______ pizza

2 ______ sunglasses

3 ______ cups

4 ______ drinks

4 Complete the sentences with the words from Exercise 3.

1 I've just bought .... shoes. Do you like them?
2 Let's have .... music styles at the party. We can have rock, blues and rap.
3 Can you pass me the knife? I'll cut you .... cake.
4 Our teacher has got .... keys for the school.

LISTENING

1 Work in pairs. Tell your partner what you like to eat on your birthday.

110
2 David and Lana are planning a birthday picnic for their friend Pia. Listen and tick (✓) the things they have already got.

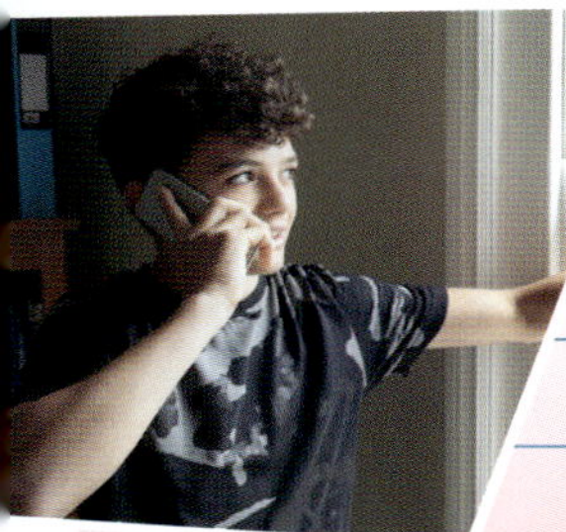

Things for Pia's Picnic

- pizzas
- fruit juice
- crisps
- water
- apples

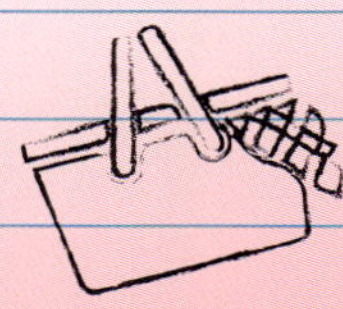

Plus

- cake
- blanket
- lemonade
- presents!

110
3 Listen again. Look at the list in Exercise 2. How much of each food and drink have they got or do they want?

4 Read the next part of Lana and David's conversation and answer the questions.

Lana: Hey, just a minute, we forgot about music. We haven't chosen the music yet. We can't have a party without music. What shall we do?
David: I <u>could</u> bring my guitar, I suppose.
Lana: Yes, and <u>I can</u> text everyone who's coming, <u>if you like</u>, and ask them to bring instruments, too. Right. Is that all?
David: Oh, I nearly forgot. The biscuits! I'll try and make them this afternoon. <u>If not</u>, I'll make them in the morning.
Lana: OK.

1 Which two <u>underlined</u> phrases make offers and suggestions?
2 Which <u>underlined</u> phrase says what the situation will be when something does not happen?

5 In pairs, write conversations. Use the ideas below and the conversation in Exercise 4 to help you. Then, in pairs, practise the conversations.

1 You're planning a day out at the beach with your friend. You forgot about the food.
2 You're planning a visit to a new shopping centre. You forgot how you're going to get there.

WRITING

PREPARE TO WRITE

Writing Part 6 An email

GET READY Read the note from David to his dad. Correct the punctuation. Add full stops, capital letters, apostrophes and question marks.

> dear dad
>
> Lana and i need to get some things for pias party please can you take us to the supermarket this morning thanks see you later
>
> david

In pairs, compare your corrected notes.

PLAN You have just bought a birthday present for your sister. Write a message about it to your English friend Sam.
In your message
- say what you have bought for your sister
- say why you chose it
- say which shop you bought it in.

WRITE 25 words or more. Make sure you include information about all three ideas in your answer. Think carefully about punctuation.

IMPROVE In pairs, read each other's notes and look for mistakes. Check that you have both included all the necessary information and that you used punctuation correctly.

CULTURE

SHOPPING AND MONEY

1 **In pairs, discuss the questions.**

1 Where do you usually go shopping?
2 Do you or your parents ever shop in markets?

2 **Match the types of markets in the box to the photos A–D. How many objects can you name that you can buy in them? Do you have similar markets in your country?**

food market	clothes market
antiques market	flower market

3 **Read about three famous markets. Which one isn't a food market?**

A

B

C

D

Amazing MARKETS

111

A You should definitely visit the Queen Victoria Market in Melbourne, Australia. The market started in the 1870s. Today, it's open every morning on Tuesdays and Thursdays to Sundays. There's also a night market on Wednesdays from 5 to 10 pm. There are more than 600 shops and stalls in the market. The fresh-food areas sell fruit and vegetables, cakes, fish and meat (including kangaroo and crocodile steaks!).

C St Lawrence Market in Toronto, Canada, started in 1803, but they built the buildings you can see today in 1904. The market is open Tuesday to Saturday from 8 am to early evening. You can buy many different things there from more than 100 stalls, especially fresh food and delicious homemade products. A fun thing to do is cookery classes in the Market Kitchen. Here, you can learn to make different dishes and take them home to eat! The farmers' market opens on Saturdays at 5 am, and local farmers come to sell meat, fruit, vegetables, eggs, etc.

B Hell's Kitchen market is an outdoor street market in New York, USA. It only opens at weekends from 9 am to 5 pm, with nearly a hundred stalls on the streets – but if the weather is bad, there aren't so many people selling or buying. It started in 1976, and you can buy antiques, such as old furniture or clothes and jewellery. If you enjoy music, it is a great place to visit because there are often jazz concerts, and you can buy musical instruments there, as well. Local artists also show their paintings, sculptures and photos.

4 **Read the text again and answer the questions.**

Which market(s) …

1 is sometimes open at 9 pm?
2 has fewer visitors if it is raining?
3 can you buy a guitar in?
4 is over 100 years old?
5 can you learn to cook in?
6 sells unusual meat?
7 is the biggest?

5 **Find words in the text that match the definitions.**

1 a kind of small shop (text A) ....
2 a piece of meat (text A) ....
3 rings, necklaces, etc. (text B) ....
4 a kind of music (text B) ....
5 constructed (text C) ....
6 food that people prepare themselves (text C) ....

112 **6** **Listen to Alice talking to her friend Dan about a market in London. Which part of the market did she like most?**

112 **7** **Listen again. Are these statements right (✓) or wrong (✗)?**

1 Alice went to Camden Lock Market last Saturday.
2 Camden Lock Market is very big.
3 You can buy fresh fruit and vegetables in the market.
4 Alice ate pizza in the market.
5 Alice bought three T-shirts and a handbag.
6 Alice's friend Lisa likes Justin Bieber.

TALKING POINTS

Which market would you like to visit: Queen Victoria, Hell's Kitchen, St Lawrence or Camden Lock? Explain why.

PROJECT

A market

Find out about a famous market in your country. Make a poster to present the information to the class. Use pictures and photos to make the poster more interesting. Include information about:

- where it is
- when it is open
- what you can buy, see and do there.

Present your poster to the class.

15 FREE TIME

ABOUT YOU

How many hours of free time do you have per week?
Is this the right amount, too much or too little?

VOCABULARY AND LISTENING

Free-time activities

1 EP In pairs, match photos A–E to activities in the questionnaire. Which of the activities do you think are most popular in your class?

Questionnaire

Activities	I do this	I'd like to try this	I'm not at all interested in this
chatting			
collecting			
cooking			
going out with friends			
going shopping			
listening to music			
making things			
photography			
playing an instrument			
playing computer games			
playing sport			
reading books			
singing, acting, dancing			
spending time online			
watching TV			

2 Do the questionnaire in your class. Walk around the room and ask people which activities they do in their free time, which they'd like to try and which they are not interested in. Write your results for each activity or hobby like this: ~~||||~~ ||

3 In small groups, look at all your results and write some sentences.

In our class, lots of / some / a few people already do these activities: ...., ..., ...
In our class, lots of / some / a few people want to try these activities: ...., ..., ...
In our class, no one likes these activities: ...., ..., ...

Were you surprised by any of your results? Why?

113 **4** **Listen to three young people talking about what they do in their free time. Write the activity or activities from the questionnaire below each speaker.**

Owen	Kyle	Erin

113 **5** **Listen again. Are the sentences right (✓) or wrong (✗)?**

1 Owen keeps his computer in his bedroom.
2 Owen thinks he uses his computer too much.
3 Kyle still collects pins and badges.
4 Kyle does two different sports.
5 Erin has got a new guitar.
6 Erin has her own camera.

GRAMMAR Present perfect with *for* and *since*

1 **Look at these examples. Then, complete the rules below with *for* or *since*.**

I've had my own computer for three years.
I haven't bought any football cards for a long time.
I've played the guitar for two years.
I've had this guitar since January.
I've had one of them since I was ten.
My dad's had his camera since he was a teenager.

1 We use ______ with an amount of time, such as a number of hours / months / years.
2 We use ______ with the time when the action started, such as a day / date / age.

» GRAMMAR REFERENCE AND PRACTICE PAGE 161

2 **Complete the sentences with *for* or *since*.**

1 Jack's lived here ______ he was three years old.
2 Mum's been asleep ______ four hours.
3 I've been a member of the club ______ last month.
4 Sophie's had her new phone ______ three days.
5 We've had our puppy ______ 31st October.
6 The students have worked together ______ Monday.
7 You've been at this school ______ six months.
8 I've had a headache ______ yesterday.
9 They've known Jules ______ a long time.

3 **Complete the sentences so they are true for you. In pairs, compare your answers.**

1 I haven't read a comic since ______.
2 I haven't watched a cartoon for ______.
3 I've played ______ for ______.
4 I've been able to ______ since I was ______.
5 I've lived in my home since ______.
6 I've had this pen for ______.
7 I've known my best friend since ______.

4 **Correct the mistakes in the sentences.**

1 It's been my hobby from I was ten years old.
2 I've needed one since a month.
3 I've had it since a year.
4 I've wanted to buy this T-shirt since several weeks.
5 It has been open since one month.

ə PRONUNCIATION Weak forms

114 **5** **Listen to the sentences and notice the pronunciation of the underlined words.**

I've had this since I <u>was</u> three.
He's played basketball <u>for</u> two years.
I've just walked home <u>from</u> school.
They haven't been <u>to</u> your house since Saturday.
I've bought <u>some</u> nice shoes.

114 **Listen again and repeat.**

6 **In pairs, ask and answer.**

Do you have a hobby?
→ Yes → What is it?
→ No → What do you do in your free time?
→ How long have you enjoyed doing it? Do you need anything special to do it?
→ Yes → What do you need? Do you usually do it with other people?
→ No

7 **Write sentences about your partner. In groups, read out your sentences. How much did your partner remember about you?**

Andrei has done karate since he was seven. He has a special white jacket and trousers called a gi. He has a blue belt. He's had it for six months.

READING

1 Look at the photos and the title of the blog. What do you think geocaching is? Read the blog once to check your ideas.

MY HOBBY – geocaching

115

Blog post written by Lucy Barton, aged 14

I started geocaching because of my uncle – he's done it for years. Geocaching is a treasure hunt that you do with an app. The 'treasure' is a box called a cache that someone else has hidden. There are 2 million of these, all over the world! It's a really fun hobby and I'm so glad my uncle told me about it. We have a great time doing it together, but if he's busy I go with friends, or do it by myself.

The app takes you quite close to the cache, and then it gives you a puzzle to help you find exactly the right place. A lot of older people are geocachers, so some of the puzzles are difficult for me as they are about movies and TV shows that I haven't seen. But I don't really mind – I can always look them up on the internet!

It's a fantastic feeling when you find a cache! You have to open the box and put your name in the little book inside. Often, there are things in the cache as well. You can take something out to keep if you want to, but if you do that, you should always put something new inside for the next person.

Next year, I'm going to start using the paid version of the app. Then, I can make and hide my own caches! I'm also going to tell all my friends and family about geocaching. It's such a great way for everyone, from adults to little kids, to spend time together, enjoy themselves and get to know their local area.

PREPARE FOR THE EXAM

Reading Part 3

2 Read the text again. For each question, choose the correct answer.

1 What do we learn about Lucy from the first paragraph?
  - **A** She has done her hobby for longer than her uncle.
  - **B** She didn't enjoy her hobby much at the beginning.
  - **C** She doesn't always do her hobby with other people.

2 What does Lucy say about the puzzles?
  - **A** They can be hard for her because she's young.
  - **B** It's a shame so many of them are about films.
  - **C** People shouldn't look online to find the answers.

3 What must you do when you find a box?
  - **A** check how many people have already found it
  - **B** leave something of yours for the next person
  - **C** write down who you are in the little book

4 What does Lucy plan to do in the future?
  - **A** spend more time geocaching in the city
  - **B** get other people interested in geocaching
  - **C** spend less money on going geocaching

5 What do we find out about geocaching from this article?
  - **A** It's becoming more popular every year.
  - **B** It takes a long time to learn how to do it.
  - **C** It's a good hobby for people of all ages.

TALKING POINTS

What makes geocaching a good hobby?

Would you like to try it? Why / Why not?

VOCABULARY Collocations about having fun

1 Look at the phrases in the box. Which ones are in the blog?

EP

have	fun a great time a laugh
spend time	with a friend doing a hobby
be feel	glad happy
enjoy	yourself an activity

a(n)	fun brilliant exciting fantastic	feeling day out hobby feeling

2 Complete the sentences with the correct form of *have*, *spend*, *be* or *enjoy*.

1 I .... a wonderful time at the party last night.
2 .... time with friends is my favourite free-time activity.
3 My brother .... playing computer games more than anything else and is really good at them.
4 I .... most of yesterday at the beach. It .... a really fun day.
5 I always .... fun when I see my cousins.
6 It .... an amazing feeling to win the race! I .... so glad I entered!
7 My dad and my brother went fishing and they really .... themselves.

3 Complete the sentences so they are true for you. In pairs, compare your answers.

1 It was a fantastic feeling when I ....
2 I love spending time with ....
3 The last time I had a good time was when ....
4 I always enjoy myself when I ....
5 My idea of a fun day out is ....
6 I was really glad when ....

LISTENING

116 **1** Listen to a girl talking about her hobby – beekeeping. Who is she speaking to? How long has she done her hobby?

116 **2** Listen again and decide if the sentences are right (✓) or wrong (✗).

1 Libby got her bees as a birthday present.
2 Libby went on a beekeeping course with some other teenagers.
3 Libby loved beekeeping as soon as she tried it.
4 Libby does more for her bees in summer than in winter.
5 Libby thinks her bees know what she looks like.
6 Libby says it's good to have lots of bees in her hive.
7 Libby says collecting the honey is her favourite part of beekeeping.

SPEAKING

1 In pairs, prepare an interview. One of you is a journalist. The other has an unusual hobby. Use the examples of unusual hobbies in the box, or you can choose your own.

dog training fencing jewellery making
remote-controlled vehicles

In the interview, the journalists must ask at least five questions:

Tell me about…
How long have you…?
When did you…?
How do you feel about…?
Why did you…?
How did you get the idea to…?
Are you glad you…?

2 Practise your interview. Then, role-play your interview in front of the class.

16 LANGUAGES OF THE WORLD

ABOUT YOU

How do you feel about learning English?
Is it a fun hobby?
Is it boring and not very useful?
Is it important for your future?

VOCABULARY AND LISTENING

Words to describe language learning

1 Complete the quiz with the words in the box.

EP

articles	exercises	guess	list	look up
meaning	mistakes	spell	topic	translate

What kind of language learner are you?

1 When do you use English outside the classroom?

A to read **(1)** ______ online
B when I'm on holiday abroad
C to watch English-language movies and TV shows
D only when I'm doing homework

2 What do you do when you find a new word in a text?

A **(2)** ______ it ______ in a dictionary
B try to **(3)** ______ what it means
C ask my teacher to **(4)** ______ it into my language
D ask my little brother for the **(5)** ______

3 What's the best way to learn vocabulary?

A from a **(6)** ______ of words
B by doing vocabulary **(7)** ______
C by reading books and magazines
D five minutes before a test

4 Which of these sentences do you agree with?

A It's important to be able to **(8)** ______ correctly.
B Making **(9)** ______ is an important part of learning.
C Pronunciation doesn't matter as much as grammar.
D I only learn if the **(10)** ______ of the lesson is interesting.

2 Now do the quiz. Choose only one answer for each question. Turn to page 137 to see your results. Do you agree with them?

3 In pairs, compare your quiz results.

PREPARE FOR THE EXAM

Listening Part 4

4 (117) For each question, choose the correct answer. Read through the questions before you listen.

1 You will hear a boy called Danny talking to his friend. How did Danny improve his Spanish?
A by writing to his penfriend
B by practising online
C by spending time in Spain

2 You will hear a teacher talking to her class. What does she want them to work harder on?
A their grammar
B their pronunciation
C their vocabulary

3 You will hear two friends talking about some homework. Why hasn't the boy done his homework?
A He forgot to make a note of it.
B He wasn't at the lesson.
C He wrote down the wrong thing.

4 You will hear a girl telling her mother about her new friend, Yumi. What languages does Yumi speak well?
A English, Russian and Swedish
B Swedish, Japanese and English
C Japanese, Swedish and Russian

5 You will hear a boy giving a classmate some important news. How did he find out about the news?
A from a family member
B he heard it on the radio
C the teacher told him

5 (117) In pairs, compare your answers. Then, listen again and check.

GRAMMAR Present perfect and past simple

1 **Look at the sentences from the recordings on page 90. Which are present perfect and which are past simple?**

1 She lived in Sweden three years ago.
2 She learned Russian last year.
3 She's spoken Japanese since she was a baby.
4 Did you go to Spain in the holidays?
5 I've already finished mine.
6 The teacher gave it to us three days ago.

2 **Complete the rules with *present perfect* or *past simple*.**

1 We use the
- **a** ________ with words and phrases like *yesterday*, *ago*, *last year*, *in the holidays*.
- **b** ________ with words like *since*, *already*, *yet*, *just*, *ever*.

2 We use the
- **a** ________ to talk about an action that began in the past but continues into the present.
- **b** ________ to talk about someone's general life experiences.
- **c** ________ to talk about an action that finished in the past.
- **d** ________ to talk about an action that finished in the past, but the result is important or interesting now.

» GRAMMAR REFERENCE AND PRACTICE PAGE 162

3 **Match the sentences to uses a–d in part 2 of Exercise 2.**

1 Have you done the German homework yet?
2 I've noticed you're all using a good level of vocabulary these days.
3 Did you meet anyone interesting?
4 I haven't missed any lessons this term.
5 She's lived all over the world!
6 She hasn't learned much English yet.
7 I've just heard some amazing news!
8 Our French teacher has won first prize in a competition!
9 We had a lesson with her this morning.

4 **Complete the text with the present perfect or past simple form of the verbs in brackets.**

An amazing language learner

Susanna Zaraysky **(1)** ________ (study) 11 languages (English, Russian, French, Spanish, Italian, Portuguese, Croatian, Ladino, Hebrew, Arabic and Hungarian) and speaks eight of them. Susanna **(2)** ________ (be) born in Russia and first **(3)** ________ (learn) English when she **(4)** ________ (move) to California. She **(5)** ________ (study) French and Spanish at school. Then, one day, she **(6)** ________ (hear) some tourists speaking in Italian and **(7)** ________ (decide) to learn that language. Portuguese came next and then all her other languages.
Susanna **(8)** ________ (write) several books and **(9)** ________ (be) on TV many times. She **(10)** ________ (have) a special interest in language and music for many years. On her blog, you'll find many interesting articles about this, as well as video clips and language-learning advice.

5 **Choose the correct verb form to complete each sentence.**

1 Yesterday, I *have watched* / *watched* a swimming competition with my brother.
2 I *already bought* / *have already bought* the tickets for the film tonight.
3 I'm in Melbourne, and I *saw* / *have seen* the beach and the sea.
4 My friend John *has watched* / *watched* the competition with me.
5 We *have arrived* / *arrived* home at eight o'clock in the evening.
6 It was a great party. We *have danced* / *danced* all night and *have eaten* / *ate* too much food!

6 **Complete the conversations with the present perfect or past simple of the verbs in brackets.**

1 **A:** ________ (do) your homework yet, Tania?
B: Yes, I ________ (finish) it an hour ago.

2 **A:** Where ________ (you go) on holiday last summer, Robin?
B: We ________ (go) to New York to visit my sister. She ________ (live) there since 2014.

3 **A:** ________ (you ever eat) curry?
B: Yes, I ________ (have) some yesterday. Delicious!

4 **A:** ________ (you enjoy) the *Toy Story* films when you were little, Sergio?
B: I ________ (never see) any of the *Toy Story* films. But I ________ (like) *Despicable Me*.

7 **In pairs, make conversations. Ask a question in the present perfect, and answer in the simple past. Use the conversations in Exercise 6 for ideas.**

READING

1 **Look at questions 1–4. In pairs, discuss the questions. Then, read the texts quickly to check your answers.**

1 How many languages are there in the world?
2 What European language family does Polish belong to?
3 Which Asian language has the most speakers?
4 What are some common second languages in Africa?

2 **Read the texts again and answer the questions.**

1 What are the three biggest languages in the world? How many speakers do they have?
2 Which continent has the most languages?
3 Which country has the largest number of languages?
4 What is special about the Basque language?
5 What has happened to some of the languages of Australia and Oceania?

LANGUAGES *of the* WORLD

118

There are around 7,000 different languages in the world today. Languages that are similar to each other are in groups or 'families'. Some languages have a lot of speakers and others have very few. Many of the smaller languages have no writing, so when the last speaker dies, the language dies too.

Europe

Europe has 284 different languages. One language family here is Romance languages, which includes Spanish, Portuguese and Italian. Another is Slavic languages, such as Russian, Polish and Czech.

English belongs to the Germanic group, and is the third largest language in the world: 335 million people speak it as a first language and 505 million speak it as a second language. The Basque language from Spain and France is very unusual. It doesn't belong to any language family!

Asia

Asia has 2,303 languages. Chinese has a billion speakers – more than any other language in the world. Hindi is the world's fourth largest language, and Arabic comes fifth. Some parts of Asia have a very large number of languages.

Australia and Oceania

This area has 1,311 languages in total. The main language of Australia and New Zealand is English, but there are a lot of smaller languages too. Papua New Guinea has only around 8 million people, but it has 832 languages – more than any other country! Unfortunately, some Aboriginal languages are very small now and have only one or two speakers.

Americas

This area has 1,060 languages. English and Spanish have the most speakers on these continents. Spanish, with 406 million speakers, is the world's second-largest language. Portuguese is spoken in Brazil. While in Canada people speak mainly English and French. There are also many other native languages, for example Mam, a Mayan language, which people speak in parts of Mexico and Guatemala.

Africa

Human language probably began on this continent. There are 2,146 languages here. Many people in Africa can speak more than one language because, as well as their own language, they also speak English, French or Portuguese.

TALKING POINTS

12 Watch the video and discuss the questions.

What languages do you speak?
What languages are you studying?
What languages do your parents speak?

PREPARE FOR THE EXAM

Speaking Part 1

1 **Ask and answer with a partner.**

1. Where do you come from?
2. What languages do people in your country speak?
3. Do you enjoy studying English?
4. Tell me something about what you do in your English lessons.

VOCABULARY Large numbers

1 **Match the numbers to the words.**

EP

176	seven billion
7,468	one hundred and seventy-six
76,000,000	seven thousand four hundred and sixty-eight
7,000,000,000	seventy-six million

2 **Find and underline all the big numbers in the text. Write them in words.**

119 **3** **Listen and check. Then, in pairs, practise saying the numbers.**

PRONUNCIATION

Word stress in numbers

120 **4** **Listen to the numbers and underline the stressed syllable. Can you make a rule about the stress in numbers?**

thirteen	thirty
fifteen	fifty
eighteen	eighty
nineteen	ninety

5 **Work in pairs. Practise saying the numbers.**

6 **Work in pairs. Student A, say a number from the text. Student B, close your book. Can you remember what the number refers to?**

Two hundred and eighty four.

That's the number of languages in Europe.

LISTENING

1 **You will hear a man giving some information about different languages. In pairs, discuss the possible answers.**

1. How many colour words are there in Russian and Greek? How many in English?
2. How many number words does the Pirahã language of Brazil have?
3. Some languages have two sets of vocabulary. Why?
4. Some languages have no words for *left*, *right*, *in front of* and *behind*. How do they say where things are?
5. How is modern technology helping small languages?

121 **Listen and check.**

WRITING

PREPARE TO WRITE

Information about your English class

GET READY **Read what a Spanish student wrote about her English class.**

My name is María and I come from Spain. Most of the people in my English class are from Spain too, but one of my classmates is from China and two are from Ecuador. The languages people speak in my class are Spanish, Catalan, Chinese and English. I like speaking in English, but I find listening difficult. I plan to spend more time learning vocabulary in the future.

Look at how she uses capital letters. Find examples of these uses:

- after a full stop
- for people's names
- for countries
- for nationalities
- for languages
- for 'I'

PLAN **Plan a paragraph about your English class. Make notes about:**

- people's nationalities
- languages people speak
- languages people in the class are learning
- your likes, dislikes, plans about learning English.

WRITE **Write 50–70 words, using all your notes.**

IMPROVE **In pairs, read each other's paragraphs. Check that you have both included all the information you need and have used capital letters correctly.**

LIFE SKILLS LEARNING TO LEARN

EFFECTIVE LEARNING

LIFE SKILLS

To learn something well, you need to

- use a notebook
- revise
- practise
- try

It's normal to make mistakes when we are doing something new. But we can learn from our mistakes as well.

1 **Think about how you learn and answer the questions.**

1. How did you learn that 2 x 2 = 4, 2 x 3 = 6, 2 x 4 = 8, etc.?
2. How did you learn to ride a bicycle?
3. How do you learn to remember names and dates in history?

2 **Match questions 1–3 in Exercise 1 to answers a–c. Then match them to one of the ideas in the *Life skills* box.**

a At first, I couldn't do it, but my brother helped me to go along our street every day until one day I could do it by myself.
b We said it in class and repeated it lots and lots of times.
c I work with a friend and we ask each other questions about the things we learn in class.

3 **Did you learn to do these things in the same way? In pairs, discuss how you learn.**

4 **Read the text. Circle the language skills it mentions.**

a reading **b** listening
c speaking **d** writing

What was the **first word** you said? 122

Have you ever thought about how babies learn to speak? For the first months of their lives, they cry and make noises, but, in general, children start forming words when they are about 12 months old. Which are the first words they say? Sometimes, they are the words they hear most often, sometimes the words for things they like. They usually start with words like *mama*, *papa* or *dada*. Some scientists say that sounds like *ma, da, pa* and *ba* are the easiest sounds to make, so when parents are very happy because their child is saying *mama*, in fact the baby is just experimenting with making noises!

All children begin learning their language first by listening and then speaking. They start with words for objects, like *car* or *dog*, then verbs for actions, like *drink* or *eat,* slowly adding other kinds of words to make sentences. They can understand more difficult words and sentences, but they can't say them. Some children speak more than others (just like adults!) and some children speak earlier than others, but by practising, they all learn in the end.

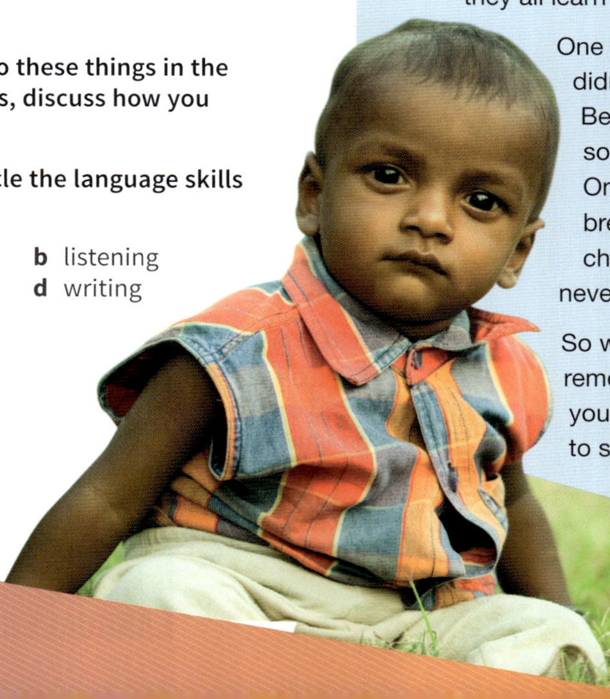

One mother tells the story of her son who didn't speak until he was four years old. Before then, he pointed when he wanted something or just made strange noises. One day, he came into the kitchen for breakfast and said, 'Can I have some chocolate cereal, please?' And then, he never stopped chatting.

So when you start to learn another language, remember that it took years for you to learn yours! If you keep listening and trying hard to speak, you improve, just like in your own language.

Did you know?

- Babies can learn any language. No language is more difficult than another.
- Most children say their first words between 11 and 14 months old.
- A boy from the USA, Michael Kearney, spoke his first words when he was four months old and finished secondary school when he was six years old.

5 **Read the text on page 94 again. Are the sentences right (✓) or wrong (✗)?**

1. Babies make their first sounds when they are about a year old.
2. Their first words are often words they have heard a lot.
3. Some scientists think that babies aren't thinking about their mother when they say *mama*.
4. Babies use verbs before nouns when they start speaking.
5. The boy who didn't speak until he was four didn't make any sounds at all.
6. You can learn a new language better if you listen more and talk less.

6 **Match the highlighted words in the text to the definitions.**

1. making an effort to do something
2. doing new things to find out something
3. repeating something again and again
4. talking
5. making the shape of something
6. increasing the number of something

123 **7** **Listen to Mario talking to his class about learning English. Why did he improve?**

123 **8** **Listen again and complete the sentences.**

1. Mario didn't like English at first because he couldn't remember the ________ and ________.
2. He met the brothers at the ________.
3. He wrote the words in a book and ________ to show the meaning.
4. After the holiday, he sent his new friends ________.
5. When he needed a new word, he used an ________.
6. He's going to ________ his friends next summer.

123 **9** **Listen again and tick (✓) the expressions Mario uses to make his presentation.**

USEFUL LANGUAGE

1. Hello, my name's Mario.
2. I'm going to talk about …
3. The first thing I want to tell you about is …
4. Next,
5. For example,
6. Finally,
7. To sum up,
8. Does anyone have any questions?

10 **Do you know any people who speak English? Do you try to talk to them in English? In pairs, discuss your experiences.**

PROJECT

Sharing resources

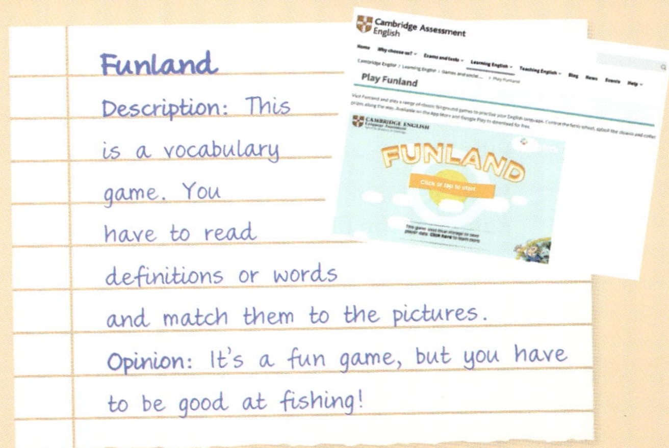

- Work in small groups.
- Individually, think of something you read in English that was interesting – a web page, a blog, a game, an article, a book, etc. or something you enjoyed watching in English – a video, a film, a series, a cartoon, an activity from your coursebook, etc.
- In your group, prepare a short information page about each idea.
- Include: the title, what it is, where you can find it (the link to a web page or a video etc.), your opinion, photos, screenshots or drawings.
- Present your idea to the class. Try to use some of the expressions from Exercise 9 and be ready to answer any questions about it.
- Create a class file for everyone and add new pages when you find other interesting things to read or watch in English.

REVIEW 4 UNITS 13–16

VOCABULARY

1 **Complete the sentences with a word from the box.**

dollars	grams	litres	metres	pair	pounds	set	slices

1 I've lost my ______ of coloured pens. Can I borrow yours?
2 There are ten of us, so let's cut the melon into ten ______.
3 I think I've lost my new ______ of gloves. My mum won't be pleased!
4 The jacket was on sale for 30 ______ and 99 cents.
5 We need 250 ______ of flour to make the cake.
6 My dad's nearly two ______ tall. That's much taller than me.
7 In our family, we drink two ______ of milk a day. We all have it on our cereal.
8 I haven't got any money for the bus. Can you lend me two ______ 50 pence, please?

2 **Match words from A to words in B to make verb phrases about life experiences.**

A	B
1 camp	a cave
2 climb	under the stars
3 explore	wild animals
4 kayak	in the snow
5 look for	down a river
6 pick	a tree
7 play	wild fruit
8 track	fossils

Now, write a sentence using each verb phrase.

3 **Look at the photos and complete the names of the places.**

1 d ______ s ______

2 s ______ s ______

3 m ______

4 c ______ s ______

5 b ______

6 s ______

GRAMMAR

1 **Choose the correct options to complete the sentences.**

1 They *have never seen* / *never don't see* a city like it.
2 My dad *has already bought* / *already buy* the paint.
3 I have had it *since* / *for* one year.
4 Last night, my sister *left* / *have left* her bag on the train.

Correct the mistakes in the sentences.

5 I never been to a wedding and I want to come.
6 Tom left his science book at school and he needs it because he doesn't do his homework yet.
7 My mum has played the violin for she was six.
8 I have texted you an hour ago, but you didn't answer.

2 **Write questions for the answers. Then, answer the questions about yourself. Use *never, just, yet* or *already* in your answers.**

0 *Have you ever done a Saturday job?*
No, I've never done a Saturday job.

1 Yes, I've just finished my homework.
2 I've lived in this town for five years.
3 Yes, I have. I visited Russia in 2018 for the World Cup!
4 Yes, I've already read three English books this year.
5 No, I've never cooked a pizza.
6 I've known my best friend since I was three years old.

3 **Complete the text with the correct form of the verbs in brackets. Use the past simple or present perfect.**

I **(1)** .... (love) languages since I **(2)** .... (be) a little boy. My dad is English and my mum is Spanish, and when I was young, they **(3)** .... (speak) both languages to me at home. So I **(4)** .... (begin) learning English and Spanish as a baby. Then we **(5)** .... (move) to Turkey for my dad's work, and I **(6)** .... (go) to primary school there. I **(7)** .... (learn) Turkish quite quickly in school. Now, we live in Japan. I **(8)** .... (not start) learning Japanese yet. But I'm going to learn it soon.

PREPARE FOR THE EXAM

Listening Part 5

1 **For each question, choose the correct answer.**

124

You will hear Ella and Tom talking about people's hobbies. What is each person's hobby?

PEOPLE	HOBBIES
0 Suzy *F*	**A** collecting things
1 Jason	**B** cooking
2 Laura	**C** doing sport
3 Tom	**D** horse riding
4 Ella	**E** listening to music
5 Maria	**F** photography
	G playing an instrument
	H shopping

Writing Part 6

2 **You would like to go camping next weekend.**

Write an email to your English friend, Sam.

- Ask Sam to come with you.
- Say where you want to go camping.
- Tell Sam what to bring.

Write **25 words** or more.

Speaking Part 1

3 **Make questions. Then, in pairs, ask and answer the questions.**

1 How many languages / you speak?
2 How long have you studied / spoken this / these languages?
3 your parents / grandparents / speak / same language?
4 What language(s) / they speak?
5 Which languages / would / like / learn? Why?
6 ever visit countries that speak / different language?
7 like / learn / English?
8 What / most difficult thing / about English?
9 What / best thing / about learning English?

17 STAYING HEALTHY

ABOUT YOU

13 **Watch the video and discuss the questions.**
Have you ever hurt yourself? What happened?
Have you ever had an accident?
Have you ever broken a bone?

VOCABULARY AND READING

Body parts

1 **Match the words in the box to the body parts 1–12.**

EP

ankle	back	blood	brain	ear	finger
heart	neck	stomach	thumb	toe	tongue

125 **Listen and check. Then repeat.**

126 **2** **Name the body parts A–H. Listen and check.**

3 **Work in pairs. One of you says a letter or a number, the other says the body part.**

4 **Match the definitions with the words from Exercise 1. You may need to make some of the words plural.**

1 You've got ten of these on your feet. ....
2 Your food goes into here when you eat. ....
3 You think with this. ....
4 This joins your leg to your foot. ....
5 You've got four of these on each hand. ....
6 This carries things that keep us healthy around our bodies. ....
7 This joins your body to your head. ....
8 You've got one of these on each hand. ....
9 You hear with these. ....
10 This is opposite to the front of your body. ....
11 This sends blood around your body. ....
12 You use this to talk. ....

5 **Read Ben's blog on page 99 about what happened to him yesterday. Which parts of his body did he hurt?**

6 **Are these sentences right (✓) or wrong (✗)?**

1 Ben got a bike for his birthday.
2 There were often quite a lot of people on the cycle path.
3 The two cyclists knocked Ben off his bike.
4 The two cyclists came back to help Ben.
5 Ben was able to ride his bike after the accident.
6 Ben had blood on his clothes when he got home.

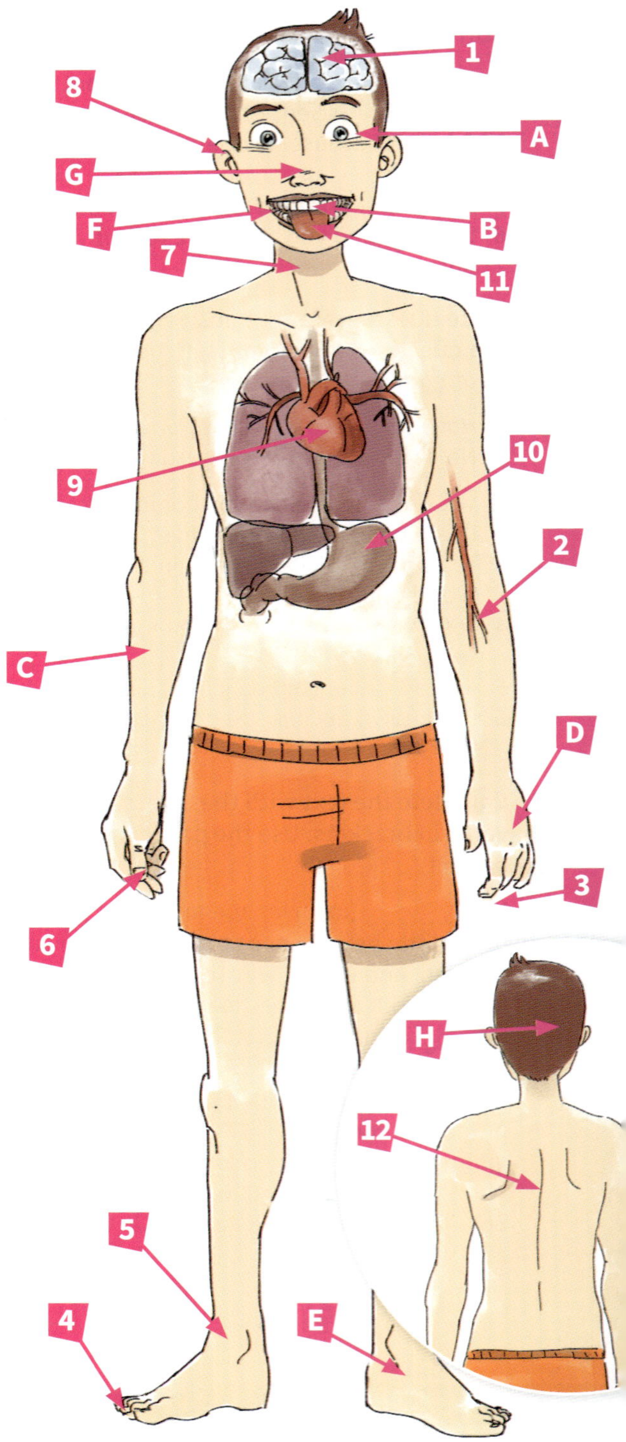

ACCIDENT!

Posted by Ben09 on Monday 13th May

127

This is me with my new bike – before the accident! Have you ever fallen off your bike and hurt yourself? Well, here's my story.

It was my birthday (thanks for all the texts) and this amazing bike was my present. I went for a ride by myself along the bike path. The path isn't usually busy. But that day there were two cyclists coming towards me. I slowed down as quickly as possible but I forgot it was a new bike with good brakes! I stopped really suddenly and fell off. I hit my ankle and it really hurt. The two cyclists rode past and didn't stop. I sat on the ground and watched their backs as they rode away. They were enjoying themselves too much to think about me! I got up by myself and picked up my bike, which luckily was OK. My heart was beating fast as I cycled slowly home and people were looking at me! When I got there I found out why – there was blood all over my T-shirt from a cut on my ear.

GRAMMAR Reflexive pronouns

1 **Look at the examples from Ben's blog and complete the Grammar box.**

Have you ever fallen off your bike and hurt yourself?
They were enjoying themselves too much.

2 **Complete the table with reflexive pronouns: *himself*, *yourselves*, *herself*, *ourselves*.**

We use *-self* when the subject and the object of the verb are *the same* / *a different* person.

I	myself	we	**c**	....
you	yourself	you	**d**	....
he	**a**	they		themselves
she	**b**			

» GRAMMAR REFERENCE AND PRACTICE PAGE 163

3 **Look at two more examples from Ben's blog and match sentences 1 and 2 to meanings a and b.**

1 I went for a ride by myself.
2 I got up by myself.

We use the expression *by myself, yourself etc.* to mean **a** *alone* or **b** *without any help*.

4 **Complete the sentences with the correct reflexive pronouns.**

1 Peter wasn't badly hurt and drove .... to the hospital.
2 Simon and I really enjoyed .... at the party.
3 I hurt .... when I fell off the chair.
4 Zoë told .... that she wasn't ill.
5 Ben and Sara prepared all the food by ....
6 Be careful! Don't cut .... with that knife!
7 'You can help .... to paper and pens,' the teacher said to the students.

5 **Correct the mistakes in the sentences.**

1 I bought a new shirt for me which was very nice.
2 Our friends had a really good time together and everybody enjoyed.
3 You need to bring a photo of you with your name.
4 She went herself. No one went with her.
5 We were both hungry, so we went out and bought us some sandwiches.

6 **Read the conversation and answer the questions.**

1 What's Sara done?
2 Where's she going?
3 Who's going with her?

Anna: Hi, Sara, are you ok?
Sara: Hi, Anna, no, not really. I've hurt my big toe. Look!
Anna: Oh no, that's horrible! Are you going to the doctor?
Sara: Yes.
Anna: Are you going by yourself?
Sara: Yes, but I'll be fine.
Anna: No, you won't. I'll come with you.

7 **In pairs, write your own conversations about an accident.**

Use the conversation in Exercise 6 to help you. Choose different sentences from the box to include in each conversation.

Practise your conversations. Then role-play a conversation in front of the class.

> Help yourselves!
> I tried it myself and it was delicious.
> They didn't enjoy themselves that day.
> He couldn't do it by himself.
> We bought ourselves new clothes after that.
> Did she cut herself?

A

Teen Health

128

C

B

Today's topics

- How much exercise should I do?
- Are some foods healthier than others?
- Can it be dangerous to listen to loud music?
- Is it OK to feel sad sometimes?

1 ....

Yes! But how do you know when it's too loud? Can someone sitting next to you on the train hear the music on your earphones? They can? Do they get upset? Do they get angry? Well, then you need to make it quieter. Remember, you need to look after your ears, so you'll be able to hear well when you're older.

D

READING

1 **Work with a partner. Look at Today's Topics on the *Teen Health* website. What do you think the answers to the questions are?**

2 **Look at the questions on the *Teen Health* website. Match them to the paragraphs.**

3 **Work with a partner. Read the texts again. Tell your partner what they say about:**

1 earphones
2 hearing well
3 too much sport
4 playing sport after meals
5 feelings
6 a friend, parent or teacher
7 a plate of chips
8 variety

4 **In pairs, ask and answer the questions.**

1 Do you listen to loud music on your headphones?
2 Do you eat healthily? What do you like to eat?
3 Do you do too little or enough exercise?

PRONUNCIATION /uː/ and /ʊ/

129 **5** **Listen and repeat the sentence. Do both the *oo* words have the same sound?**

These types of food are good for you.

What other words sound like:

a *food?*   b *good?*

6 **In pairs, discuss whether you agree with the website's answers to the teenagers' questions.**

TALKING POINTS

Do you worry about any of these things?
What do people your age usually worry about?
What do you worry about? Why?

VOCABULARY Adjectives to express emotion

1 **Match the words in the box to photos A–J.**

EP

angry	confident	embarrassed
friendly	lazy	lonely
surprised	unhappy	upset
worried		

2 **Complete the sentences with the adjectives in Exercise 1.**

1 I feel very .... today. All I want to do is sit here and read my book. I don't want to do any exercise.
2 I was so .... when the teacher asked me to read my story. My face went red!
3 It was my first day at the new school today and everyone was really .... It was great!
4 I read a lot of French magazines, so I'm really .... about my French exam.
5 My brother doesn't have any friends and he gets very .... by himself.
6 You look .... You didn't think you'd get 100% in that test did you?
7 That woman over there is very .... She's shouting really loudly.
8 I can't find my phone anywhere. I'm really .... that I've lost it.
9 You look .... today. Usually, you're smiling and laughing! What's the matter?
10 He was very .... when he failed the exam. He didn't want to talk to anyone.

3 **In pairs, tell each other about different situations when you had some of the feelings in Exercise 1.**

2 ....

Everyone tells you it's not healthy to sit at the computer all day. For one thing, it's very lonely and can make you feel lazy. But doing too much sport can also be bad for you. Your body is still young, so you shouldn't do too much exercise. You can easily hurt something. About an hour of sport a day is right for a teenager. You should also think about when you do sport. For example, you can get a stomach ache if you play tennis just after you've eaten.

3 ....

Everyone feels unhappy from time to time, so you're not alone. Don't be surprised. It's normal for your feelings to change at your age. Is there something you're worried about? Find a friendly person to talk to, like your mum or dad or a teacher. You might get a bit embarrassed, but you'll be glad that you did. If you talk about your problems, they aren't so bad.

4 ....

The answer to this is yes! I'm sure you know that a plate of fruit is better for you than a plate of chips! But what your growing body, your heart and your brain need is variety. If you are careful and eat a bit of everything, then you are healthier. Don't forget fresh fruit, vegetables and eggs! Eating a variety of healthy food gives you energy and can help you feel confident about studying and doing exams.

LISTENING

PREPARE FOR THE EXAM

Listening Part 1

1 **Look at the pictures. In pairs, discuss what you can see in each one.**

2 **For each question, choose the correct picture.**

130

1 What time is basketball practice today?

2 Which food does the girl choose?

3 Which earphones does the boy buy?

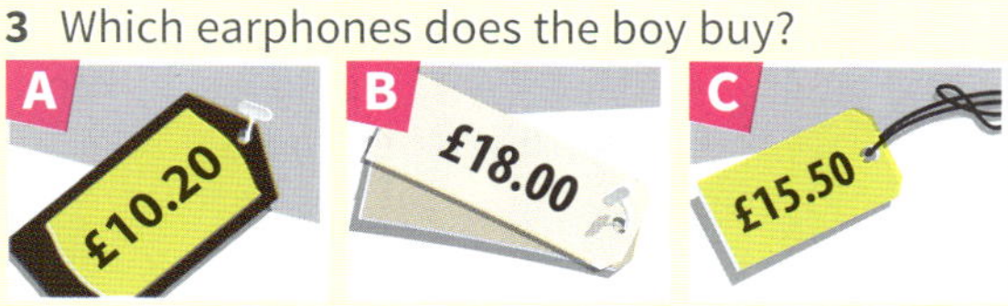

4 What's the weather like?

5 What are they going to do?

SPEAKING

1 **Look at photos A–D below and match them to the things the teenagers are worried about 1–4.**

1 I failed my exam.
2 They haven't picked me for the team.
3 My parents don't understand me.
4 I think it's broken.

2 **Work in pairs. Take turns to be the teenager asking a question about one of the problems in Exercise 1 and the person giving advice. Use the ideas in the *Teen Health* website and the phrases in the box to help you.**

How about …	Why don't you …
Why not …	You should …

I failed my exam. What can I do?

You should ask the teacher what you need to work on. You're always listening to music. Maybe you should spend more time studying.

18 FROM COVER TO COVER

ABOUT YOU

Write a list of all the things you've read in the last three days.
How many books are included in your list? What kind of books are they?

VOCABULARY AND READING

Books and reading

1 **Look at the messages, signs and notices. Where would you see 3, 4, 5 and 6?**

1

Kat
I've just finished an amazing book – the kind you pick up and then can't put down again! I'll lend it to you, if you want.
Amber

131

2

To: All students
From: School secretary
Reply Forward

Everyone – please remember! If you don't return your library books by the end of term, you will have to pay for them.

3

HILLCREST SCHOOL

The writer Jill Hadfield is speaking here next Tuesday! If you buy a book after her talk, she'll write in it for you.

4

Put books back on the right shelves when you've finished with them.
Library receptionist

5

If you buy two books today, we'll give you another from this table **FOR FREE!**

6

Class 9A
Everyone who took a maths textbook home, please bring it back to school tomorrow. If you don't, I won't be able to lend them to 9B.
Miss Taylor

PREPARE FOR THE EXAM

Reading Part 1

2 **For each question choose the correct answer.**

1 What is Amber doing in this message?
  A telling Kat when she'll finish her book
  B asking Kat for some advice about a book
  C finding out if Kat wants to borrow a book

2 What must students do?
  A take the books they've borrowed back to the library
  B collect the books they've ordered from the library
  C choose which books they want to take out of the library

3 Next Tuesday, students will be able to
  A find out how to write a book.
  B listen to a well-known writer.
  C get some books at a special price.

4 The receptionist wants people to
  A ask if they cannot find the right book.
  B return books to the correct place after using them.
  C give books back to him when they've finished them.

5 **A** Every customer will get a free book today.
  B There's a discount on all books for today only.
  C You can get three books for the price of two today.

6 **A** Miss Taylor wants to give the books to another class.
  B Miss Taylor has new maths books to lend to the class.
  C Miss Taylor would like to know who borrowed her books.

3 **In pairs, compare your answers. Discuss why you chose each answer and change any you think are wrong.**

4 Find and underline the phrasal verbs in the texts in Exercises 1 and 2. Then match each one to its meaning a–h.

EP

bring back	find out	give back
pick up	put back	put down
take back	take out	

a return something to a person
b lift something with your hands
c return from somewhere with something
d learn something new
e return something to the place you borrowed or bought it from
f put something you are holding onto the floor or a table, for example
g return something to a place
h remove something from somewhere

5 Complete the sentences with phrasal verbs from Exercise 4 in the correct tense.

1 Did you ________ what we need to do for homework?
2 Can you ________ all the books and clothes from the floor, please?
3 My mum went to China and ________ some great presents for us.
4 How many books are you allowed to ________ of the school library?
5 My book is so exciting. I can't ________ it ________!
6 Thanks for lending me this magazine! I'll ________ it ________ to you tomorrow.
7 My new book had several pages missing, so I'm going to ________ it ________ to the shop.
8 When you've finished with my book, can you ________ it ________ in my room?

6 » In pairs, go to page 138. Choose one of the situations and write a short conversation. Use at least three phrasal verbs in your conversation.

7 In small groups, ask and answer the questions.

1 What's your school library like? What sort of books can you borrow from it?
2 Is there a library in your town? Do you borrow books from it? What else do you do there?
3 How do you feel about lending other people your books or other things?
4 Do you ever borrow books or other things from friends? Do you look after them carefully?

GRAMMAR First conditional

1 Look at the examples of first conditional sentences. Then, find and underline all the examples in Exercise 1 on page 102.

If you buy two books today, **we'll give** you another from this table for free!
I'll lend it to you, **if you want**.

2 Read the information and choose the correct answers to the questions.

Sentences in the first conditional have two clauses:
if + verb … , *will* + infinitive
1 Does the *if* clause have to come first?
Yes, it does. / No, it doesn't.
2 What tense do we use after *if*?
Present simple / Future simple

We use first conditional sentences to talk about a possible future.
3 How sure are we about that future?
Very sure / Not very sure

» GRAMMAR REFERENCE AND PRACTICE PAGE 164

3 Match the two halves of the sentences.

1 We'll miss the film	a I'll give it to the teacher.
2 If I find your book,	b if you don't hurry.
3 I won't tell anyone	c if you can't find yours.
4 If you don't eat fast food,	d you'll be healthier.
5 I'll lend you my earphones	e if you don't want me to.

4 Complete these sentences with your own ideas.

1 You won't get into the football team if …
2 If our team get into the final, …
3 If I have time this weekend, …
4 I'll lend you my jacket if …

5 Correct the mistakes in the sentences.

1 If I will go, I will play with my friends.
2 I'm happy if you come to my party.
3 If you join this class, you like it.
4 If you like, we would go by car.
5 My mum is angry if I don't wear these trousers.

ə PRONUNCIATION Sentence stress

6 Listen to the sentences. Mark the stressed words, then practise the sentences.

132

0 I'll bring cake if you bring sandwiches.
1 They'll come if you invite them.
2 If you pass the exam, I'll buy you a present.
3 You'll miss the bus if you don't hurry.
4 If you help Tom, I'll help Pete.

7 » In pairs, go to page 138 and play the *If* game.

READING

1 Look at the pictures of the books and try to guess what they are about. Read the texts quickly to check your ideas.

133

BOOKS TO MAKE YOU laugh this summer

We asked three readers to tell us about a funny book they enjoyed – here's what they told us.

A NATALIE

My mum bought this for me for my birthday and I knew from the picture on the front and the title that I was going to love it. I read it in just two days and I was really sad when I got to the end. The story is about a girl who has to help her family by getting back some stolen paintings – I found it really exciting! I'm now a huge fan of the author, Ally Carter – I have all her other books on my shelf ready for the summer.

B HEIDI

In my opinion, this is one of the funniest books ever written for teenagers. It's about a 15-year-old boy who wants to start a rock band, but the adults in his life all try to stop him. Nothing goes right for him until the very end of the story. The writer is also an artist and the clever drawings on each page help the story along. Unfortunately, the cover makes it look like it's for little kids, which is a shame as it might stop some teenagers from picking it up.

C DAVINA

I got this book for a great price in my local store. It's a funny story about a terrible girl who has to learn to be a better person. It's the first time I've tried this kind of book, but I really enjoyed it. Of course, it's not perfect – I wasn't happy with what happens in the last few pages. But it was a lot of fun, and I think I'll probably read more like it in the future.

PREPARE FOR THE EXAM

Reading Part 2

2 **For each question, choose the correct answer. Write *A* for Natalie, *B* for Heidi or *C* for Davina.**

1 Who didn't like the way the book ended?
2 Who plans to read more books by the same writer?
3 Who explains where she bought the book?
4 Who thought the pictures inside were excellent?
5 Who says the book is different from what she usually reads?
6 Who thinks some people may get the wrong idea about the book?
7 Who says it didn't take her long to read the book?

TALKING POINTS

Do you like reading? If yes, what sort of books?
What's the best book you've ever read?

VOCABULARY Words about books

1 EP **Read the texts again and underline the words from the box. Then, match them to the definitions 1–9.**

author	chapter	cover	drawings
end	opinion	pages	shelf	title

1 This is the last part of the book.
2 The words and pictures on this help you decide if you want to read it.
3 This is the name the writer gives to the book.
4 These pictures are done with a pen or pencil.
5 You can put your books on this.
6 You turn these as you read.
7 This person writes books.
8 This is what you think or believe about something.
9 This is one of the sections of a book that usually has a number or title.

2 **Complete the questions with words from Exercise 1. Then, in pairs, ask and answer the questions.**

1 Do you listen to other people's ________ when you choose a book to read?
2 Do you think books with ________ in them are just for little kids?
3 Have you ever chosen a book because you think the ________ or ________ look interesting?
4 Do you like books with hundreds of ________ or do you prefer shorter ones?
5 Have you ever got to the ________ of a book and felt sad that it was finished?

LISTENING

134 **1** **Listen to the teacher talking to his class. Which of these is he talking about?**

a new book   a competition   a website   a writer

134 **2** **Read the sentences. Then, listen again. Are the sentences right (✓) or wrong (✗)?**

1 If you're under 12, you can enter the competition.
2 To win, you need to read more books than anyone else.
3 If you enter, you'll have to buy lots of books.
4 The teacher will give the students all the instructions they need.
5 One of the prizes is a writing course.
6 You can see people's opinions of books on the competition website.
7 You might save money if you buy a book from the website.
8 The website blog is written by teenagers who like writing stories.

3 **In pairs, ask and answer the questions.**

1 How many books do you usually read in the long school holiday?
2 Would you like to enter a competition like this?

WRITING

PREPARE TO WRITE

Writing Part 7 A story

GET READY

Look at the pictures and read the sentences. Put the sentences in the correct order to tell the story.

a He started to feel a bit bored, so he took his book out of his bag and started reading it.
b Unfortunately, Tom was enjoying the book so much that he missed his bus, and he had to wait for the next one.
c Tom was waiting for his bus, but it was late. There was lots of traffic because the weather was bad.

Complete each sentence with one of the linking words in blue above.

1 I'm tired this morning .... I read my book until midnight last night.
2 I lost my library book .... I had to pay for a new one.
3 I liked the writer's first book .... I hated her second one.
4 .... the shop didn't have the book I wanted.
5 I like books that can make me laugh .... cry.

PLAN **You are going to write a story about the pictures on page 139.**

- Look at the pictures carefully.
- Make notes about the story. Answer the questions *Who?*, *Where?* and *What is happening?*
- Write down key vocabulary and decide what tense to use.

WRITE **Now write the story shown in the pictures on page 139. Remember to write about every picture and use linkers. Write 35 words or more.**

IMPROVE **In pairs, read each other's stories and check you have both used linking words correctly.**

CULTURE

ENGLISH LITERATURE

1 **In pairs, ask and answer the questions.**

1 What books do you like?
2 Who wrote them?
3 Can you name some famous authors from your country?

2 **Have you heard of R. J. Palacio? Have you read any of her books or seen films of them? Read the text and complete the fact file.**

R.J. Palacio

R. J. PALACIO was born in New York and still lives there with her husband, two sons and two dogs. She studied at the High School of Art and Design and worked for many years as a graphic designer, creating book covers. She wrote her first book, *Wonder*, in 2012. R. J. is also the author of several short stories and has recently published a picture book for younger readers called *We're All Wonders*, combining her writing and artistic talents. She wanted to be a writer for many years but never found the time until one day she decided to write *Wonder*. She says, 'This story was something that I wanted to say and I needed to say.' The book is about a boy who looks very different to other teenagers and his experiences when he first goes to school. The film of the book came out in 2017.

135

FACT FILE R. J. Palacio

Nationality: (1) ....
First job: (2) ....
First book (name and date): (3) ....
Other books: (4) ....
Date of film: (5) ....

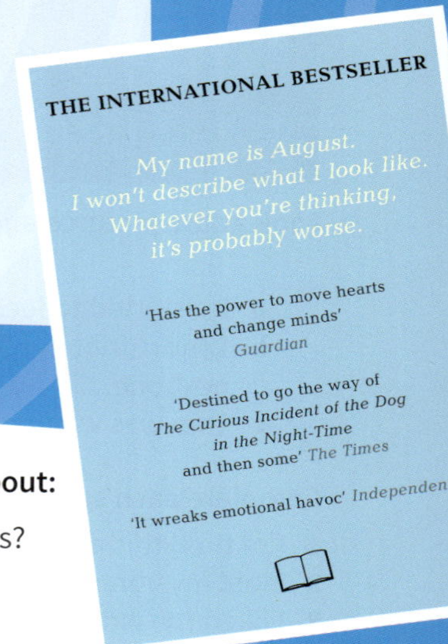

3 **Look at the cover of *Wonder* and the words on the back cover. What do they tell you about:**

1 the main character's name? 2 what he looks like? 3 how good the book is?

4 **Put the sentences about the beginning of the story in the correct order.**

a ☐ He feels lonely sitting on his own, but then he meets a friendly girl called Summer.
b ☐ Jack is sorry and he and August become friends again.
c ☐ When he arrives, the principal of the school asks three students to look after him,
d 1 It's August's first day at his first school.
e ☐ He also meets another boy, Jack,
f ☐ who is nice to him at first but then is horrible.
g ☐ but they don't sit with him at lunch.
h ☐ August is upset because his friend isn't nice to him and runs away from school.

5 **Read and listen to part of Chapter 2 of *Wonder*. Guess any words you don't know, or ignore them! Answer the questions.**

1. Why didn't August go to school before fifth grade?
2. Where did he study before?
3. Why doesn't his mother draw anything now?

Why I didn't go to school

136

Next week, I start fifth grade. Since I've never been to a real school before, I am pretty much totally and completely petrified. People think I haven't gone to school because of the way I look, but it's not that. It's because of all the surgeries I've had. Twenty-seven since I was born. The bigger ones happened before I was even four years old, so I don't remember those. But I've had two or three surgeries every year since then (some big, some small), and because I'm little for my age, and I have some other medical mysteries that doctors never really figured out, I used to get sick a lot. That's why my parents decided it was better if I didn't go to school. I'm much stronger now, though. The last surgery I had was eight months ago, and I probably won't have to have any more for another couple of years.

Mom homeschools me. She used to be a children's-book illustrator. She draws really great fairies and mermaids. Her boy stuff isn't so hot, though. She once tried to draw me a Darth Vader, but it ended up looking like some weird mushroom-shaped robot. I haven't seen her draw anything in a long time. I think she's too busy taking care of me and Via.

I can't say I always wanted to go to school because that wouldn't be exactly true. What I wanted was to go to school, but only if I could be like every other kid going to school. Have lots of friends and hang out after school and stuff like that.

6 **Read the text again and choose the correct options.**

1. August feels *worried* / *confident* about going to school.
2. He has spent a lot of his life in *hotels* / *hospitals*.
3. He didn't go to school because he was often *ill* / *unhappy*.
4. His mother is good at drawing pictures for *girls* / *boys*.
5. August wants to go to school to *make friends* / *learn more*.

TALKING POINTS

Would you like to read the book? Why / Why not?

PROJECT

A book blurb and author fact file

A blurb is a short description about a book on the back of its cover. It should make you want to read the book! Write a blurb of no more than 50 words about your favourite book.

Include:

- an outline of what happens in the book
- why it is a good book

Find out about the book's author and write a fact file to go with your blurb. Tell your class about your favourite author and read your blurb.

14 NOW WATCH THE CULTURE VIDEO

19 DIFFERENT INGREDIENTS

Breakfast cereals

137

Breakfast cereals are popular in many countries. They are made from grains, such as corn, wheat and rice. They are usually eaten with milk, or with yogurt and fruit. In the beginning, cereals were health foods, but these days some children's cereals are 50% sugar, and doctors say we shouldn't eat them too often.

There are lots of kinds of cereal. This is how cereals in different shapes, like stars and balls, are made.

- First, the grain is taken to the factory, where it is cleaned and checked.
- Then it is **prepared** for cooking. It is made into flour and **mixed** with other ingredients. Water is **added** and the mixture is **boiled**.
- When it is soft, it is put into special machines which make it into shapes like stars, circles, or even letters of the alphabet.
- The shapes are **baked** in an oven to dry them. Then, they are 'puffed' in another machine to make them light and full of air.
- After that, they are **covered** with sugar or honey. Some are **filled** with chocolate. The cereal pieces are then **dried** in hot air.
- Finally, the cereal is packed into boxes, ready for the shops.

A

B

C

VOCABULARY AND READING

Words to describe cooking

ABOUT YOU

Do you eat breakfast cereals?
How often do you eat them?
What kinds do you like?
Do you think they are healthy?

1 **Read the text and put photos A–C in the correct order.**

2 **Look at the verbs in the text. Match them to the definitions below. Write the verbs in the infinitive.**

EP

1. Put one thing with another thing.
2. Make something ready.
3. Take the water out of something.
4. Join two or more things together using a spoon or a machine.
5. Cook something like a cake in an oven.
6. Cook in water.
7. Put something on top of something else.
8. Make an empty space full.

3 **In pairs, ask and answer the questions.**

1. What other kinds of food do you eat for breakfast?
2. How do you prepare them?
3. Describe the best breakfast you have ever had.

PRONUNCIATION Ways to pronounce *ea*

138 **4** **Listen to the different ways to say the letters *ea*.**

/ɪə/ ear /e/ head /iː/ seat

5 **In pairs, put these words into the correct column of the table.**

beach	bread	breakfast	
clean	eat	healthy	meal
near	ready	teacher	wheat

/ɪə/ **ear**	/e/ **head**	/iː/ **seat**

139 **Listen and check. Then repeat.**

GRAMMAR Present simple passive

1 **Look at the sentence from the article. The verbs are in the present simple passive. Find other examples of the present simple passive in the text on page 108 and complete the rules.**

The grain is taken to the factory, where it is cleaned and checked.

1 To make the passive, we use the verb .... and the .... of the main verb.
2 When we use the passive, we *always have to* / *don't always have to* say who does the action.

» GRAMMAR REFERENCE AND PRACTICE PAGE 165

2 **Complete the text with the present simple or present simple passive form of the verbs in brackets.**

How orange juice is made

The oranges (1) .... (pull off) the trees and then they (2) .... (put) into boxes. These (3) .... (send) to a factory which (4) .... (make) juice.

At the factory, the fruit (5) .... (wash and dry) and any bad oranges (6) .... (throw away). After that, the fruit (7) .... (cut) in half and the juice (8) .... (remove) by a machine. Most factories then (9) .... (heat) the juice to 94 °C. This makes it last a lot longer (6–8 months outside the fridge). The hot juice (10) .... (put) into cartons or bottles and then left to cool. Finally, lorries (11) .... (take) the cartons to supermarkets, where they (12) .... (sell).

3 **Rewrite the sentences in the passive. You don't need to say who does the action.**

0 People throw away a lot of food these days.
A lot of food is thrown away these days.
1 They play loud rock music in my favourite café.
2 People often eat bread with butter and jam.
3 At my school, they serve lunch at 12.30 every day.
4 Our teacher always puts our paintings on the classroom wall.
5 People in Britain eat a lot of sweets and chocolates.

4 **Choose the correct options to complete each sentence.**

1 My house *paints* / *is painted* red and blue.
2 These trousers *are cost* / *cost* only £15!
3 Do you know that girl? She *calls* / *is called* Sarah.
4 My sister's children *call* / *are called* Charlie and Karen.
5 The kitchen drawer *breaks* / *is broken* and the cooker is not working.
6 The price of the ticket *includes* / *is included* lunch.
7 Dinner *is always cooked* / *always cooks* by my dad.

5 **Work with a partner. Invent a snack, for example a new kind of ice cream, cake or biscuit. Draw a picture of it and describe what it is like and how it is made. Read your description to the class.**

6 **While you are listening to the other students' descriptions, imagine you are the manager of a food company. Decide which new snack you are going to make in your factory.**

READING

1 Look at the website. Whose blog is this? What is it about? What information can you find on the website?

140

THE TASTE TEST

About me

Hello everyone!

Thank **(0)** *you* for visiting my blog. My name's Caitlin and I'm 14. I've always loved cooking. **(1)** ________ I was nine, I told my parents I wanted to be **(2)** ________ chef and that's still my plan today. I especially love making cakes and baking.

On this blog, I want to show people **(3)** ________ much fun it is to cook. I also want to show them that cooking a meal can **(4)** ________ quick and easy, and that it tastes better **(5)** ________ food that is made in a factory.

And remember, if you do the cooking, you don't have to do the washing-up. That's my rule anyway. So go on – make a mess! I always do.

Don't forget **(6)** ________ leave me a message if you like anything on my website. Happy reading!

The best steak!

YOU NEED:

1 steak per person
some garlic
a little butter
salt and pepper

HOW TO MAKE IT

1. Cover the steak in salt and pepper.
2. Heat the grill. It needs to be hot!
3. Grill the steak for two or three minutes on each side.
4. Fry the garlic in the butter.
5. Serve the steak with garlic butter, fried potatoes and green beans or carrots.

Pancakes

YOU NEED:

2 eggs
300 ml milk
100 g flour

HOW TO MAKE THEM

1. Mix the eggs and milk together.
2. Add the eggs and milk to the flour.
3. Put some oil in a pan.
4. Cook the pancake on both sides.
5. Cover it with lemon and sugar, chocolate sauce or cream, or with pieces of fresh fruit, such as banana and raspberries.

3 Read the two recipes. Match each recipe to one of the photos A–G. Which recipe would you like to make? Do you know any other recipes?

PREPARE FOR THE EXAM

Reading Part 5

2 Complete the *About me* text on the web page. For each question, write the correct answer. Write one word for each gap.

TALKING POINTS

15 Watch the video, then discuss the questions.

What's your favourite food?
Do you like to cook?
Tell me about your favourite breakfast.

VOCABULARY Ingredients; *make* and *do*

1 Match the words in the box to photos A–H below.

EP

beans carrots garlic melon pears
potatoes salt and pepper steak

141 Listen and check. Then repeat.

2 Now, write them in the table under the correct headings. Add more words you know to each column.

Meat	Fruit	Vegetables	Other
steak			

3 Check the meaning of these words in a dictionary. Can you find pictures of foods cooked like this on the web page on page 110?

EP

baked boiled fried grilled roast

4 In pairs, say what you use each thing for.

1 knife / fork / spoon
You use a knife to cut food. You use a fork to pick food up. You use a spoon to …
2 mug / glass / cup
3 bowl / plate / dish

5 Put the words and phrases with *make* and *do* in the correct column in the table.

EP

the bed a cake ~~the cleaning~~
~~a cup of tea~~ the dishes your homework
a mess a mistake the shopping
the washing

make	do
a cup of tea	*the cleaning*

6 Which of the things in Exercise 5 do you sometimes/often/never do?

A

B

C

D

E

F

G

H

LISTENING

PREPARE FOR THE EXAM

Listening Part 2

1 For each question, write the correct answer in the gap. Write one word or a number or a date or a time.

142

You will hear a woman giving information about a cooking competition.

SCHOOL CHEF COMPETITION	
For students aged:	12–15
Last date to enter:	**(1)** .... June
Number of teams:	**(2)** ....
Where competition will be:	**(3)** the ....
Name of chef:	**(4)** John ....
Prizes:	**(5)** T-shirts, cookbooks and ....

2 In pairs, compare your answers. Then, listen again and check.

142

SPEAKING

1 You are going to enter the Junior Chef cooking competition. Work in teams of three or four and decide on your recipe.

- What ingredients will you need for your recipe? Make a list together.
- How you will cook it? Write a simple recipe. Look at the ones on page 110 to help you.
- Who will do the different jobs, such as shopping, cutting the vegetables, cooking on the day of the competition, washing up … ?
- Why is it a good meal to serve in a school café? Try to think of three reasons.

USEFUL LANGUAGE

Can you cut the vegetables?
I'd prefer not to do the dishes.
I'll buy the ingredients.
I'm not sure about that.
Let's …
That's a great idea.
That sounds good!
What about …?
Why don't we …?

2 Present your ideas to the class. Choose the best dish for your school café.

20 LIFE CHANGES

ABOUT YOU

Have you moved house or changed schools recently? Talk to your partner about it.

VOCABULARY AND READING

change as a verb and noun

1 **Match sentences 1–4 to the meanings of *change* a–d.**

EP
1. I'm sorry, I can't change a ten-pound note.
2. You've really changed your life.
3. Please can I change this jacket? It's too small.
4. We had to change planes in San Francisco.

a take something back to a shop and get something else in its place
b give someone smaller coins when they have paid with a larger coin or note
c move from one kind of transport to another
d do something very different from when you were younger

Now look at sentences with the noun *change* (5–8) and match them to meanings e–h.

5. Remember to bring a change of shoes. It might be wet.
6. I'll email you my change of address.
7. That will make a change.
8. My grandparents hate change.

e new contact details
f something interesting because it's new
g something becoming different
h another item of similar clothing

2 » Go to page 139.

3 **Look at pictures A–F in the article. In pairs, discuss the life changes they show.**

4 **Read the article. Which picture is about Joe's life change?**

5 **Read the post again and answer the questions.**

1. What did Joe remember about his bedtimes as a little boy?
2. Why did they move from London?
3. How did Joe feel about the move?
4. What happened in Dublin that changed their lives?
5. Did people like his mum's first album? How do you know?
6. What was the new apartment like?
7. Which does he prefer, his new life or his old life?

LIFE CHANGES

143

Hi, my name's Joe and I'm 15. I want to tell you about something which changed my life. My mum always sang me songs at bedtime when I was a little boy. The songs weren't written by other people. They were all her own work. Anyway, Mum changed her job and it meant we had to move from London to New York. I was very excited but sad to leave my friends. When we were changing planes in Dublin my mum started talking to a man who worked for a record company. She told him about her songs, and he asked her to send him some of them. When we got to New York, Mum sent him some songs, and he loved them. A year later, her first album was released and it sold a million copies in a week! She recorded another and soon she was rich.

Our old apartment wasn't very comfortable and because mum had lots of money we moved to a really big apartment with a great view of Central Park. Then, our lives really changed. Suddenly, everything was done for us, our food was cooked by someone else, our apartment was cleaned, I was driven to school, Mum and I were flown everywhere in a private plane. I know it sounds amazing and it is, but actually I'd like to go back to my old life in London.

GRAMMAR Past simple passive

1 **Look at the example sentences from the article. Choose the correct words to complete the rule.**

1 Everything **was done** for us.
2 Mum and I **were flown** everywhere in a private plane.

The past simple passive is formed with the *present simple / past simple* of the verb 'be' plus the *past simple / past participle* of the main verb.

» GRAMMAR REFERENCE AND PRACTICE PAGE 166

2 **Find other examples of the past simple passive in Joe's post. How many examples tell you who did the action? Why isn't it always necessary to say who did the action?**

3 **Write sentences in the past simple passive about what happened before the day of Joe's 16th birthday.**

0 The guests / invite.
The guests were invited.
1 The clothes / make.
2 The music / chose.
3 The cake / decorate.
4 The food / prepare.
5 The presents / buy.

4 **Rewrite the text, changing the verbs in italics into the past simple passive. Decide if you need to say who did the action. Which of the four photos is best for the new text?**

A CHANGING GARDEN

The Qing Emperor Qianlong (1) *designed* the Garden of Clear Ripples in the middle of the sixteenth century. But there was a war about 100 years later and people (2) *destroyed* some of the garden. So the Emperor Guangxu (3) *built* the garden and the buildings again and he (4) *gave* them a new name: the Summer Palace. Empress Dowager Cixi (5) *used* the Summer Palace. In 1924, someone (6) *changed* it into a public park.

Empress Dowager Cixi

Garden of Clear Ripples

Emperor Qianlong

Emperor Guangxu

5 **Correct the mistakes in the sentences.**

1 It gave to me by my uncle.
2 My bike is stolen last year.
3 They were cost £25.
4 All those things are sold in yesterday's sale.
5 The school open five years ago.

PRONUNCIATION Sounds and spelling

6 **Choose the word in each group which has a different sound to the other words.**

1	buy	boy	by
2	which	witch	watch
3	hear	hair	here
4	would	word	wood
5	know	now	no
6	meat	meet	met
7	own	one	won
8	their	there	they
9	toe	too	to
10	were	wear	where

144 **In pairs, compare your answers. Then listen and check.**

7 **In pairs, take turns to read these sentences aloud.**

1 The boys went to buy some food in the shop by the river.
2 Did you see which witch had a watch?
3 Did you hear that? You can get your hair cut here.
4 Would you write a word on the wood, please?
5 I know there are no books there now.
6 You met Sophie at that café, but we can't meet there because I don't eat meat.
7 She won one of her own.
8 They arrived there in their car.
9 My toe hurts too much to put on those shoes.
10 Where were you yesterday? Did you wear that coat?

8 » **Work with a partner. Go to page 139.**

READING

1 Look at the photos. What do you learn about Kevin Pearce from the fact file?

2 Read the fact file to check your ideas from Exercise 1.

FACT FILE Kevin Pearce

Born: New Hampshire, 1st November 1987
January 1997: entered first snowboarding competition
2002: moved to California with brother Adam
August 2006: won Slopestyle event in New Zealand
January 2008: won open halfpipe in Switzerland.
December 2009: received serious brain injury training in Utah
2010: had to relearn how to walk, talk and swallow
2010: his brother Adam left work to help look after Kevin
2013: the Sundance Film Festival showed documentary film about his life, *The Crash Reel*
2014: Adam and Kevin set up *Love Your Brain Foundation*
2014 – today: giving talks at schools and hospitals
2017: moved back to Vermont

145

KEVIN PEARCE was born in **(1)** ______ on 1st November 1987. He grew up where there was plenty of snow in the winter and loved snowboarding from when he was young. He entered his first snowboarding competition when he was **(2)** ______ years old. He moved to California with his brother in **(3)** ______ and started training full-time at Mammoth Mountain. Over the next **(4)** ______ years, he travelled a lot and won events in New Zealand and Switzerland. He was a star of the snowboarding world.

In December 2009, when Kevin was training in Utah, he crashed and was very badly **(5)** ______. He spent three months in hospital and it took him a year to learn basic skills like **(6)** ______, talking and swallowing again. His brother Adam left work to help look after Kevin.

Kevin slowly got better, but he was not able to take part in snowboarding competitions any more. In 2013, a documentary film about his life called *The Crash Reel* was **(7)** ______. A year later, a foundation called **(8)** ______ was started by Kevin and his brother Adam. This helps people who have had brain injuries and teaches activities like yoga and meditation.

(9) ______ 2014, Kevin has been busy visiting schools and hospitals. He talks about how important it is for people to look after their brains and to wear helmets. In 2017, he moved to **(10)** ______ in Vermont.

3 Read the fact file again and complete Kevin's biography.

4 Answer the questions about Kevin.

1. What sport did he start doing when he was a small boy?
2. Who did he go to California with?
3. What did he do at Mammoth Mountain?
4. How well known was he in the sport of snowboarding before his accident?
5. Which part of his body did he hurt worst in the crash?
6. How long did it take before he could do basic things again?
7. Was Kevin able to return to competition snowboarding after his accident?
8. What is *The Crash Reel*?
9. What kinds of things does *Love Your Brain* teach?

TALKING POINTS

How has Kevin's life changed from when he was a teenager? In pairs, discuss what you think he learned from the accident.

VOCABULARY Life changes

1 **Look at the phrases about things that happen in people's lives. Can you put them in order? Some might happen more than once. Work with a partner and then compare your list with another pair.**

EP

be born become a teenager
change schools find part-time work
get married go to high school
learn to walk and talk move house
take exams travel start school
start working or training

2 **In pairs, compare your lists. Now, invent a story of someone's life which uses all these phrases. Use the text about Kevin Pearce to help you. Tell your story to another pair.**

LISTENING

PREPARE FOR THE EXAM

Listening Part 3

1 **For each question, choose the correct answer. You will hear Tanya talking to her friend Jon about her new school.**

146

1 What time did Tanya arrive for her exam at her new school?
A 8.30
B 8.40
C 9.00

2 How does Tanya get to her new school at the moment?
A by bike
B on foot
C by car

3 What can Tanya take home from school?
A a musical instrument
B sports kit
C a science textbook

4 What has Jon just started doing?
A playing in a band
B playing hockey
C working

5 What reason does Jon give for wanting to stay at his school next year?
A friends
B a school trip
C his mum and dad

WRITING

PREPARE TO WRITE

A biography

GET READY **Look at the text about Kevin Pearce again.**

1 How many paragraphs are there?
2 What are the topics of each paragraph?
3 When in each paragraph is Kevin's name used?
4 When is his full name used?
5 When is the pronoun *he* used instead of *Kevin*?

FACT FILE Serena Williams

Born: 26th September 1981 in Michigan in the USA
Early 80s: family moved to Los Angeles
1984: began to play tennis
1995: her father became her coach
1999: won her first tournament, the US Open tennis title
2002: won the Wimbledon tennis tournament
2002: became the number one player in the world
2004: started her own designer label, Aneres (Serena spelt backwards)
2005 & 2007: won the Australian Open
2008: opened Serena Williams Secondary School in Kenya
2011: made International Goodwill Ambassador for UNICEF
2012: won the singles gold medal at the Olympic Games
Languages: English, some French, Spanish and Italian
Family: husband – Alexis Ohanian, one daughter, born 1st September 2017

PLAN **Read the fact file for Serena Williams. You are going to write a short biography about her. Think about:**

- how many paragraphs you will write
- what the topic of each paragraph will be
- when you will use her full name, first name and the pronoun *she*.

WRITE **Write your biography. Use the passive as well as the active in your writing.**

IMPROVE **In pairs, read each other's biography and check for mistakes. Check that you have both included all the necessary information and that you used paragraphs and pronouns correctly.**

LIFE SKILLS STUDY SKILLS

TAKING EXAMS

LIFE SKILLS

When you have an exam you should:

- organise your time
- prepare what you need
- keep calm and don't worry!

Taking exams can make you feel nervous or worried. If you prepare well and relax, you will do your best.

1 **Look at the statements. Are they true for you?**

1 I have a good memory.
2 I find some exams difficult.
3 I don't worry about exams.
4 I can never finish exams in the time.
5 I like doing exams.

In pairs, compare your answers.

2 **Do you think these ideas are important when you have to study for exams?**

1 how much you sleep
2 what you eat
3 preparing what you need for the exam
4 organising your time
5 talking to your teacher
6 doing physical exercise

Read the text and tick the ideas that are mentioned.

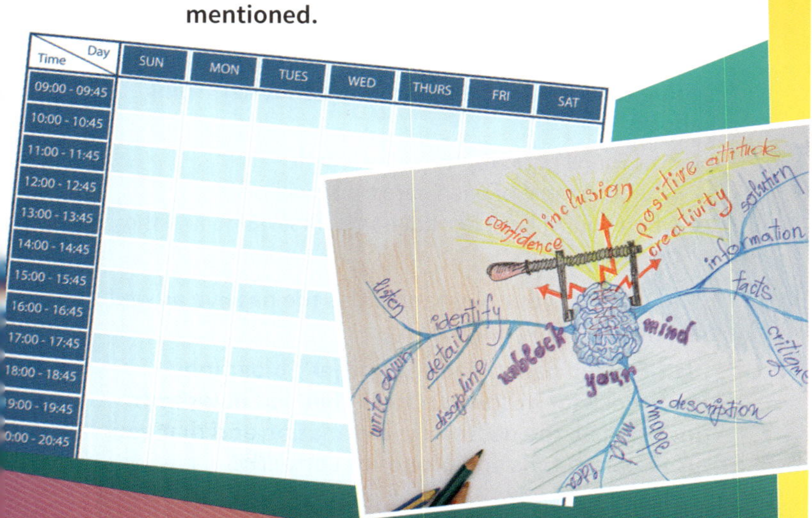

ADVICE – studying for exams

1 ________ : Don't spend too long on one topic, but do a little of each subject every day or week. Make a timetable for the afternoons or evenings, with study time, eating time and include some free moments.

2 ________ : It's difficult to remember too many things at the same time, so if you have a lot of information to learn, divide it into sections.

3 ________ : For example, draw a picture next to a foreign word you want to remember. Or, to remember the formula $E=mc^2$, you could write *The elephant made cakes twice*.

4 ________ : We often remember better if we can see a kind of picture of the most important points. This makes it easier to connect the information in our minds.

5 ________ : Healthy food gives you energy and helps you to concentrate.

6 ________ Stand up every hour and move around. Have a small snack or a short walk to clear your mind.

7 ________ : Don't stay up late to send messages on your phone or play video games. It's better to go to bed not too late, get up early the next day and review what you studied the day before.

8 ________ : You can test each other on what you need to know. For example, if you are studying history, say the name of an important event and then your friend can say the date, or say the date and he/she can try to say the event.

9 ________ : Find time to do some physical activity at the weekend or during the week.

3 **Complete the texts 1–9 with the sentences a-i.**

- **a** Make mind maps with important information
- **b** Get plenty of sleep
- **c** Organise your study time
- **d** Exercise regularly to help your brain
- **e** Have a good breakfast before you go to school
- **f** Make sure you have breaks
- **g** Try and learn information in small blocks
- **h** Draw pictures or create sentences about information you have to learn
- **i** Revise with a friend

4 **Answer the questions. Use ideas from the text on page 116.**

1. What information should you put in a study timetable?
2. What can you do to remember foreign words?
3. What can you do in the morning when you have an exam?
4. What should you do when you take a break from studying?
5. What shouldn't you do at night instead of sleeping?
6. How can friends help each other to study?

5 **What do you do when you have to prepare for exams? Talk to your partner.**

148 **6** **Listen to the conversations and answer the questions.**

Conversation 1: What things did Peter and Matty need for the exam?
Conversation 2: Why did Meg fail her exam?
Conversation 3: Did Sam answer all the questions in the exam?
Conversation 4: What did Tim forget to do in the exam?
Conversation 5: What advice does the teacher give Sophie?

148 **7** **Listen again. Complete the expressions for giving advice.**

USEFUL LANGUAGE

1. You ________ remember to bring an extra pen.
2. ________ I help you study for the next test?
3. You know that you ________ guess?
4. You ________ make sure you've done everything.
5. If I ________ you, I'd look at the clock.

PROJECT

A video presentation

Make a video presentation, giving advice and suggestions for exams.

- Work in small groups.
- Think about what you need to do before an exam, during an exam or at the end of an exam.
- In your group, prepare a short video presentation with the best advice for your class. You can record this on your phones, and you can have a conversation or explain the ideas individually.
- Show your video to the class and be ready to answer any questions about it.
- After you see the video, tell the other groups the ideas you liked.

REVIEW 5 UNITS 17–20

VOCABULARY

1 Put the letters in order to make words for parts of the body.

1 outhm	**7** eadh ....
2 mtuhb	**8** ranib ....
3 grinfse	**9** thare ....
4 cekn	**10** dolob ....
5 esto	**11** cakb ....
6 are	**12** nekal ....

2 Look at the words. Which words are used to talk about books (*B*) and which words are used to talk about preparing food (*F*)?

bowl	chapter	cover	knife
plate	shelf	spoon	title

Now, match the words to the definitions.

1 This is a section of a book that has a number or title. ....
2 We put soup in this. ....
3 We use this to cut our food. ....
4 We put books on this. ....
5 We eat our food off this. ....
6 This is the name of a book. ....
7 This is the front and back of a book. ....
8 We use this to eat soup and ice cream. ....

3 Complete the sentences with the correct form of the words in the box.

be born	change schools	find out
find part-time work	give back	
take back	take exams	take out

1 He only .... the name of the book yesterday. He didn't know it before.
2 Please can I borrow your maths book? I .... it .... to you tomorrow.
3 We .... our English .... last week. I hope everyone passed.
4 I (not) .... last year. We moved house, but I stayed at the same school.
5 Please can you .... the forks from the drawer and put them on the table?
6 My grandmother .... on 15th June 1962.
7 Some teenagers like to .... in the holidays so they have money to buy things.
8 (you) .... your library book yesterday?

GRAMMAR

1 Choose the correct options to complete the sentences.

1 You must bring your pyjamas and clean clothes for *you* / *yourself*.
2 If it *will be* / *is* all right, I'll meet you in the restaurant.
3 The batteries *include* / *are included* in the price.
4 This present *gave* / *was given* to me by my father.

Correct the mistakes in the sentences.

5 I bought a blue shirt for me, which is very nice.
6 If you like, we go by car.
7 You like the class if you come.
8 You need to bring a photo of you with your name on the back.

2 Complete the sentences with the verbs in the box. Use the past passive.

bake	find	make	open	sell	write

1 That book .... by my mother. She's an author.
2 Her bike .... in the park after she lost it.
3 The cakes .... for too long!
4 The new school .... last week.
5 My phone .... (not) in this country. It's from South Korea.
6 The paintings .... for a lot of money.

3 Complete the text with the correct form of the verbs in brackets. Use the present simple active or present simple passive.

WHAT HAPPENS IN AN ICE CREAM FACTORY?

First, the cream, eggs and sugar **(1)** .... (mix) together in a big machine. Then, the mixture **(2)** .... (cook) to kill any bacteria and make it safe to eat. After this, the flavourings **(3)** .... (add). These **(4)** .... (include) chocolate, vanilla, coffee, mint and of course fruit of all kinds. Some ice cream makers also **(5)** .... (put) pieces of marshmallow or whole nuts in their ice cream.

The next step is very important. The ice cream **(6)** .... (freeze) and mixed at the same time in a special machine. After it **(7)** .... (come) out of the machine, it **(8)** .... (put) into boxes and then into a big freezer. When it is very cold and hard, it **(9)** .... (send) to the shops for us to buy. Around 13 billion litres of ice cream **(10)** .... (sell) every year around the world.

PREPARE FOR THE EXAM

Reading Part 5

1 For each question, write the correct answer.

Write one word for each gap.

Example: **0** *of*

To: Dave
From: Sally
Subject:

I'm sorry I didn't see you on the last day **(0)** .... term to say goodbye. I hope you have a really lovely summer holiday in the mountains **(1)** .... your family. I'm sure it **(2)** .... be sunny and warm. We're going to London for a week. I'm very excited because it's my first visit there. I want **(3)** .... see all the famous places. We went to Madrid last year, and that was really interesting, **(4)** .... it was too hot for me. I hope London won't **(5)** .... so warm.

See **(6)** .... next term!

Sally

Speaking Part 1

2 Work with a partner. Take turns to ask and answer the questions.

Tell your partner about health and fitness.
What exercise do you do to stay healthy?
Which foods keep you healthy?
Have you ever hurt any part of your body?
How do you get to school every day?

Tell your partner about books.
What kind of books or comics do you like reading?
Where is your favourite place to read?
Do you prefer reading on a screen to reading real books? Why?
What is the best book you have read?

Tell your partner about food.
Describe your favourite meal.
What food can you cook?
Who's the best cook in your family?
Which country's food do you like best?

Listening Part 2

3 For each question, write the correct answer in the gap. Write one word or a number or a date or a time.

149

You will hear a woman talking to a class of students about the history of her town.

Mrs Smith's town

Years Mrs Smith has lived in the town: **(0)** *60* years

Age of town: **(1)** .... years

Town in 1980

Number of people: **(2)** ....

Day shops closed: **(3)** ....

Name of old cinema: **(4)** the ....

Cost of cinema seat: £ **(5)** ....

PREPARE FOR THE EXAM
A2 KEY FOR SCHOOLS

READING AND WRITING

Reading Part 1 Multiple-choice signs, notices and messages (Unit 11, Unit 18, Review 3)

EXAM INFORMATION

What is Part 1?

There are six short texts to read. They may be emails, text messages, signs, notices, postcards, etc.

What do I have to do?

Each text has a multiple-choice question for you to answer.

EXAM TIPS

- Look at each text and think about where you would see it.
- Decide what the main message of the text is.
- Read all the options carefully. Think about the meaning of each one. Don't just choose an option because it has words or ideas from the text.

1 **Look at the exam task and read question 1. What kind of message is it? Which option is the correct answer? Why are the other two wrong?**

1

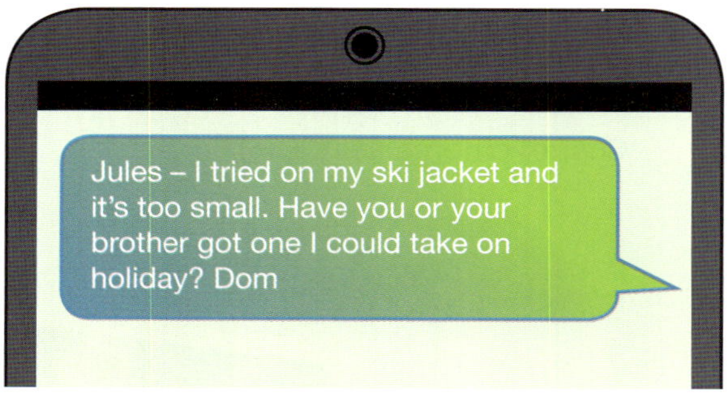

Dom would like Jules to

A find a jacket that Dom can borrow.

B tell Dom what size jacket is best.

C ask his brother to return Dom's jacket.

2 **Now you try. Complete the Reading Part 1 task. Use the *Exam tips* to help you.**

For each question, choose the correct answer.

2

A Students can get information about the new menu here.

B The café is asking for ideas for new dishes to add to the menu.

C This is how students can give their opinion of the menu.

3

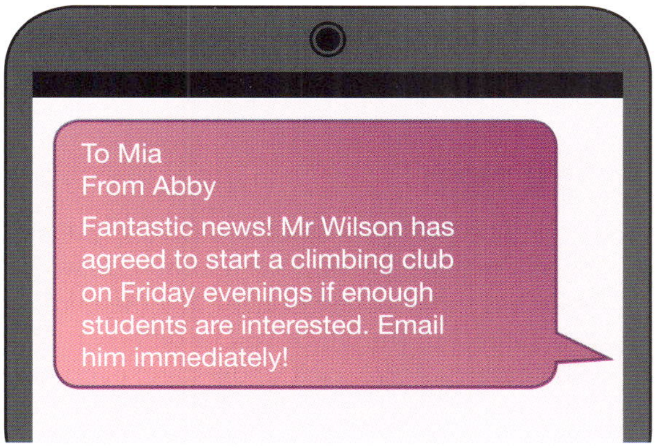

A Abby is excited about how good the climbing club was.

B Abby wants Mia to contact Mr Wilson as soon as possible.

C Abby and Mia are the only students who like climbing.

4

What do students find out from this message?

A what kind of painting can go into the exhibition

B how long they've got to finish their paintings

C why the art exhibition is taking place in July

5

A The shopping centre closes later than usual two days a week.

B You can see films here from Tuesday to Thursday.

C Some places in the centre close earlier than others.

6

A Isobel will ask her mum if she can go to the park.

B Isobel won't be able to meet Zoe this weekend.

C Isobel will see Zoe later than they planned.

PREPARE FOR THE EXAM
A2 KEY FOR SCHOOLS

Reading Part 2 Multiple-choice three short texts (Unit 3, Unit 12, Unit 18)

EXAM INFORMATION

What is Part 2?

There are three short texts to read. They might be about people, places, books, films, etc.

What do I have to do?

There are seven questions to answer. You match each question to one of the texts.

EXAM TIPS

- Underline the important words in the questions.
- Read the texts and find the information which matches the question exactly. The meaning will be the same, but the words will be different.
- Don't worry if you don't understand every word in the text.

1 **Look at the title of the article and read the questions. Then, read the article and find the answer to question 1. Underline the part of the text that gives you the answer.**

2 **Now you try. Complete the Reading Part 2 task. Use the *Exam tips* to help you.**

For each question, choose the correct answer.

		Sarah	Andrea	Trudi
1	Who knows other people who live in homes like hers?	**A**	**B**	**C**
2	Who says that she feels safe in her home?	**A**	**B**	**C**
3	Who is happy with the size of her home?	**A**	**B**	**C**
4	Who says that her house is bright?	**A**	**B**	**C**
5	Who says that guests enjoy spending the night in her home?	**A**	**B**	**C**
6	Who needs a lift when she wants to visit friends?	**A**	**B**	**C**
7	Who feels less comfortable when she is in other people's homes?	**A**	**B**	**C**

THREE *UNUSUAL* HOMES

SARAH

My home is a houseboat on a river. My parents and I have lived here since I was four, and I can't remember living anywhere else. Lots of my friends live on houseboats too, so it feels normal to me. We haven't got much space, but we don't mind – it's enough for us. Visitors love staying here and are surprised by how comfortable it is. They always sleep really well and love being on the water.

ANDREA

My friends at school think my lighthouse home is very cool. I like it, but it's not easy living here. The rooms are round, so it's hard to fit furniture in, and they're not very big. Also, my parents have to drive me everywhere as we are so far from town. The sea is only about 10 metres away, so it gets very exciting when there is a storm. But the building is very strong, and I never feel afraid.

TRUDI

My dad built our house. It took him four years because he did most of it by himself. The sides and the top are covered with earth and grass, but the front of the house has big windows. Lots of light comes in and it's lovely and quiet. There's always lots of fresh air, too. When I am at my friends' houses, I often get too hot and want to open a window.

Reading Part 3 Multiple-choice one long text (Unit 5, Unit 9, Unit 15)

EXAM INFORMATION

What is Part 3?

There is a newspaper, magazine or website article to read.

What do I have to do?

You have five multiple-choice questions to answer.

EXAM TIPS

- One or two questions will test your understanding of the text as a whole.
- The other questions will test details, opinions or feelings in the text.
- The detail questions will follow the order of information in the text.
- Don't just match words in the options with words in the text. Think carefully about the meaning.

1 **Read the text and the questions, but don't answer the questions yet. One question tests your understanding of the whole text. Which question is it?**

2 **For each question, choose the correct answer. Use the *Exam tips* to help you.**

Luke Thill

When he was 12, Luke Thill was at home during the school holidays. He was bored and looking for a fun activity, but he didn't want to play computer games or ride his bike. Then, he heard about people who build, and live in, very small wooden houses. 'I decided that I wanted to build one in my garden,' he said. 'I thought if I made enough money doing jobs for my neighbours, it might be possible.'

Luke's dad agreed to help, but he had a few rules. Luke had to pay for everything himself and had to do most of the work. Luke describes his dad as his 'coach' and says that working as a team brought them closer together. It took them a year and a half to finish the house and it cost $1,500.

The house is three metres long and two metres wide. Downstairs, it has a kitchen and sitting area with a TV, and upstairs there's a little bedroom. When he began, Luke was already quite good at repairing things, but there was a lot he didn't know. 'It all seems very simple to me now,' he said. 'But at the time, I had no idea what to do.'

Luke sleeps in his house about twice a week, does homework there after school and invites friends round. He enjoyed building his little house so much that he plans to build a second, bigger one soon, and in a few years' time he'd like to live in it full time.

1 What is the writer doing in this text?
A giving advice to teenage builders
B describing an interesting project
C saying why small houses are popular

2 Why did Luke decide to build a little house?
A He needed something to do.
B He liked the one his neighbour had.
C It was a way to meet new people.

3 Luke's dad was happy to
A do most of the building work.
B lend Luke money for the house.
C show Luke how to do things.

4 What does Luke say about building the house?
A He was surprised it was so easy.
B He learned a lot while he was doing it.
C He broke some things at the beginning.

5 What would Luke like to do next?
A make another little house
B build houses for his friends
C move out of the family home

PREPARE FOR THE EXAM
A2 KEY FOR SCHOOLS

Reading Part 4 Multiple-choice cloze factual text
(Unit 8, Unit 10, Review 2)

EXAM INFORMATION

What is Part 4?

There is a short newspaper, magazine, website or encyclopaedia article to read.

What do I have to do?

Complete the text by choosing the correct word for each gap.

There are six multiple-choice questions.

EXAM TIPS

- Before choosing an answer, read the whole sentence so you understand what it is about.
- Look at the words around the space carefully before choosing the one you think is best.
- With some questions, you need to think about grammar as well.

1 **Read the article and try question 1. What is the answer? Why?**

2 **Now you try. Complete the Reading Part 4 task. Use the *Exam tips* to help you.**

For each question, choose the correct answer.

THE CITY WHERE PEOPLE CAN SEND EMAILS TO TREES

A few years ago, workers in Melbourne, Australia, gave each of the city's 70,000 trees ID numbers and email addresses. They did this so that people had a way of **(1)** ________ workers know when there was a **(2)** ________ with a tree or if it was dangerous. They could then send someone to work on it and make it **(3)** ________.

The emails soon started arriving. However, workers got a big **(4)** ________ when they read them because many people were using the email addresses to send love letters to the trees. They **(5)** ________ the trees stories, asked them questions and said how beautiful they were. The workers joined in by sending replies from the trees. The email conversations are **(6)** ________ to read and show how important trees are to the people of Melbourne.

1	**A** making	**B** letting	**C** getting
2	**A** mistake	**B** trouble	**C** problem
3	**A** safe	**B** correct	**C** well
4	**A** adventure	**B** surprise	**C** experience
5	**A** spoke	**B** told	**C** explained
6	**A** popular	**B** glad	**C** wonderful

Reading Part 5 Open cloze email (Unit 13, Unit 19, Review 5)

EXAM INFORMATION

What is Part 5?

There is a short text, such as an email, postcard or internet post. Sometimes, there may be two emails.

What do I have to do?

You have to complete the text by writing one word in each space.

EXAM TIPS

Read the text once without thinking about the gaps, so you know what it is about.

- Think about what kind of word is needed for the gap, e.g. preposition, pronoun, article.
- Read the whole sentence carefully.
- Only write one word in each space or you will not get the mark.
- Spell each word perfectly or you will not get the mark.

1 **Read the texts once. What kind of words are missing, grammar or vocabulary?**

2 **Now you try. Complete the Reading Part 5 task. Use the *Exam tips* to help you.**

For each question, write the correct answer.
Write **one** word for each gap.

Example: **0** *my*

To:	Bart
From:	Shammi

Guess what? Mum says I can paint the walls in **(0)** .... bedroom. I'm really happy **(1)** .... I hate the colour it is now! **(2)** .... you want to come and help me? I'm free on Saturday afternoon and **(3)** .... day on Sunday.

To:	Shammi
From:	Bart

Of course! I know **(4)** .... much you hate your pink walls! Is it OK **(5)** .... I come at ten on Sunday morning? By the way, **(6)** .... colour are we going to use? I painted my room black a few weeks ago, and it looks fantastic!

PREPARE FOR THE EXAM
A2 KEY FOR SCHOOLS

Writing Part 6 Guided writing email or note (Unit 10, Unit 14, Review 4)

EXAM INFORMATION

What is Part 6?

There is a short writing task.

What do I have to do?

You have to write a short email or note to a friend. You may get some instructions to follow, or you may have part of a message with some questions to reply to.

EXAM TIPS

- Underline the important words in the email so you understand the topic and the three questions.
- When you have finished, check for spelling and grammar mistakes and that your email or note clearly includes answers to all three questions.
- Check you have written at least 25 words.

1 **Read the exam task question and the four example answers. Which one is perfect? What is wrong with the other three?**

Read the email from your English friend, Danny.

To:
From: Danny

Reply Forward

Tell me about your birthday presents! What's the best thing you got? Who gave it to you? Why do you like it?

Write an email to Danny and answer the questions.
Write **25 words** or more.

A *I got lots of fantastic presents for my birthday. The best thing was my bike, which my parents gave me. I love it because it's fast and a really cool colour. Lets go for a ride together soon!*

B *My birthday was great. All my friends came to my party and we had a great time. We all missed you a lot! When can we see you?*

C *I got lots of presents including a new mobile phone it's the best one I've ever had*

D *My best present is earring from my frend. is bautiful I loving it and waring always*

2 Now you try. Write your own answer to the Writing Part 6 task. Use the *Exam tips* to help you.

Writing Part 7 Picture story
(Unit 4, Unit 18, Review 1)

EXAM INFORMATION

What is Part 7?

There is a story writing task.

What do I have to do?

You have to write a story based on three pictures.

EXAM TIPS

- Look at all three pictures and get an idea of the whole story before you begin.
- Include something about every picture in your story.
- Use the past tense for the events of the story.
- Try to use linking words such as *so, and, but, because,* etc. in your story.

1 **Read the exam task and the sample answer. Is there something about every picture? What tense is the story in? Why?**

Look at the three pictures.
Write the story shown in the pictures.
Write **35 words** or more.

Last week, Jim saw a poster at school about a cooking competition. He loves baking, so he decided to enter it. He went home and baked an amazing chocolate cake. Jim took his cake to the competition and was very happy and surprised when he got first prize for it.

2 **Now you try. Do the Writing Part 7 task below. Use the *Exam tips* to help you.**

Look at the three pictures.
Write the story shown in the pictures.
Write **35 words** or more.

PREPARE FOR THE EXAM
A2 KEY FOR SCHOOLS

LISTENING

Listening Part 1 3-option multiple choice five short dialogues (Unit 4, Unit 17, Review 1)

EXAM INFORMATION

What is Part 1?

There are five short conversations.

What do I have to do?

Each conversation has a multiple-choice question for you to answer. The options are pictures.

EXAM TIPS

- You will hear something about each picture, but only one picture answers the question, so only give one answer.
- You hear the conversation twice, so don't worry if you miss the answer the first time.

1 **Look at the pictures for question 1. Write down some words you think you are going to hear in the conversation.**

150 **2** **Read the question carefully. Is it asking about what Ted has got or what he wants? Now, listen and answer the question.**

1 What would Ted like to get for his room?

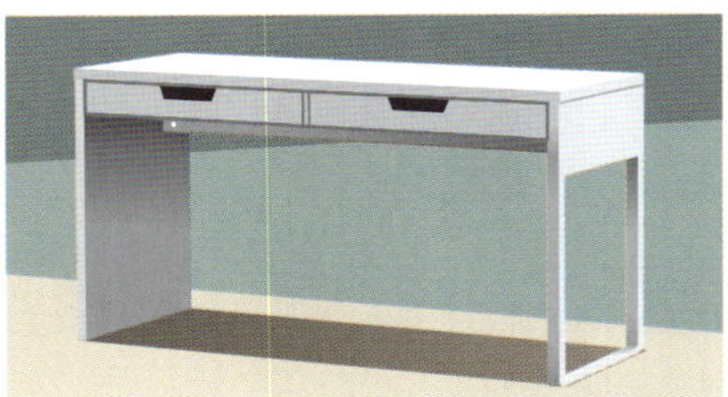

A

B

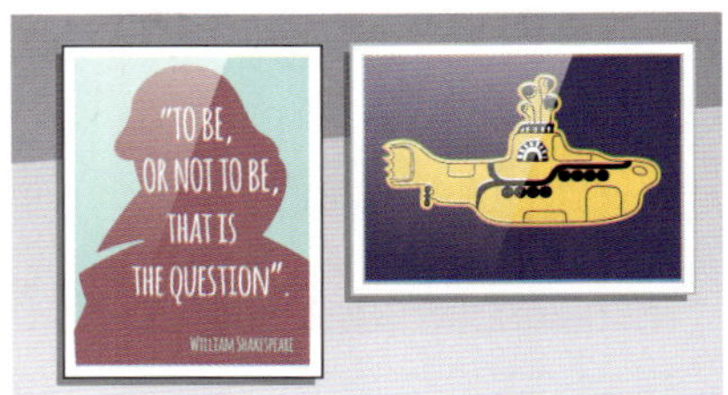

C

150 **Listen again to check your answer.**

151 **3** **Now you try. Complete the Listening Part 1 task. Use the *Exam tips* to help you.**

For each question, choose the correct picture.

2 What is still in the car?

A

B

C

3 How much is the bag?

A

B

C

4 Where did they go camping last year?

A

B

C

5 What are the boys going to do now?

A

B

C

Listening Part 2 Gap fill notes (Unit 7, Unit 19, Review 5)

EXAM INFORMATION

What is Part 2?

There is a person giving some information on a subject.

What do I have to do?

You need to listen and complete some notes. There are five pieces of information you need to write down. These will be words, numbers or spellings.

EXAM TIPS

- Before you listen, think about the kind of information you need for the gap.
- Sometimes, you will hear two possible answers. Listen carefully to understand which one is correct.
- It's best to write numbers as numbers and not as words, so you don't make a mistake with spelling.
- You hear the recording twice, so don't worry if you miss the answer the first time.

152 **1 Read the exam task. Then, listen to the first part and look at the example. You hear two days – Saturday and Friday. Why is Saturday correct and Friday wrong?**

153 **2 Now you try. Complete the Listening Part 2 task. Use the *Exam tips* to help you.**

For each question, write the correct answer in each gap. You will hear someone talking about a gym. Write one **word**, or a **number** or a **date** or a **time**.

Bodyfit Gym

Club for teenagers

Day:	*Saturday*	Teacher's name:	**(3)** ________
Price:	**(1)** £ ________ per month	What **not** to wear:	**(4)** ________
Start time:	**(2)** ________ am	What to bring:	**(5)** ________

PREPARE FOR THE EXAM
A2 KEY FOR SCHOOLS

Listening Part 3 3-option multiple choice dialogue (Unit 12, Unit 20, Review 3)

EXAM INFORMATION

What is Part 3?

There is a conversation between two people.

What do I have to do?

Listen and answer five multiple-choice questions.

EXAM TIPS

- Read the questions before you listen so you know what information to listen for.
- You will hear something about all three options, so listen carefully to catch the meaning of what the people are saying.
- The answer can come from either speaker.
- At least one question will ask about the opinion or feelings of one of the speakers.
- You hear the conversation twice, so don't worry if you miss the answer the first time.

154 **1** **Read the questions and the instructions so you know what the conversation will be about. Then, look at question 1. Listen to the first part of the recording and answer the question below.**

Why is C the answer? Why are A and B wrong?

155 **2** **Now you try. Complete the Listening Part 3 task. Use the Exam Tips to help you.**

For each question, choose the correct answer.
You will hear Callum talking to his friend Stella about going to a skatepark.

1 Callum says the new skatepark is close to
A the cinema.
B Callum's house.
C the swimming pool.

2 Stella does not like skateparks that are
A old.
B small.
C dirty.

3 What will the skatepark have in the future?
A a shop
B a roof
C a café

4 How much does it cost to use the skatepark at the moment?
A £7
B £5
C £3

5 The friends will see each other at the skatepark at
A 10 o'clock.
B 12 o'clock.
C 1 o'clock.

Listening Part 4 3-option multiple choice main idea, message, gist or topic (Unit 8, Unit 16, Review 2)

EXAM INFORMATION

What is Part 4?

There are five short conversations or monologues.

What do I have to do?

Listen and answer five multiple-choice questions.

EXAM TIPS

- Read the focus question carefully as this will tell you what to listen for.
- The kind of things you'll be listening for include the topic, an opinion, someone's reasons for doing something, someone's likes and dislikes, activities, events, etc.
- Don't worry if you don't understand every word.
- Listen for the meaning, don't just match words in the question and answer.
- You hear the recordings twice, so don't worry if you miss the answer the first time.

156 **1** **Look at question 1. Then listen and choose the correct answer. Compare with a partner and say why you chose the answer you did.**

157 **2** **Now you try. Complete the Listening Part 4 task. Use the *Exam tips* to help you.**

For each question, choose the correct answer.

1 You will hear a girl talking to her mother. What does she want to eat?
A a sandwich
B some biscuits
C a large meal

2 You will hear a girl talking to a friend about a TV programme. What does she say about it?
A It was funny.
B It was long.
C It was exciting.

3 You will hear two friends talking about a walk they did together. What happened on the walk?
A They got wet.
B They got lost.
C They hurt themselves.

4 You will hear a boy leaving a message for a friend. Where would he like to meet his friend?
A at the bus stop
B at the ticket office
C at the big stage

5 You will hear a teacher talking to her class. What is she talking about?
A a story they'll write
B a book they'll read
C a film they'll watch

PREPARE FOR THE EXAM
A2 KEY FOR SCHOOLS

Listening Part 5 Matching
(Unit 2, Unit 6, Review 4)

EXAM INFORMATION

What is Part 5?

There is a longer dialogue.

What do I have to do?

You need to listen and match five people / days / times, etc. to eight possible answers.

EXAM TIPS

- Before you listen, read the list A–H carefully and think about the kinds of words you may hear.
- Often the words in A–H will be different in the listening, e.g. *get ready for the concert* = *music practice*.
- You will hear the conversation twice, so don't worry if you cannot answer all the questions the first time.
- The information in the recording will be in the same order as the questions.

158 **1 Read the exam task instructions and the example. Then, listen to the first part of the dialogue while you read the recording. Underline the part of the text that gives you the answer to the example.**

Grandma:	How was your half-term holiday, Jasmin? What did you and your friends do?
Jasmin:	Well, Grandma, I played the guitar a lot. I'm in the school concert next week and I need to get ready for it.

159 **2 Now you try. Complete the Listening Part 5 task. Use the *Exam tips* to help you.**

For each question, choose the correct answer.

You will hear Jasmin telling her grandmother about her half-term holiday. What activity did each person do?

Example: **0** Jasmin C

People

1 Sophie ☐
2 Sam ☐
3 Joe ☐
4 Emily ☐
5 Gemma ☐

Activities

A cooking
B going online
C music practice
D photography
E shopping
F studying
G sport
H travelling

SPEAKING

Speaking Part 1 Examiner led questions (Unit 1, Unit 16, Review 1, Review 4, Review 5)

EXAM INFORMATION

What is Part 1?

There are questions about you.

What do I have to do?

You need to talk to the examiner and answer the questions you are asked.

EXAM TIPS

- Listen carefully to the examiner's questions. You and your partner will get questions on different topics.
- You can ask the examiner to say the question again if you don't understand.
- When the examiner says *Tell me about* … try to answer in two or three sentences.
- This part will take three to four minutes.

1 The examiner will ask you questions like these. Which need short answers and which need longer answers?

1 What's your name?
2 Where do you come from?
3 What's your best subject at school?
4 Do you like studying science?
5 What do you wear to school?
6 How much homework do you get?
7 Tell me something about your favourite teacher.
8 How much free time do you have?
9 Who do you spend your free time with?
10 Do you play computer games?
11 Do you like reading?
12 Tell me something about a hobby you enjoy.

2 Match the answers a–e to the questions in Exercise 1. Which are good answers and which are not so good? Why?

a No, I don't.

b No, not really. I find it quite difficult.

c Just my normal clothes. I don't have to wear a uniform.

d She's nice. I like her.

e I haven't got any hobbies.

160 **3** Listen to some more answers and match them to the questions in Exercise 1.

4 Now you try. Take turns to ask and answer the Speaking Part 1 questions. Use the *Exam tips* to help you.

PREPARE FOR THE EXAM
A2 KEY FOR SCHOOLS

Speaking Part 2 Discussion with visual stimulus (Unit 3, Unit 7, Review 2)

EXAM INFORMATION

What is Part 2?

There is a conversation with your partner and the examiner about some pictures.

What do I have to do?

You need to answer the examiner's questions and talk to your partner as well.

EXAM TIPS

- Don't forget to say what you can see in the pictures. Let the examiner see how much vocabulary you know. Don't just say *yes* or *no*. Use some adjectives.
- Try to make correct sentences and questions if you can. Don't worry about making small mistakes.
- Let your partner speak too and ask him/her questions. You will get marks for that, too.
- Try to relax and enjoy yourself!

1 **Look at the pictures. They are all places you can visit. Work with a partner and say what each one is.**

161 **2** **Listen to two students doing this exam task. Number the pictures in the order the students speak about them.**

161 **3** **Write the places in the table in the correct order. Then listen again and complete the table with (✓) for 'likes it' and (✗) for 'doesn't like it'. The first one has been done for you as an example.**

Place	Girl	Boy
Shopping centre	✓	✗

4 **What adjectives did you hear the speakers use about each place?**

5 **Now you try. Take turns to ask and answer the Speaking Part 2 questions. Look at the pictures on the opposite page. Use the *Exam tips* to help you.**

Here are some pictures that show different places to visit. Do you like these different places to visit? Say why or why not.

6 **Now ask and answer these questions together.**

Do you think:
going to a museum is boring?
visiting a castle is interesting?
going to the cinema is expensive?
shopping is fun?
going to a park is pleasant?

Which of these places do you like visiting best? Say why.

162 **7** **Listen to the last part of the test. Number the questions below in the order you hear them.**

- ☐ Do you prefer visiting places that are inside or outside? Why?
- ☐ Do you like places that teach you about history? Why?
- ☐ Do you prefer visiting places on your own or with other people? Why?

162 **8** **Listen again. What happens if the candidate gives a very short answer to a question?**

9 **Ask and answer the questions in Exercise 6 with your partner. Ask Why? / Why not? if your partner gives a short answer.**

Do you like these different places to visit?

EXTRA ACTIVITIES

UNIT 2 PAGE 17, EXERCISE 3

Student A

Ask your partner for information about the sand cat to write a fact file. Make a note of the answers. Then, answer your partner's questions about the kakapo. Use the information on the right:

FACT FILE Kakapo

What is it: A kind of parrot

From: New Zealand

Lives: only on two small islands

Eats: plants, fruit and nuts

Adult weight: 2–4 kg

Numbers: about 127 kakapos left in the wild, none in zoos

Kakapo babies are called chicks. Females have 2–3 chicks every two years. The chicks stay with their mother for 10 weeks.

UNIT 5 PAGE 33, EXERCISE 6

Work with a partner. Take turns to make sentences.

Use one of the verbs in box A and the correct form of a comparative or superlative adverb made from the adjectives in box B.

A

dance, eat, laugh, learn, run, sing, speak, study, walk, write

B

bad, careful, dangerous, fast, good, loud, noisy, quick, quiet, slow

UNIT 8 PAGE 49, EXERCISE 3

Complete the sentences with the words in the box. Use each word twice.

book kind picture ring watch

1 Sorry, I'm busy now. I'll .... you later.
2 You can draw a .... of your time capsule, if you like.
3 She's really .... She lent me her favourite jacket for the party.
4 I don't want to .... TV. I'd prefer to listen to some music.
5 When you phone the cinema, can you .... a ticket for me, too, please?
6 What .... of soup would you like? Vegetable or chicken?
7 That's a beautiful .... you've got on your finger.
8 Can I borrow your maths .... ? I left mine at home.
9 I'll take a .... of it with my phone.
10 I'm sorry, I don't know what the time is. My .... is broken.

UNIT 9 PAGE 55, EXERCISE 10

In pairs, imagine you are setting up a sport or activity club at your school. Choose the sport or activity, then think of a name for your club. Write some rules for your club. Tell another pair about your club. Whose club sounds most fun?

UNIT 11 PAGE 67, EXERCISE 3

Play this game. Work in pairs. Student A chooses an uncountable noun from Exercise 1. Student B must ask a question beginning *How many …?* using a related countable noun. Student A answers the question.

A: *homework*
B: *How many maths exercises did you do last night?*
A: *Eight!*

UNIT 12 PAGE 69, EXERCISE 7

In small groups, design your own cinema. Think about:

- where your cinema will be
- the kind of films you'd like to show
- extra activities you might offer
- what you could sell
- the kind of seats you'll have.

Choose one person from your group to present your ideas to the class.

We'll have shops that sell …
We'll show films that …
People who come to our cinema will …
Our cinema will be in a place which …

UNIT 16 PAGE 90, EXERCISE 2

Scores:

Add up your scores

A 4
B 3
C 2
D 1

12–16 You are a very serious language learner. You will do very well in your studies, but remember you can have fun when you are learning English! It's not all about getting the best mark in the class.

8–11 You enjoy learning English. You are happy to try new ways of learning and you are not afraid to make mistakes. You like using the language in real situations.

4–7 English probably isn't your favourite subject, but if you work hard, you can be good at it. Study a little but often and you'll soon see the difference!

EXTRA ACTIVITIES

UNIT 2 PAGE 17, EXERCISE 3

Student B
Answer your partner's questions about the sand cat. Use the information on the right. Then ask your partner for information about the kakapo to write a fact file. Make a note of the answers.

FACT FILE Sand cat

What is it: a kind of cat
From: Africa, Asia
Lives: in deserts
Eats: insects, birds and other small animals
Adult weight: 1–3 kg
Numbers: No one knows how many there are in the wild; 200 in zoos.
Sand cat babies are called kittens.
Females have 18 kittens every year. The kittens stay with their mother for about six months.

UNIT 18 PAGE 103, EXERCISE 6

1 Student A Student B has got one of your books and you want it back by tomorrow at the latest.
Student B You don't know where the book is! Don't tell Student A the truth! Try to get more time to return the book.

2 Student A You want a book that Student B has borrowed from the library. You think Student B has had it for a very long time and want him/her to return it to the library so you can borrow it.
Student B You borrowed a book from the school library and Student A wants it. You haven't finished with it yet and want to keep it for as long as possible.

UNIT 18 PAGE 103, EXERCISE 7

The *If* game. Choose a sentence from 1–3 below and complete it.
Then start a new sentence with the second part of your first sentence. Then write two more sentences.

If I have a party on my birthday, I'll …
If I have a party on my birthday, I'll ask all my friends.
If I ask all my friends, we'll make a lot of noise.

1 If I have enough money, I'll buy …
2 If I pass all my exams, I'll …
3 If I move to a new class next year, I'll …

In pairs, compare your answers.

UNIT 18 PAGE 105, WRITING

UNIT 20 PAGE 112, EXERCISE 2

Write a sentence for each of these situations.

A time when you:

- changed something in a shop.
- changed from one kind of transport to another of the same type.
- made a big or small change in your life, either because you wanted to or because someone else made it happen. For example, had a hair cut, moved things around in your bedroom.
- had to take a change of clothes somewhere.
- had to give someone a change of email address or change of phone number.
- enjoyed something because it was new or different.
- talked to someone who liked things in the past and didn't like life changing today, e.g computers, smartphones.
  Last year, my parents bought me a jacket for my birthday, but I didn't like it. So, I changed it for a different jacket that I really liked.

In groups, discuss your sentences for Exercise 2. Are any of them the same?

UNIT 20 PAGE 113, EXERCISE 8

All these things have changed people's lives. In pairs, discuss each one and decide how important it is for our lives today. Decide which is the most important. What other things would you add to the list?

DNA was discovered.
The internet was created.
Electricity was discovered.
The steam engine was developed.
Air conditioning was invented.

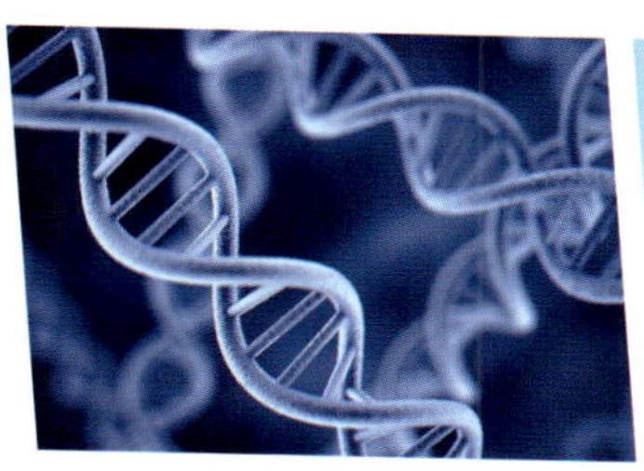

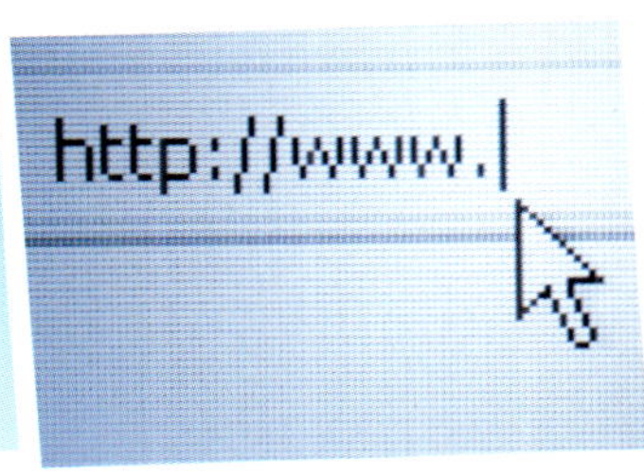

VOCABULARY LIST

UNIT 1

ADJECTIVES OF PERSONALITY

active /'æktɪv/ *adjective*
creative /kri'eɪtɪv/ *adjective*
friendly /'frendli/ *adjective*
funny /'fʌni/ *adjective*
helpful /'helpfəl/ *adjective*
kind /kaɪnd/ *adjective*
lazy /'leɪzi/ *adjective*
polite /pə'laɪt/ *adjective*
popular /'pɒpjələ/ *adjective*
quiet /kwaɪət/ *adjective*

PERSONAL DETAILS

address /ə'dres/ *noun*
age /eɪdʒ/ *noun*
email address /'iːmeɪl ə'dres/ *noun*
first language /'fɜːst 'læŋgwɪdʒ/ *noun*
first name /'fɜːst neɪm/ *noun*
home telephone /'həʊm 'telɪfəʊn/ *noun*
mobile /'məʊbaɪl/ *noun*
surname /'sɜːneɪm/ *noun*

UNIT 2

GEOGRAPHICAL FEATURES

desert /'dezət/ *noun*
forest /'fɒrɪst/ *noun*
hill /hɪl/ *noun*
lake /leɪk/ *noun*
mountain /'maʊntɪn/ *noun*
river /'rɪvə/ *noun*
sea /siː/ *noun*
valley /'væli/ *noun*
volcano /vɒl'keɪnəʊ/ *noun*

ANIMALS

dolphin /'dɒlfɪn/ *noun*
elephant /'elɪfənt/ *noun*
giraffe /dʒɪ'rɑːf/ *noun*
monkey /'mʌŋki/ *noun*
parrot /'pærət/ *noun*
penguin /'peŋgwɪn/ *noun*
polar bear /'pəʊlə beə/ *noun*
snake /sneɪk/ *noun*
tiger /'taɪgə/ *noun*
whale /weɪl/ *noun*

UNIT 3

HOLIDAYS: WAYS OF TRAVELLING

by bike /baɪ 'baɪk/ *adverb*
by boat /baɪ 'bəʊt/ *adverb*
by coach /baɪ 'kəʊtʃ/ *adverb*
by helicopter /baɪ 'helɪkɒptə/ *adverb*
by motorbike /baɪ 'məʊtəbaɪk/ *adverb*
by plane /baɪ 'pleɪn/ *adverb*
by scooter /baɪ 'skuːtə/ *adverb*
by ship /baɪ 'ʃɪp/ *adverb*
by tram /baɪ 'træm/ *adverb*
by underground /baɪ 'ʌndəgraʊnd/ *adverb*

HOLIDAY VOCABULARY

guest /gest/ *noun*
guidebook /'gaɪdbʊk/ *noun*
luggage /'lʌgɪdʒ/ *noun*
map /mæp/ *noun*
on foot /ɒn 'fʊt/ *adverb*
receptionist /rɪ'sepʃənɪst/ *noun*
suitcase /'suːtkeɪs/ *noun*
tourist /'tʊərɪst/ *noun*
visitor /'vɪzɪtə/ *noun*

UNIT 4

HOMES

balcony /'bælkəni/ *noun*
ceiling /'siːlɪŋ/ *noun*
cooker /'kʊkə/ *noun*
cupboard /'kʌbəd/ *noun*
entrance /'entrəns/ *noun*
first floor /'fɜːst flɔː/ *noun*
garage /'gærɑːʒ/ *noun*

ground floor /ˈgraʊnd flɔː/ *noun*
lamp /læmp/ *noun*
sink /sɪŋk/ *noun*
sofa /ˈsəʊfə/ *noun*

ADJECTIVES TO DESCRIBE HOMES

attractive /əˈtræktɪv/ *adjective*
bright /braɪt/ *adjective*
cold /kəʊld/ *adjective*
comfortable /ˈkʌmftəbl/ *adjective*
cool /kuːl/ *adjective*
cosy /ˈkəʊzi/ *adjective*
dark /dɑːk/ *adjective*
light /laɪt/ *adjective*
peaceful /ˈpiːsfəl/ *adjective*
tiny /ˈtaɪni/ *adjective*
unusual /ʌnˈjuːʒuəl/ *adjective*
warm /wɔːm/ *adjective*

UNIT 5

SCHOOL SUBJECTS

biology /baɪˈɒlədʒi/ *noun*
chemistry /ˈkemɪstri/ *noun*
design and technology /dɪˈzaɪn ən tekˈnɒlədʒi/ *noun*
drama /ˈdrɑːmə/ *noun*
foreign languages /ˈfɒrɪn ˈlæŋgwɪdʒɪz/ *noun*
geography /dʒiˈɒgrəfi/ *noun*
history /ˈhɪstəri/ *noun*
ICT /ˌaɪsiːˈti/ *noun*
maths /mæθs/ *noun*
PE /ˌpiːˈiː/ *noun*
physics /ˈfɪzɪks/ *noun*
science /ˈsaɪəns/ *noun*

TAKE

take [= carry, e.g. an umbrella] /teɪk/ *verb*
take [= catch, e.g. a train] /teɪk/ *verb*
take [= do, e.g. exams] /teɪk/ *verb*
take [= go along, e.g. the second turning] /teɪk/ *verb*
take [= make, e.g. a photo/picture] /teɪk/ *verb*
take [= study, e.g. maths] /teɪk/ *verb*
take [= use, e.g. medicine] /teɪk/ *verb*

UNIT 6

MATERIALS

cotton /ˈkɒtən/ *noun / adjective*
glass /glɑːs/ *noun / adjective*
gold /gəʊld/ *noun / adjective*
leather /ˈleðə/ *noun / adjective*
metal /ˈmetəl/ *noun / adjective*
paper /ˈpeɪpə/ *noun / adjective*
plastic /ˈplæstɪk/ *noun / adjective*
silver /ˈsɪlvə/ *noun / adjective*
wood /wʊd/ *noun*
wool /wʊl/ *noun / adjective*

ADJECTIVES FOR DESCRIBING OBJECTS

colourful /ˈkʌləfəl/ *adjective*
hard /hɑːd/ *adjective*
heavy /ˈhevi/ *adjective*
large /lɑːdʒ/ *adjective*
little /ˈlɪtl/ *adjective*
lovely /ˈlʌvli/ *adjective*
old /əʊld/ *adjective*
pretty /ˈprɪti/ *adjective*
round /raʊnd/ *adjective*
small /smɔːl/ *adjective*
smooth /smuːð/ *adjective*
soft /sɒft/ *adjective*
wooden /ˈwʊdən/ *adjective*

UNIT 7

GET

get back [= arrive home] /get ˈbæk/ *phrasal verb*
get lost /get ˈlɒst/ *phrasal verb*
get on [+ form of transport] /ˈget ɒn/ *phrasal verb*
get to [= arrive at] /ˈget tə/ *phrasal verb*
get up [= leave the bed] /get ˈʌp/ *phrasal verb*

HOLIDAY ACTIVITIES

camping /ˈkæmpɪŋ/ *noun*
diving /ˈdaɪvɪŋ/ *noun*
hiking /ˈhaɪkɪŋ/ *noun*

EP VOCABULARY LIST

horse riding /ˈhɔːs ˈraɪdɪŋ/ *noun*
kite surfing /ˈkaɪt ˈsɜːfɪŋ/ *noun*
mountain biking /ˈmaʊntɪn ˈbaɪkɪŋ/ *noun*
paddle boarding /ˈpædl ˈbɔːdɪŋ/ *noun*
sailing /ˈseɪlɪŋ/ *noun*
waterskiing /ˈwɔːtəˌskiːɪŋ/ *noun*
zip wiring /ˈzɪp ˈwaɪərɪŋ/ *noun*

THINGS TO TAKE ON AN ADVENTURE HOLIDAY

backpack /ˈbækpæk/ *noun*
first-aid kit fɜːst ˈeɪd kɪt/ *noun*
map and compass /ˈmæp ən ˈkʌmpəs/ *noun*
sleeping bag /ˈsliːpɪŋ bæg/ *noun*
snacks /snæks/ *noun*
sun cream /ˈsʌn kriːm/ *noun*
tent /tent/ *noun*
torch /tɔːtʃ/ *noun*
trainers /ˈtreɪnəz/ *noun*
walking boots /ˈwɔːkɪŋ buːts/ *noun*
wash bag /ˈwɒʃbæg/ *noun*
waterproof trousers and jacket /ˈwɔːtəpruːf ˈtraʊzəz ən ˈdʒækɪt/ *noun*

UNIT 8

FURNITURE AND HOUSEHOLD APPLIANCES

air conditioning /eə kənˈdɪʃənɪŋ/ *noun*
barbecue /ˈbɑːbɪkjuː/ *noun*
bin /bɪn/ *noun*
bookcase /ˈbʊkkeɪs/ *noun*
drawer /drɔː/ *noun*
fridge /frɪdʒ/ *noun*
heating /ˈhiːtɪŋ/ *noun*
lights /laɪts/ *noun*
roof /ruːf/ *noun*
seat /siːt/ *noun*
stairs /steəz/ *noun*
washing machine /ˈwɒʃɪŋ məˈʃiːn/ *noun*

WORDS WITH TWO MEANINGS

book [= for reading] /bʊk/ *noun*
book [= reserve] /bʊk/ *verb*
kind [= nice] /kaɪnd/ *adjective*
kind [= variety] /kaɪnd/ *noun*
letter [= in the mail] /ˈletə/ *noun*
letter [= part of writing] /ˈletə/ *noun*
picture [= drawing] /ˈpɪktʃə/ *noun*
picture [= photo] /ˈpɪktʃə/ *noun*
ring [= jewellery] /rɪŋ/ *noun*
ring [= phone] /rɪŋ/ *verb*
watch [= for the time] /wɒtʃ/ *noun*
watch [= look at] /wɒtʃ/ *verb*

UNIT 9

SPORTS AND ACTIVITIES

badminton /ˈbædmɪntən/ *noun*
board game /ˈbɔːd geɪm/ *noun*
card game /ˈkɑːd geɪm/ *noun*
climbing /ˈklaɪmɪŋ/ *noun*
cricket /ˈkrɪkɪt/ *noun*
dance class /ˈdɑːns klɑːs/ *noun*
diving /ˈdaɪvɪŋ/ *noun*
fishing /ˈfɪʃɪŋ/ *noun*
fitness class /ˈfɪtnəs klɑːs/ *noun*
golf /gɒlf/ *noun*
karate /kəˈrɑːti/ *noun*
puzzle /ˈpʌzl/ *noun*
skateboarding /ˈskeɪtbɔːdɪŋ/ *noun*
skiing /ˈskiːɪŋ/ *noun*
video game /ˈvɪdiəʊ geɪm/ *noun*

SPORTS VOCABULARY

champion /ˈtʃæmpiən/ *noun*
fan /fæn/ *noun*
prize /praɪz/ *noun*
professional /prəˈfeʃənəl/ *adjective*
take part /teɪk ˈpɑːt/ *verb*
tournament /ˈtʊənəmənt/ *noun*

SUFFIX *-ER*

cleaner /ˈkliːnə/ *noun*
climber /ˈklaɪmə/ *noun*
dancer /ˈdɑːnsə/ *noun*
diver /ˈdaɪvə/ *noun*
golfer /ˈgɒlfə/ *noun*
photographer /fəˈtɒgrəfə/ *noun*
runner /ˈrʌnə/ *noun*
singer /ˈsɪŋə/ *noun*
skier /ˈskiːə/ *noun*
swimmer /ˈswɪmə/ *noun*
teacher /ˈtiːtʃə/ *noun*
worker /ˈwɜːkə/ *noun*

UNIT 10

PEOPLE

best friend /ˈbest ˈfrend/ *noun*
classmate /ˈklɑːsmeɪt/ *noun*
close friend /ˈkləʊs ˈfrend/ *noun*
contact [= person you know] /ˈkɒntækt/ *noun*
guest /gest/ *noun*
member /ˈmembə/ *noun*
neighbour /ˈneɪbə/ *noun*
ˈold, friend /əʊld frend/ *noun*
penfriend /ˈpenfrend/ *noun*
relative /ˈrelətɪv/ *noun*

INTERNET NOUNS AND VERBS

blog /blɒg/ *noun*
download /ˌdaʊnˈləʊd/ *verb*
link /lɪŋk/ *noun*
menu /ˈmenjuː/ *noun*
message board /ˈmesɪdʒ bɔːd/ *noun*
post /pəʊst/ *verb*
record /rɪˈkɔːd/ *verb*
save /seɪv/ *verb*
search /sɜːtʃ/ *verb*
site /saɪt/ *noun*
the web /ðə ˈweb/ *noun*
upload /ʌpˈləʊd/ *verb*

UNIT 11

PLACES IN A CITY

art gallery /ˈɑːt ˈgæləri/ *noun*
cathedral /kəˈθiːdrəl/ *noun*
embassy /ˈembəsi/ *noun*
fountain /ˈfaʊntɪn/ *noun*
mosque /mɒsk/ *noun*
old town /ˈəʊld ˈtaʊn ˈsentə / *noun*
palace /ˈpælɪs/ *noun*
shopping area /ˈʃɒpɪŋ ˈeəriə/ *noun*
skyscraper /ˈskaɪˌskreɪpə/ *noun*
sports centre /ˈspɔːts ˈsentə/ *noun*
stadium /ˈsteɪdiəm/ *noun*
statue /ˈstætʃuː/ *noun*
temple /ˈtempl/ *noun*

UNCOUNTABLE NOUNS

electricity /ɪˌlekˈtrɪsəti/ *noun*
food /fuːd/ *noun*
furniture /ˈfɜːnɪtʃə/ *noun*
homework /ˈhəʊmwɜːk/ *noun*
information /ˌɪnfəˈmeɪʃən/ *noun*
jewellery /ˈdʒuːəlri/ *noun*
luggage /ˈlʌgɪdʒ/ *noun*
money /ˈmʌni/ *noun*
news /njuːz/ *noun*
staff /stɑːf/ *noun*
traffic /ˈtræfɪk/ *noun*
wildlife /ˈwaɪldlaɪf/ *noun*

UNIT 12

TYPES OF FILM

a comedy /ə ˈkɒmədi/ *noun*
a drama /ə ˈdrɑːmə/ *noun*
a horror film /ə ˈhɒrə fɪlm/ *noun*
a musical /ə ˈmjuːzɪkəl/ *noun*
a science-fiction film /ə ˌsaɪəns ˈfɪkʃən fɪlm/ *noun*
a thriller /ə ˈθrɪlə/ *noun*

VOCABULARY LIST

an action film /ən 'ækʃən fɪlm/ *noun*
an adventure film /ən əd'ventʃə fɪlm/ *noun*
an animated film /ən 'ænɪmeɪtɪd fɪlm/ *noun*

CONJUNCTIONS

and /ənd/ *conjunction*
because /bɪ'kəz/ *conjunction*
but /bʌt/ *conjunction*
if /ɪf/ *conjunction*
or /ɔː/ *conjunction*
so /səʊ/ *conjunction*
that /ðæt/ *conjunction*
when /wen/ *conjunction*
where /weə/ *conjunction*
while /waɪl/ *conjunction*

UNIT 13

OUTDOOR ACTIVITIES

camp under the stars /'kæmp 'ʌndə ðə 'stɑːz/ *verb phrase*
climb a tree /'klaɪm ə 'triː/ *verb phrase*
explore a cave /ɪk'splɔːr ə 'keɪv/ *verb phrase*
kayak down a river /'kaɪæk daʊn ə 'rɪvə/ *verb phrase*
look for fossils /'lʊk fə 'fɒsəlz/ *verb phrase*
pick wild fruit /'pɪk 'waɪld 'fruːt/ *verb phrase*
play in the snow /'pleɪ ɪn ðə 'snəʊ/ *verb phrase*
record birdsong /rɪ'kɔːd 'bɜːdsɒŋ/ *verb phrase*
track wild animals /'træk 'waɪld 'ænɪməlz/ *verb phrase*
try rock climbing /traɪ 'rɒk 'klaɪmɪŋ/ *verb phrase*

PAST PARTICIPLES

be /biː/ *verb* → **been** / biːn/ *verb*
break /breɪk/ *verb* → **broken** /'brəʊkən/ *verb*
eat /iːt/ *verb* → **eaten** /iːtən/ *verb*
fly /flaɪ/ *verb* → **flown** /fləʊn/ *verb*
grow /grəʊ/ *verb* → **grown** /grəʊn/ *verb*
have /hæv/ *verb* → **had** /hæd/ *verb*
make /meɪk/ *verb* → **made** /meɪd/ *verb*
meet /miːt/ *verb* → **met** /met/ *verb*
ride /raɪd/ *verb* → **ridden** /'rɪdən/ *verb*
send /send/ *verb* → **sent** /sent/ *verb*
sleep /sliːp/ *verb* → **slept** /slept/ *verb*
swim /swɪm/ *verb* → **swum** /swʌm/ *verb*

UNIT 14

SHOPS

bakery /'beɪkəri/ *noun*
bookshop /'bʊkʃɒp/ *noun*
butcher's /'bʊtʃəz/ *noun*
café /'kæfeɪ/ *noun*
chemist's /'kemɪsts/ *noun*
clothes shop /kləʊðz ʃɒp/ *noun*
department store /dɪ'pɑːtmənt 'stɔː/ *noun*
market /'mɑːkɪt/ *noun*
newsagent's /'njuːzˌeɪdʒənts/ *noun*
shoe shop /'ʃuː ʃɒp/ *noun*
supermarket /'suːpəˌmɑːkɪt/ *noun*
sweet shop /'swiːt ʃɒp/ *noun*

UNITS OF MEASUREMENT

a pair of /ə 'peər əv/ *noun*
a set of /ə 'set əv/ *noun*
a slice of /ə 'slaɪs əv/ *noun*
a variety of /ə və'raɪəti əv/ *noun*
centimetres /'sentɪˌmiːtəz/ *noun*
dollars and cents /'dɒləz ən 'sents/ *noun*
euros and cents /'jʊərəʊz ən 'sents/ *noun*
grams /græmz/ *noun*
kilograms /'kɪləʊgræmz/ *noun*
kilometres /'kɪləˌmiːtəz/ *noun*
litres /'liːtəz/ *noun*
metres /'miːtəz/ *noun*
millilitres /'mɪlɪˌliːtəz/ *noun*
pounds and pence /'paʊndz ən 'pens/ *noun*

UNIT 15

FREE-TIME ACTIVITIES

chatting /'tʃætɪŋ/ *noun*
collecting things /kə'lektɪŋ 'θɪŋz/ *noun phrase*
cooking /'kʊkɪŋ/ *noun*
dancing /'dɑːnsɪŋ/ *noun*
going out with friends /'gəʊɪŋ aʊt wɪð 'frendz/ *noun phrase*
going shopping /'gəʊɪŋ 'ʃɒpɪŋ/ *noun phrase*

listening to music /ˈlɪsənɪŋ tə ˈmjuːzɪk/ *noun phrase*

photography /fəˈtɒgrəfi/ *noun*

playing an instrument /ˈpleɪɪŋ ən ˈɪnstrəmənt/ *noun phrase*

playing computer games /ˈpleɪɪŋ kəmˈpjuːtə geɪmz/ *noun phrase*

playing sport /ˈpleɪɪŋ ˈspɔːt/ *noun phrase*

reading books /ˈriːdɪŋ ˈbʊks/ *noun phrase*

singing /ˈsɪŋɪŋ/ *noun*

spend time doing something /spend taɪm ˈduːɪŋ ˈsʌmθɪŋ/ *verb phrase*

spending time online /ˈspendɪŋ taɪm ɒnˈlaɪn/ *noun phrase*

watching TV /ˈwɒtʃɪŋ ˌtiːˈviː/ *noun phrase*

COLLOCATIONS ABOUT HAVING FUN

a brilliant day out /ə ˈbrɪliənt deɪ ˈaʊt/ *collocation*

a brilliant hobby /ə ˈbrɪliənt ˈhɒbi/ *collocation*

a fantastic feeling /ə fænˈtæstɪk ˈfiːlɪŋ/ *collocation*

a fun day out /ə ˈfʌn deɪ ˈaʊt/ *collocation*

a fun hobby /ə ˈfʌn ˈhɒbi/ *collocation*

an exciting day out /ən ɪkˈsaɪtɪŋ deɪ ˈaʊt/ *collocation*

an exciting hobby /ən ɪkˈsaɪtɪŋ ˈhɒbi / *collocation*

be glad /biː ˈglæd/ *collocation*

be happy /biː ˈhæpi/ *collocation*

enjoy an activity /ɪnˈdʒɔɪ ən ækˈtɪvəti/ *collocation*

enjoy yourself /ɪnˈdʒɔɪ jɔːˈself/ *collocation*

feel happy /ˈfiːl ˈhæpi/ *collocation*

have a great time /ˈhæv ə ˈgreɪt ˈtaɪm/ *collocation*

have a laugh /ˈhæv ə ˈlɑːf/ *collocation*

have fun /ˈhæv ˈfʌn/ *collocation*

making things /ˈmeɪkɪŋ ˈθɪŋz/ *noun phrase*

spend time with someone /spend ˈtaɪm wɪð ˈsʌmwʌn/ *collocation*

UNIT 16

WORDS TO DESCRIBE LANGUAGE LEARNING

article /ˈɑːtɪkl/ *noun*

exercise /ˈeksəsaɪz/ *noun*

guess /ges/ *verb*

list /lɪst/ *noun*

look up /ˈlʊk ʌp/ *verb*

meaning /ˈmiːnɪŋ/ *noun*

mistake /mɪˈsteɪk/ *noun*

spell /spel/ *verb*

topic /ˈtɒpɪk/ *noun*

translate /trænzˈleɪt/ *verb*

LARGE NUMBERS

billion /ˈbɪliən/ *noun*

hundred /ˈhʌndrəd/ *noun*

million /ˈmɪljən/ *noun*

thousand /ˈθaʊzənd/ *noun*

UNIT 17

BODY PARTS

ankle /ˈæŋkl/ *noun*

back /bæk/ *noun*

blood /blʌd/ *noun*

brain /breɪn/ *noun*

ear /ɪə/ *noun*

finger /ˈfɪŋgə/ *noun*

heart /hɑːt/ *noun*

mouth /maʊθ/ *noun*

neck /nek/ *noun*

stomach /ˈstʌmək/ *noun*

thumb /θʌm/ *noun*

toe /təʊ/ *noun*

tongue /tʌŋ/ *noun*

ADJECTIVES TO EXPRESS EMOTION

angry /ˈæŋgri/ *adjective*

confident /ˈkɒnfɪdənt/ *adjective*

embarrassed /ɪmˈbærəst/ *adjective*

friendly /ˈfrendli/ *adjective*

lazy /ˈleɪzi/ *adjective*

lonely /ˈləʊnli/ *adjective*

surprised /səˈpraɪzd/ *adjective*

unhappy /ʌnˈhæpi/ *adjective*

upset /ʌpˈset/ *adjective*

worried /ˈwʌrid/ *adjective*

VOCABULARY LIST

UNIT 18

BOOKS AND READING

bring back /brɪŋ ˈbæk/ *phrasal verb*
find out /faɪnd ˈaʊt/ *phrasal verb*
give back /gɪv ˈbæk/ *phrasal verb*
pick up /pɪk ˈʌp/ *verb phrase*
put back /pʊt ˈbæk/ *phrasal verb*
put down /pʊt ˈdaʊn/ *phrasal verb*
take back /teɪk ˈbæk/ *phrasal verb*
take out /teɪk ˈaʊt/ *phrasal verb*

WORDS ABOUT BOOKS

author /ˈɔːθə/ *noun*
chapter /ˈtʃæptə/ *noun*
cover /ˈkʌvə/ *noun*
drawings /ˈdrɔːɪŋz/ *noun*
end /end/ *noun*
fan /fæn/ *noun*
opinion /əˈpɪnjən/ *noun*
pages /ˈpeɪdʒɪz/ *noun*
shelf /ʃelf/ *noun*
title /ˈtaɪtl/ *noun*

UNIT 19

WORDS TO DESCRIBE COOKING

add /æd/ *verb*
bake /beɪk/ *verb*
boil /bɔɪl/ *verb*
cover /ˈkʌvə/ *verb*
dry /draɪ/ *verb*
fill /fɪl/ *verb*
fried /fraɪd/ *adjective*
grilled /grɪld/ *adjective*
mix /mɪks/ *verb*
prepare /prɪˈpeə/ *verb*
roast /rəʊst/ *adjective*

INGREDIENTS

beans /biːnz/ *noun*
carrots /ˈkærəts/ *noun*
garlic /ˈgɑːlɪk/ *noun*
melon /ˈmelən/ *noun*
pears /peəz/ *noun*
potatoes /pəˈteɪtəʊz/ *noun*
salt and pepper /ˈsɒlt ən ˈpepə/ *noun phrase*
steak /steɪk/ *noun*

MAKE AND *DO*

do the cleaning /ˈduː ðə ˈkliːnɪŋ/ *collocation*
do the dishes /ˈduː ðə ˈdɪʃɪz/ *collocation*
do the shopping /ˈduː ðə ˈʃɒpɪŋ/ *collocation*
do the washing /ˈduː ðə ˈwɒʃɪŋ/ *collocation*
do your homework /ˈduː jə ˈhəʊmwɜːk/ *collocation*
make a cake /ˈmeɪk ə ˈkeɪk/ *collocation*
make a cup of tea /ˈmeɪk ə ˈkʌp əv ˈtiː/ *collocation*
make a mess /ˈmeɪk ə ˈmes/ *collocation*
make a mistake /ˈmeɪk ə mɪˈsteɪk/ *collocation*
make the bed /ˈmeɪk ðə ˈbed/ *collocation*

UNIT 20

CHANGE AS A VERB AND NOUN

change [= alternative clothes] /tʃeɪndʒ/ *noun*
change [= become something different] /tʃeɪndʒ/ *verb*
change [= give money back when buying something] /tʃeɪndʒ/ *verb*
change [= something in a shop] /tʃeɪndʒ/ *verb*
change [= something new] /tʃeɪndʒ/ *noun*
change [= transport] /tʃeɪndʒ/ *verb*
change schools /ˈtʃeɪndʒ ˈskuːlz/ *verb phrase*

LIFE CHANGES

be ˈborn /biː bɔːn/ *verb phrase*
become a teenager /bɪˈkʌm ə ˈtiːnˌeɪdʒə/ *verb phrase*
find part-time work /faɪnd ˈpɑːt taɪm ˈwɜːk/ *verb phrase*
get married /get ˈmærid/ *verb phrase*
go to high school /gəʊ tə ˈhaɪ skuːl/ *verb phrase*
learn to walk and talk /lɜːn tə ˈwɔːk ən ˈtɔːk/ *verb phrase*
move house /ˈmuːv ˈhaʊs/ *verb phrase*
start school /ˈstɑːt ˈskuːl/ *verb phrase*
start working or training /stɑːt ˈwɜːkɪŋ ɔː ˈtreɪnɪŋ/ *verb phrase*
take exams /teɪk ɪgˈzæmz/ *verb phrase*
travel /ˈtrævəl/ *verb*

GRAMMAR REFERENCE AND PRACTICE

UNIT 1 PRESENT SIMPLE AND PRESENT CONTINUOUS

Present simple

We use the **present simple** to talk about things that are always true or that happen regularly. We often use it with words like *often*, *usually*, *every day*, *twice a week*, etc.

*I usually **work** hard.*
*She **learns** English at school.*
***Does** he **work** here? No, he **doesn't**.*
***Do** they often **go** to the cinema? Yes, they **do**.*

Spelling: third person -*s*

Most verbs, add –*s*	*learn**s**, work**s**, live**s**, walk**s***
verbs that end in -*o*, -*s*, -*sh*, -*ch*, -*x* and -*zz* add -*es*	*go**es**, miss**es**, watch**es**, box**es**, buzz**es***
verbs that end in consonant + -*y*, remove the -*y* and add -*ies*	*stud**ies**, carr**ies***
irregular verbs	*have* → ***has***

Present continuous

We use the **present continuous** to talk about things that are happening now or at the moment. We often use it with words like *now*, *at the moment*, *today*, *this week*, etc.

***I'm teaching** my brother to swim **at the moment**.*
*They**'re playing** tennis now.*
*You **aren't practising** the piano much this week.*
***Are** we **getting** fitter? Yes, we **are**.*

Spelling: -*ing* form

Most verbs add -*ing*	*play**ing**, go**ing**, learn**ing***
verbs ending in -*e*, remove -*e* and add -*ing*	*live* → *liv**ing**,* *make* → *mak**ing***
verbs ending in -*ie*, change the -*ie* to -*y* and add -*ing*	*lie* → ***ly**ing*
one-syllable verbs ending in a vowel + a consonant (except *w*, *x* or *y*), double the consonant and add -*ing*	*sit* → *si**tting**,* *swim* → *swi**mming***
two-syllable verbs ending in a stressed vowel + a consonant, double the consonant and add -*ing*	*begin* → *begi**nning*** (**but** *open* → *opening*)
In British English, we double the final *l* in *travel*	*travel* → *trave**lling*** (American English: *travel* → *traveling*)

1 **Complete the conversation with the present simple or present continuous form of the verb in brackets.**

Sara: What **(0)** *are you doing* (do)?
Martina: I **(1)** .... (paint) a picture of the trees.
Sara: But you **(2)** .... (not like) art!
Martina: Yes, I know, but my friends **(3)** .... (play) football at the moment and I **(4)** .... (hate) that.
Sara: What sports **(5)** .... you .... (enjoy) doing?
Martina: I **(6)** .... (go) swimming twice a week. What about you?
Sara: My best friend **(7)** .... (play) *hockey*, but I **(8)** .... (prefer) basketball.
Martina: I **(9)** .... (not do) anything now. Let's go for a walk.
Sara: Good idea!

2 **Write complete sentences in the present simple or present continuous.**

0 I / play tennis / at the moment.
I'm playing tennis at the moment.
1 My dad / usually go to work by car.
....
2 We / learn how to play the guitar / today.
....
3 I / always watch TV / after dinner.
....
4 My friends / not swim in the sea / now.
....
5 My cousin / not have breakfast / every day.
....

GRAMMAR REFERENCE AND PRACTICE

UNIT 2 VERBS WE DON'T USUALLY USE IN THE CONTINUOUS

There are some verbs which we don't normally use in the present continuous:

- Verbs of thinking: *believe, understand, know, think, mean, hope*.
  *Scientists **believe** the Earth is 4.6 billion years old.*
  (**not** ~~*Scientists are believing*~~ *…*)
- Verbs of liking and not liking: *like, hate, love, want, need, prefer*.
  *I **like** those monkeys over there.* (**not** ~~*I'm liking*~~ *…*)
- Verbs of owning: *own, belong, have*.
  *That coat **belongs** to me.* (**not** ~~*That coat's belonging*~~ *…*)
- Verbs to describe sensations: *see, feel, hear, smell, taste*.
  *The water **feels** very cold.*
  However, we can use the present continuous to say how someone looks or feels now.
  *How **do** you **feel** today? I **feel** better.*
  or *How **are** you **feeling** today? I'**m feeling** better.*
  We often use *can* with these verbs.
  *I **can hear** the sea from my bedroom.* (**not** ~~*I'm hearing*~~)
- When *think* means 'have an opinion' about something, we do not use the continuous.
  *Scientists **think** there are about 1,000 wild pandas left.* (**not** ~~*Scientists are thinking*~~ *…*)
  However, when *think* means 'consider', we use the continuous.
  *I'**m thinking** of working in a zoo when I'm older.*

Practice

1 Complete the table with the verbs.

believe buy climb feel
hate like make mean
~~need~~ own ~~run~~ sing
understand want work

Verbs we can use in the continuous	Verbs we don't normally use in the continuous
run	*need*

2 Choose the correct words to complete the sentences.

0 Jack's behind that tree. I *(can see)* / *'m seeing* him.
1 I *know* / *'m knowing* the names of all the rivers in my country.
2 My brother *learns* / *'s learning* about the weather at the moment.
3 You *need* / *'re needing* to do your homework before Tuesday.
4 You're very quiet. What *do you think* / *are you thinking* about?
5 My friends *don't play* / *aren't playing* football today. It's cold.
6 Can you say that again? We *don't understand* / *aren't understanding*.
7 *Can you hear* / *Are you hearing* that strange noise?

3 Write complete sentences. Use the present simple or the present continuous.

0 Shh! I / think.
Shh! I'm thinking.
1 I / not understand / this exercise.
2 My friends / think football is boring.
3 What / you / do right now?
4 We / not want to watch the film.
5 That dog / belong to my cousin.
6 Penguins / not feel / the cold weather.
7 I / not like this book very much.

UNIT 3 PAST SIMPLE

Be

Positive	I / He / She / It **was** at home. You / We / They **were** at school.
Negative	I / He / She / It **wasn't** at school. You / We / They **weren't** at home.
Questions	**Was** I / he / she / it at home? **Were** you / we / they at school?
Short answers	Yes, I / he / she / it **was**. No, I / he / she / it **wasn't**. Yes, you / we / they **were**. No, you / we / they **weren't**.

Regular and irregular verbs

Positive	I / You / He / She / It / We / They **climbed** … I / You / He / She / It / We / They **knew** …
Negative	I / You / He / She / It / We / They **didn't want** … I / You / He / She / It / We / They **didn't write** …
Questions	**Did** I / you / he / she / it / we / they **travel**? **Did** I / you / he / she / it / we / they **fly**?
Short answers	Yes, I / you / he / she / it / we / they **did**. No, I / you / he / she / it /we / they **didn't**.

- We use the past simple to talk about things that happened or didn't happen in the past.
  *Simon and I **travelled** by tram to the bus station.*
  *We **didn't want** my parents to drive us.*

Spelling: regular verbs

Most verbs add *-ed*	*play → played* *climb → climbed*
verbs that end *in -e*, add *-d*	*decide → decided* *arrive → arrived*
verbs that end in consonant + *-y*, change *-y* to -i and add *-ed*	*carry → carried*
one-syllable verbs ending in a vowel + a consonant (except *w*, *x* or *y*), double the consonant and add *-ed*	*stop → stopped*
two-syllable verbs ending in a stressed vowel + consonant, double the consonant and add *-ed*	*prefer → preferred*
In British English, we double the final *l* in *travel*	*travel → travelled* (America English: *travel → traveled*)

» FOR IRREGULAR VERBS SEE PAGE 167

1 Complete the paragraph with the past simple form of the verb in brackets.

Last summer, I **(0)** *visited* (visit) Moscow with my family. We **(1)** ________ (fly) from London. On the first day, we **(2)** ________ (go) to the tourist information office and we **(3)** ________ (ask) for information about the city. My sister **(4)** ________ (want) to go to the zoo. My dad **(5)** ________ (not want) to go there, so he **(6)** ________ (go) shopping. The next day, we **(7)** ________ (walk) to Red Square and we **(8)** ________ (see) the Kremlin. We **(9)** ________ (not go) inside the museum because it **(10)** ________ (be) closed. We **(11)** ________ (have) a fantastic holiday there.

SUBJECT QUESTIONS

We normally use *do* or *did* in questions.
*Where **do** you live?*
*What **did** you eat yesterday?*
However, we don't use *do* or *did* if the question word (*who*, *what*, etc.) is the subject. Look at these questions:

Subject: *Who helped you? **My mum** helped me.*

Object: *Who did you help? I helped **my sister**.*

2 Choose the correct words to complete the questions.

0 Who *did lend* / *lent* Fred money for the coach?
1 What *did the boy see* / *saw the boy* at the cinema?
2 What *did happen* / *happened* to you? You're late!
3 Who *did eat* / *ate* the cake?
4 Where *did you go* / *went you* on holiday?
5 Who *did do* / *did* their homework last night?

GRAMMAR REFERENCE AND PRACTICE

UNIT 4 PAST CONTINUOUS AND PAST SIMPLE

Past continuous

Positive	I / He / She / It **was eating** a sandwich. You / We / They **were standing** on the balcony.
Negative	I / He / She / It **wasn't working** in the garden. You / We / They **weren't reading** a book.
Questions	**Was** I / he / she / it **building** some cupboards? **Were** you / we / they **painting** the gate?
Short answers	Yes, I / he / she / it **was**. No, he / she / it **wasn't**. Yes, you / we / they **were**. No, you / we / they **weren't**.

FOR THE SPELLING OF THE *-ING* FORM, SEE UNIT 1 PAGE 147

Past continuous and past simple

We use the **past continuous**:

- to describe activities happening at a particular moment in the past. Sometimes, these activities happen at the same time. We're not interested when the activities started or finished.
  *Mum and Dad **were cooking**, my brother **was playing** and I **was doing** my homework.*
- after *while* to refer to a longer action or event that happened at the same time as another action.
  *While Gary **was painting** the bedroom, Paula **was painting** the living room.*

We use the **past simple**:

- when one action follows another.
  *I **put** on my coat and I **left** the house. Then, it **started** to rain.*
- after *when* to refer to a shorter action or event that happened in the middle of a longer one or interrupted it.
  *I **was putting** on my coat when it **started** to rain.*

FOR THE PAST SIMPLE, SEE UNIT 3 PAGE 149

Practice

1 Use the past continuous to write complete sentences.

At 7.30 last night …

0 Mum / drive / her car into the garage.
Mum was driving her car into the garage.

1 it / rain.
....

2 Dad / cook / dinner.
....

3 my brother and I / watch TV in the living room.
....

4 my sister / read.
....

5 my grandparents / leave their apartment.
....

2 Choose the correct options to complete the sentences.

0 I was studying in my bedroom when I (*heard*) / *was hearing* a strange noise.
1 While I was surfing, it *started* / *was starting* to rain.
2 My friends *played* / *were playing* football in the classroom when the teacher came in.
3 We walked to the park and then we *had* / *were having* a game of football.
4 Ed rang me while I *did* / *was doing* my homework.
5 We *packed* / *were packing* our suitcases when the phone rang.

3 Complete the email with the past simple or past continuous form of the verb in brackets.

To: Mark
From: Tim
Reply Forward

Hi, Mark!

We **(0)** *arrived* (arrive) here in New York yesterday. When we **(1)** .... (get up) this morning, the sun **(2)** .... (shine).

It was a beautiful day, so we **(3)** .... (decide) to walk to Central Park. While we **(4)** .... (sit) on the grass, I **(5)** .... (see) my teacher! She **(6)** .... (not be) pleased to see me.

See you soon!

Tim

UNIT 5 COMPARATIVE AND SUPERLATIVE ADVERBS

Adjective	Adverb	Comparative	Superlative
		Regular	
slow	slowly	more slowly	the most slowly
easy	easily	more easily	the most easily
simple	simply	more simply	the most simply
beautiful	beautifully	more beautifully	the most beautifully
		Irregular	
good	well	better	the best
fast	fast	faster	the fastest
hard	hard	harder	the hardest
late	late	later	the latest

We use **adjectives** to describe a noun and **adverbs** to describe a verb.

- We form most adverbs by adding *-ly* to the adjective.
  bad → badly, careful → carefully, easy → easily
- Some adverbs do not end in *-ly*.
  good → well, fast → fast, hard → hard, late → late

We use **comparative adverbs** to compare two things.
My brother talks ***more quickly*** *than me.*

- We use *more* with adjectives that finish in *-ly*.
  Jack did the exam ***more carefully*** *than Nick.*
- The opposite of *more* is *less*.
  Nick did the exam ***less carefully*** *than Jack.*
- We add *-er* to *fast*, *hard* and *late*.
  Peter swims ***faster*** *than Mike. Jim arrived* ***later*** *than me.*
- The comparative form of the adverb *well* is *better*.
  My sister speaks French ***better*** *than my mum.*
- The comparative form of the adverb *badly* is *worse*.
  I did much ***worse*** *in my exam than Theo.*
- We can also use *often* to compare things.
  I play tennis ***more often*** *than basketball.*
- We can also use *(not) as* + adverb + *as* to compare things.
  Oliver talks ***as loudly as*** *Phil.* (= They both talk loudly.)
  Jane doesn't write ***as quickly as*** *Paula.* (= Paula writes more quickly than Jane.)

We use **superlative adverbs** to compare one thing with two or more other things.
My dad walks ***the most slowly*** *in our family.*

- We use *most* with adverbs that finish in *-ly*.
  Of all our teachers, our maths teacher speaks ***the most quickly****.*
- The opposite of *most* is *least*.
  Kevin did his exam ***the least carefully****.*
- We add *-est* to *fast*, *hard* and *late*.
  Jason ran ***the fastest****, so he won the race.*
- The superlative form of the adverb *well* is *the best*.
  My grandma cooks ***the best*** *in my house.*
- The superlative form of the adverb *badly* is *the worst*.
  None of the teams played very well, but our team played ***the worst****.*
- We can also use *often* to compare things.
  When I was young, I played football ***the most often****.*

Practice

1 **Write the adverb, comparative and superlative adverbs of the adjective.**

1 cheap, *cheaply*, ______, ______
2 heavy, ______, ______, ______
3 fast, ______, ______, ______
4 bad, ______, ______, ______
5 serious, ______, ______, ______
6 wonderful, ______, ______, ______

2 **Complete the sentences with the comparative or superlative form of the adverb in brackets.**

0 Natalie ran *the fastest* (fast), so she won the race.
1 Laura won the competition because she danced ______ (beautiful).
2 I watch f lms ______ (often) than sports programmes.
3 My sister plays the guitar ______ (well) than me.
4 Matt's mum helped him, so he finished the homework ______ (easily) than us.
5 Luke's teacher was happy with him because he did the exercise ______ (quickly).

3 **Complete the sentences with *as* + adverb + *as*.**

0 We all finished the exam quickly. I finished the exam *as quickly as* my friends.
1 I arrived home late, but my brother arrived home later. I didn't arrive home ______ my brother.
2 My best friend speaks more quietly than me. I don't speak ______ my best friend.
3 My parents eat very slowly. My dad eats ______ my mum.
4 William watches TV more often than his sister. W lliam's sister doesn't watch TV ______ William.
5 My cousin is the best guitar player in my school. Nobody plays it ______ him.

GRAMMAR REFERENCE AND PRACTICE

UNIT 6 POSSESSION

's (apostrophe + *s*)

- We use *'s* (apostrophe + *s*) for people and animals.
  That's my brother's hat. (**not** ~~*the hat of my brother*~~)
  Where's the cat's bowl? (**not** ~~*the bowl of the cat*~~)
- With singular nouns, we use *'s*.
  my mum's necklace, my teacher's ring
- With plural nouns, we put the apostrophe (') at the end of the plural noun.
  my friends' shoes (**not** ~~*the shoes of my friends*~~)
  my cousins' jackets (**not** ~~*the jackets of my cousins*~~)
- If the plural noun does not end in *-s* (e.g. *children, men, women, people*), we use *'s*.
  The children's bedroom is over there.

Determiners and pronouns

Determiners	Pronouns
my	mine
your	yours
his	his
her	hers
our	ours
their	theirs

- We use pronouns instead of determiner + noun.
  *Is that my pencil on your desk? No, **yours** is over there.* (= your pencil)
  *Is this your jacket? No, it's **hers**.* (= her jacket)
  *Who do these books belong to? They're **ours**.* (= our books)
- We can use '*a friend of mine/yours/his,* etc.' instead of '*one of my/your/his, etc. friends*'.
  *This ball belongs to **a friend of mine**. He lent it to me.* (**not** ~~*a friend of me*~~)
  *Neil finished his homework. **A classmate of his** helped him.* (**not** ~~*a classmate of him*~~)

1 Rewrite the sentences with the apostrophe (').

0 The dogs bowl is empty.
The dog's bowl is empty.
1 Terrys gold coins are on the table.
....
2 The childrens shoes are near the door.
....
3 Both boys lunches are in the kitchen.
....
4 I can't find my sisters necklace. She'll be angry.
....
5 My cousins names are Ana and Eva.
....

2 Choose the correct words to complete the sentences.

0 That isn't Ben's book. *He* / (*His*) / *Him* is on the teacher's desk.
1 Nora saw Sue at the cinema. She's a friend of *she* / *her* / *hers*.
2 We don't live here. *We* / *Our* / *Ours* house is near the park.
3 I've got two cats. *They* / *Their* / *Theirs* names are Leo and Tiger.
4 Who does this jumper belong to? Is it *you* / *your* / *yours*?
5 I was shopping when I saw a classmate of *me* / *my* / *mine*.

3 Complete the second sentence with the correct pronoun.

0 I saw one of my friends yesterday.
I saw a friend of *mine* yesterday.
1 Jane went on holiday with one of her friends.
Jane went on holiday with a friend of ....
2 We played football with one of our neighbours.
We played football with a neighbour of ....
3 My sister borrowed one of my necklaces.
My sister borrowed a necklace of ....
4 My parents had dinner with some of their friends.
My parents had dinner with some friends of ....
5 I found some money in one of your shoes.
I found some money in a shoe of ....

UNIT 7 PRESENT CONTINUOUS FOR FUTURE

» FOR THE PRESENT CONTINUOUS, SEE UNIT 1 PAGE 147

- We often use the present continuous to talk about things that are happening now or at this moment (see Unit 1).
  *Tim's in the park. He's **climbing** a tree.*
- We can also use the present continuous to talk about our future plans and arrangements.
  *I'm **meeting** Julie later. We're **playing** tennis.*
- When we use the present continuous for the future, we usually use a future time expression (*later, on Monday morning, at 6 pm tomorrow,* etc.) to show we're talking about the future and not now.
  *We're **learning** how to ski.* (= now, at this moment)
  *We're **learning** how to ski next weekend.* (= future arrangement)

1 Complete these sentences with the present continuous form of the verb in brackets. Then, read the sentences again. Are we talking about now or the future? Write *N* (now) or *F* (future).

0 My friends *are hiking* (hike) in the mountains. *N*
1 We ________ (go paddle boarding) with Mia and Alfie on Friday.
2 ________ you ________ (listen) to me?
3 My dad ________ (not come) with us on holiday next week.
4 Be quiet! I ________ (do) my homework.
5 How ________ you and your friends (get) to football practice later?

2 Sara is talking to Vicky. Look at Sara's diary and complete their conversation.

DIARY

Thursday:	**am** **pm** help Max with homework
Friday:	**am** **pm** go to dentist
Saturday:	**am** Dad's birthday, have pizza at Paolo's Pizzas **pm**
Sunday:	**am** play basketball **pm** study
Monday:	**am** maths test! **pm**

Vicky: Would you like to come to my house after school today?
Sara: I can't,
(0) *I'm helping Max with his homework*.
Vicky: How about Friday afternoon?
Sara: No, **(1)** ________.
Vicky: Are you free on Saturday?
Sara: It's my dad's birthday and we **(2)** ________.
Vicky: And on Sunday?
Sara: In the morning, **(3)** ________.
Vicky: What about the afternoon?
Sara: Oh no, I can't! **(4)** ________. We've got a maths test on Monday!

3 What are you doing at these times this week? Complete these sentences so they are true for you.

0 (after school)
I'm doing my homework after school.
1 (tomorrow morning)
____
2 (Friday afternoon)
____
3 (Saturday morning)
____
4 (on Sunday)
____
5 (next week)
____

GRAMMAR REFERENCE AND PRACTICE

UNIT 8

FUTURE WITH *WILL*

Positive	I / You / He / She / It / We / They**'ll** (**will**) be very different in the future.
Negative	I / You / He / She / It / We / They **won't** (**will not**) live in big houses.
Questions	**Will** I / you / he / she / it / we / they drive cars?
Short answers	Yes, I / you / he / she / it / we / they **will**. No, I / you / he / she / it / we / they **won't** (**will not**).

- We use *will* to talk about things which we think are certain to happen in the future.
  *Everyone **will live** in big cities in the future.*
  *We **won't live** in small towns.*
- We often use expressions like *I think*, *I hope*, *I'm sure* or *certain* with *will*.
  *I **think** I'**ll work** in a big bank.*
  *I'm **sure** my friends **won't live** in the same town.*

1 Complete the predictions with *will* or *won't*.

0 We / live / to be 120 years old.
We'll live to be 120 years old.
1 I / have / a big house and a fast car.
____
2 My friends / move away.
____
3 My cousin / become / a famous film star.
____
4 There / be / cities on other planets.
____
5 We / not buy / things in shops.
____

2 Complete the questions with *will* and the verb in brackets, and then write your own answers.

0 Where *will* people *build* (build) houses in the future?
I think *they will build houses under the sea.*
1 _______ students _______ (go) to school in the future?
I'm sure _______________.
2 Where _______ we _______ (buy) clothes and shoes in the future?
I think _______________.
3 How _______ people _______ (travel) from one place to another?
I'm certain _______________.
4 _______ there _______ (be) more wars?
I hope _______________.
5 _______ scientists _______ (discover) new things?
I'm sure _______________.

FUTURE WITH *MAY / MIGHT*

Positive	I / You / He / She / It / We / They **may** / **might book** the hotel today.
Negative	I / You / He / She / It / We / They **may not** / **might not ring** you later.

- We use *may* and *might* to talk about future possibilities.
  *It **may rain** tomorrow.* (= I'm not sure.)
  *We **might go** for a walk later.* (= We aren't certain.)
- When we talk about future possibilities, *may* and *might* have the same meaning.
  *I **may** / **might** buy some new trainers tomorrow. Mine are very old.*
  *Jack's feeling ill. He **may not** / **might not** go to school tomorrow.*
- We don't often use *may* or *might* to ask questions about future possibilities. We usually use *will*.
  *What **will** you **take** on the school trip?*
  *I **may take** my sun hat and I **might take** my sunglasses.*

1 Choose the correct words to complete the sentences.

1 I'm sure I*'ll* / *may* go swimming. It's really hot.
2 We*'ll* / *may* have pizza or we*'ll* / *may* have a hamburger. We haven't decided yet.
3 My mum*'ll* / *might* be able to drive us to the concert, but she isn't sure.
4 Don't worry. I'm certain they *won't* / *may not* be late. They left 45 minutes ago.
5 Where *will* / *may* you go on holiday? We may go to South Africa.

2 Write complete sentences with *may* or *might* and one of the verbs in the box.

buy	~~go~~	not go	not rain
turn off	not understand		

0 I don't know what we're doing this evening.
We *might go* to Molly's barbecue party.
1 I haven't got any sun cream.
I _______ to the beach.
2 I'm really cold.
I _______ the air conditioning.
3 Look! The clouds are moving.
It _______ later.
4 It's my cousin's birthday. Her parents _______ her a new smartphone.
5 You _______ this teacher because she talks very fast.

UNIT 9 MUST, MUST NOT (MUSTN'T), HAVE TO, DON'T HAVE TO

must / mustn't

Positive	I / You / He / She / It / We / They **must** go.
Negative	I / You / He / She / It / We / They **mustn't** go.

- We use *must* and *mustn't* to talk about rules and obligations.
  *You **must** switch off your mobile phone in class.*
  *You **mustn't** eat or drink in the classroom.*
- We don't often use *must* in the question form. We prefer to use *Do* (*I, you,* etc.) *have to ... ?*
  ***Do** I **have to** wear a swimming hat?*

Practice

1 Write complete sentences with *must* or *mustn't*.

0 ✗ you / walk on the grass
You mustn't walk on the grass.

1 ✓they / fill in the form

2 ✗ we / forget Mum's birthday

3 ✗ my cousin / wear large earrings to school

4 ✓you / practise for an hour every day

5 ✓you / be careful

have to / don't have to

Positive	I / You / We / They **have to** go. He / She / It / **has to** go.
Negative	I / You / We / They **don't** (**do not**) **have to** go. He / She / It **doesn't** (**does not**) **have to** go.
Questions	**Do** I / you / we / they **have to** go? **Does** he / she / it **have to** go?
Short answers	Yes, I / you / we / they **do**. Yes, he / she / it **does**. No, I / you / we / they **don't**. No, he / she / it **doesn't**.

- We use *have to* to say something is necessary and *don't have to* to say something isn't necessary.
  *You **have to** bring sandwiches.* (= you need to bring) but *You **don't have to** bring a drink.* (= you don't need to bring)

2 Complete the sentences and questions with the correct form of *have to* and the verb in brackets.

0 *Do* you *have to join* (join) a club to play this sport?
1 Today's Saturday. I ______ (not go) to bed early.
2 My mum ______ (work) in London this week.
3 What time ______ your sister ______ (come) home when she goes out?
4 My uncle has got problems with his back.
He ______ (go) swimming every day.
5 We ______ (not watch) the film, we can play a game instead.

must and have to

- *Must* and *have to* are similar.
  *I've got a test tomorrow. I **must** study. or I **have to** study.*
- *Mustn't* and *don't have to* are different.
  *You **mustn't** be late for class.* (= you can't be late. It's the rule.)
  *You **don't have to** bring your own equipment.* (= it isn't necessary but you can if you want.)
- In the past, we use *had to* for *must* and *have to*.
  *I didn't watch the film because I **had to** study.*
- The past of *don't have to* and *do you have to* is *didn't have to* and *did you have to*.
  ***Did** you **have to** stay at school late yesterday? No, I didn't.*
  *My mum **didn't have to** go to work this morning, so she drove me to school.*

3 Choose the correct words to complete the sentences.

0 You *(don't have to)* / *mustn't* help me but you can if you want.
1 When I was younger, I *had to* / *must* go to bed at 8 pm.
2 No ball games, please! You *don't have to* / *mustn't* play football here.
3 *Do you have to* / *Must* you leave now? It's very early.
4 I *don't have to* / *mustn't* wear a swimming cap at my pool, but I usually wear one.
5 Shh! My sister's sleeping! We *don't have to* / *mustn't* wake her.

GRAMMAR REFERENCE AND PRACTICE

UNIT 10 VERB PATTERNS – GERUNDS AND INFINITIVES

- When we use two verbs together in a sentence, the second verb is usually **a gerund** (*sleeping, swimming,* etc.) or an infinitive (*to sleep, to swim*).
  *I **want to meet** my new neighbours.*
  *I **don't mind helping** close friends.*
- We use **an infinitive** after some verbs.
  *We **hope to see** you soon.*
  *He's **learning to play** the guitar.*
- We use **a gerund** after other verbs.
  *He **finished doing** his homework and watched TV.*
  *My dad **enjoys playing** chess.*
- We can use **a gerund** or **an infinitive** after these verbs: *start, begin, prefer, like, love*.
  *We went to the beach, but then it **started raining**.*
  or *… **it started to rain**.*
  *My friends **began playing** that game two hours ago.*
  or *My friends **began to play** …*
- We also use **a gerund** after prepositions (*at, in, for*, etc.).
  *Thank you **for inviting** me to your party.*
  *I'm thinking **of buying** a new bike.*

verb + gerund	finish, don't mind, enjoy, miss
verb + infinitive	decide, choose, learn, help, hope, plan, want, need
verb + gerund or verb + infinitive	start, begin, prefer, like, love

- We can use **a gerund** as the subject of a verb.
  ***Joining** the film club was a really good idea.*

1 Complete the sentences with the infinitive or gerund form of the verb in brackets.

0 I need *to buy* (buy) some new trainers.
1 I missed ________ (see) you at the party.
2 My brother decided ________ (study) maths at university.
3 I don't mind ________ (get up) early at the weekend.
4 ________ (make) friends isn't always easy.
5 My friends enjoy ________ (write) their blogs.
6 We finished ________ (download) the film and then we watched it.

2 Complete the sentences with the correct form of the verbs in the box.

~~do~~ fail join make play upload

0 I've found a new app for *doing homework*.
1 I'm interested in ________ new friends.
2 My brother is very good at ________ the guitar.
3 Don't worry about ________ the exam. It's easy!
4 My mum's getting better at ________ photos onto her blog.
5 I'm thinking of ________ a computer club.

3 Complete the sentences with a verb in the gerund or infinitive form so they are true for you.

0 My friends and I are interested in *sharing photos and stories*.
1 When I leave school, I hope ________.
2 I don't mind ________, but I don't like ________.
3 I started ________ when I was younger.
4 I prefer ________ to ________.
5 I'm thinking of ________ next weekend.

UNIT 11 DETERMINERS

a/an / the

We use ***a*** or ***an*** when we introduce something for the first time and when we talk about things in general.
*I visited **a** museum in Paris.*
*I bought **an** ice cream and **a** can of lemonade.*
We use ***the***:

- when we talk about something already mentioned.
  *I visited a museum in Paris. **The** museum was very old.*
- before superlatives.
  *London is **the biggest** city in England.*
- before *first, second*, etc.
  ***The first** man to walk on the moon was Neil Armstrong.*
- when there is only one of something.
  *I went to **the sea** to swim.* (There's only one near.)

1 Complete the conversation with *a/an* or *the*.

Matt: Where did you go on holiday?
Jane: We went to St Malo. It's **(1)** ________ town in France.
Matt: Did you have a good time?
Jane: Yes, we went to **(2)** ________ beach every day and we swam in **(3)** ________ sea. In the evening, we ate in **(4)** ________ very good restaurant near our hotel.
Matt: What was the name of **(5)** ________ restaurant?
Jane: I can't remember. I bought you **(6)** ________ T-shirt. It was **(7)** ________ nicest one in the shop.
Matt: Thank you, Jane. You're **(8)** ________ first person to buy me a present from their holiday.

both / all

- We use *both* to talk about two things.
  ***Both** Rachel and Ruth enjoy going to the theatre.*
  (**not** ~~*The both Rachel and Ruth*~~ *…*)
- We use *all* to talk about a total number of people or things.
  *We visited **all** the museums in the city.*

another / other

- We use *another* with a singular noun to talk about 'one other' person or thing. We write it as one word.
  *This café is closed. There's **another** one over there.*
- We use *other* with plural nouns and uncountable nouns to talk about people or things in general which are different from the ones we are talking about.
  *We wanted to see the palace and the cathedral, but my sister wanted to visit **other** places.*
  (**not** ~~*another places*~~)
  *Were there **other** people there?*
- We use *the other* with singular or plural nouns to talk about one or more things already mentioned.
  *We didn't eat in **the other** restaurant.* (= We know there are only two restaurants.)
  ***The other** famous places to visit are all in the old town.* (= We are talking about a list of famous places.)

2 Choose the correct word to complete the sentences.

1 This pencil is broken. Can I have *another / other* one?
2 *All / Both* my parents work in the city centre.
3 My friends want to write about their last holiday, but I've got *another / other* idea.
4 They built a new bridge because *another / the other* bridge is very old.
5 My dad's got five brothers and sisters. They *all / both* live near us.
6 I'd like to study *all / both* maths and science when I go to university.

3 Complete the sentences with the words in the box.

all	an	another	both
other	the		

1 The website didn't give me much information, so I had to look at ________ websites.
2 I don't know what to get Sam for his birthday. Can you give me ________ idea?
3 ________ the cheaper hotels were full, so we stayed in a really expensive one.
4 She's lost her map, so she'll need to buy ________ one.
5 We didn't spend much time in ________ art gallery because there were a lot of people inside.
6 'Do you prefer the green or the blue scarf?' 'I think ________ scarves are nice.'

UNIT 12 RELATIVE PRONOUNS *WHO, WHICH, THAT*

- We use *who*, *which* and *that* with a short sentence (or clause) to give more information about people or things.
  *An actor is a person **who** plays a part in a film or play.*
  *A thriller is a type of film **which** is very exciting.*
- We use *who* with people.
  *A fan is a person **who** loves watching, reading or listening to something.*
- We use *which* with things.
  *Horror is a type of film **which** is too frightening for young children.*
- We can use *that* for people or things.
  *My sister is someone **that** loves all science fiction stories.*
  *3D films are films **that** make everything on screen seem more real.*

1 Complete the sentences with *who* or *which*.

1 There are now cinemas .... are more like hotels.
2 A guest is a person .... visits your house.
3 A fim star is someone .... is a very successful and famous film actor.
4 A park is a place .... often has lakes, woods and gardens.
5 This is a website .... tells you how good films are.
6 It's best to go to the cinema with a friend .... likes the same type of films as you.

2 Use *who*, *that* or *which* to make one sentence.

0 A singer was singing. He was very good.
The singer *who was singing* was very good.
1 A film festival is here in summer. It is good fun.
The film festival .... is good fun.
2 A friend went to see a musical. He had a good time.
The friend .... had a good time.
3 There's a shop near my house. It sells jazz CDs.
There's a shop near my house ....
4 We went to a cinema. It had 12 screens.
We went to a cinema ....
5 A neighbour likes watching drama films. She acts as a hobby.
The neighbour .... acts as a hobby.

3 Match the two halves of the sentences and add *who* or *which*.

1 I know a person
2 There's a new film
3 Acting is a job
4 We've got two friends
5 I'd love to see that cinema

a only watch musicals.
b looks very easy, but isn't.
c has met Steven Spielberg.
d has beds instead of seats.
e I really want to see.

1 ....
2 ....
3 ....
4 ....
5 ....

UNIT 13 PRESENT PERFECT WITH *EVER* AND *NEVER*

Present perfect

Positive	I / You / We / They**'ve** (**have**) **talked**. He / She / It**'s** (**has**) **decided**.
Negative	I / You / We / They **haven't** (**have not**) **gone**. He / She / It **hasn't** (**has not**) **taken**.
Questions	**Have** I / you / we / they **painted**? **Has** he / she / it **worked**?
Short answers	Yes, I / you / we / they **have**. No, I / you / we / they **haven't**. Yes, he / she / it **has**. No, he / she / it **hasn't**.

- We can use the present perfect to talk about our experiences before now.
  *I**'ve tried** rock climbing.*
- We use *have/has* + past participle.
  *My sister **hasn't slept** in a tent.*
- With regular verbs, we write the past participle in the same way as regular past simple verbs. (For spelling, see *Grammar reference and practice* Unit 3.)
  *My mum **has worked** for a famous magazine.*
- With irregular verbs, the past participle does not end in *-ed*.
  *I **have spoken** to a film star.*
- We sometimes use *ever* with present perfect questions to say 'in your life'.
  ***Have** you **ever climbed** a tree?*
- We sometimes use *never* with present perfect statements to say 'not ever in my life'.
  *My grandparents **have never flown** in a plane.*
- We don't use past time expressions like *yesterday, last weekend, two days ago*, etc. with the present perfect. We use them with the past simple.
  *I **played** tennis **yesterday**.* (**not** ~~*I've played tennis yesterday*~~.)

» FOR PAST PARTICIPLES, SEE PAGE 167

Practice

1 Write the past participle.

1 arrive
2 enjoy
3 repair
4 stop
5 travel
6 walk
7 break
8 buy
9 fall
10 grow
11 lend
12 wear

2 Complete the sentences with the present perfect with *never* and these verbs.

explore grow kayak learn meet ~~pick~~

0 I *have never picked* wild fruit.
1 We .... down a river.
2 My parents have got a big garden, but they .... vegetables there.
3 My friends .... a famous person.
4 My grandma .... to speak English.
5 I .... a cave.

3 Write complete questions in the present perfect with *ever*. Then write the short answer.

0 you / swim / in a cold lake?
Have you ever swum in a cold lake?
Yes, *I have.*
1 your brother / write / a blog?
No, ...
2 your friends / ride / a horse?
Yes, ...
3 your teacher / forget / your name?
Yes, ...
4 you / sell / things you don't want?
No, ...
5 you and your friends / win / a competition?
No, ...

UNIT 14 PRESENT PERFECT WITH *JUST*, *YET* AND *ALREADY*

FOR THE PRESENT PERFECT, SEE UNIT 13 PAGE 159

- We can use the present perfect with *just*, *yet* and *already*.
  *I've **just bought** a new pair of shoes. Do you like them?*
  *I'm full. I've **already eaten** five slices of pizza.*
  ***Have** you **seen** that film **yet**?*
  *No, I **haven't seen** it **yet**, but I'm going to see it tomorrow.*
- We use the present perfect with *just* to say that something happened a very short time ago. *Just* goes between *have* and the past participle.
  *Would you like something to eat? No, thanks. **I've just eaten**.* (= I ate something a very short time ago.)
- We use the present perfect with *already* to say that something happened before now, often sooner than we expected. We often use *already* in the positive. It usually goes between *have* and the past participle.
  Mum: *You should do your homework.*
  Son: *I've already done it.* (= The son has done his homework sooner than his mum expected.)
- We use the present perfect with *yet* to ask or talk about time until now. We often expect that something might happen in the future. We often use *yet* at the end of questions or negative sentences.
  Dave: ***Have** you **been** to the new café **yet**?*
  Sue: *No, I **haven't been yet**.* (= Sue might go to the café in the future.)

1 Rewrite the sentences with the word in brackets.

0 The new sports shop hasn't opened. (yet)
The new sports shop hasn't opened yet.

1 I've seen my best friend outside the library. (just)
____

2 Let's see a different film. I've seen that one. (already)
____

3 I'm hungry. I haven't eaten. (yet)
____

4 Rob can't play football. He's broken his foot. (just)
____

5 Have your friends arrived? (yet)
____

2 Choose the correct words to complete the sentences.

1 Can you lend me a pencil? I've *just* / *yet* broken mine.
2 We're having a lovely time in Paris. We've *already* / *yet* seen the Eiffel Tower and the Louvre museum.
3 It's Grandad's birthday. Have you phoned him *yet* / *just*?
4 Wait a moment! We haven't finished *yet* / *already*.
5 Dad's *just* / *yet* phoned. He's going to be late.
6 I've *already* / *yet* tidied my room. I'm not going to do it again.

3 Read the situations and write questions or sentences in the present perfect with *just*, *yet* or *already* and the verbs in brackets.

0 Your friend fell and hurt her leg two minutes ago. What does she say?
I can't move. I *have just hurt my leg.* (hurt)

1 You are in New York. You visited the Empire State Building yesterday, but you'd like to see the Statue of Liberty. What do you say?
I ________ (not/see)

2 A friend comes to your house and you are going to have lunch. What do you ask?
________ you ________? (have lunch)

3 A friend lends you a book, but you read it last month. What do you say?
I ________ (read)

4 Your mum asks you to buy some bread from the bakery, but you did it earlier. What do you say?
________ (buy)

5 Your friends are choosing a film to watch. What do you ask them?
________ you ________? (choose)

UNIT 15 PRESENT PERFECT WITH *SINCE* AND *FOR*

FOR THE PRESENT PERFECT, SEE UNIT 13 PAGE 159

- We can use the present perfect to talk about an action or situation which started in the past and continues in the present. We use *since* and *for* to say how long something has been happening.
  *We'**ve lived** in this house **since** March.*
  *We'**ve lived** in this house **for** four months.*
- We use *since* with the time when the action or situation started.
  *I'**ve had** this computer **since** 2013, January, my birthday, etc.*
- We use *for* with an amount of time, such as the number of hours, months, years, etc.
  *My dad's worked in that bank **for** eight weeks, six months, two years, etc.*
- We usually use *how long* with the present perfect to ask questions.
  ***How long have** you **had** your dog?*
  *We'**ve had** it **since** last year / **for** 11 months.*

1 Complete the table with the time expressions in the box.

~~10 o'clock~~	~~10 seconds~~	13th April, 2011	
ages	breakfast	ever	five days
four months	I was young	May	
my birthday	three minutes	Tuesday	
two hours	two weeks	a year	years

Since	For
10 o'clock,	*10 seconds,*

2 Complete the sentences with the present perfect form of the verbs in brackets and *for* or *since*.

0 My neighbours *have lived* (live) in their house *for* five years.
1 My aunt .... (have) her cat .... 2007.
2 My brother .... (not eat) meat .... a long time.
3 I .... (like) playing tennis .... I was young.
4 We .... (not see) our cousins .... months.
5 My mum and dad .... (be) married .... 1996.

3 Write complete sentences with the present perfect and *for* or *since* so they are true for you.

0 I / not play computer games
I haven't played computer games since yesterday.
1 We / not have maths
....
2 my best friend / live in his or her house
....
3 my mum / not cook a meal
....
4 my friends / know each other
....
5 I / not eat anything
....

4 Write complete questions with *How long …?* and the present perfect. Then, write your own answers with the present perfect and *for* or *since*.

0 you / know / your best friend?
How long have you known your best friend?
I've known him for four years.
1 your parents / live / here?
....
....
2 your best friend / have / his or her school bag?
....
....
3 you / study / in this school?
....
....
4 your favourite shop / be / open?
....
....
5 your English teacher / work / in your school?
....

GRAMMAR REFERENCE AND PRACTICE

UNIT 16 PRESENT PERFECT AND PAST SIMPLE

FOR THE PAST SIMPLE, SEE UNIT 3 PAGE 149

FOR THE PRESENT PERFECT, SEE UNITS 13, 14 AND 15 PAGES 159–161

We use the **present perfect**:

- to talk about an action that finished in the past, but the result is important now. We are not interested in when the action happened.
  My brother's happy because he ***has won*** *a competition.*

We can also use the **present perfect**:

- with *ever* and *never* to talk about our experiences until now.
  I've never learned *French.* (= until now, but I may learn it in the future)
- with *just, already* and *yet* to talk about things we have or haven't done recently.
  *We****'ve just finished*** *eating. I* ***haven't read*** *that book* ***yet****.*
- to talk about an action or situation which started in the past and continues into the present. We use *for* and *since* to say how long it has been happening.
  How long have *you* ***lived*** *here?*
  *I****'ve lived*** *here* ***since*** *2005.*

We use the **past simple**:

- to talk about an action that happened in the past.
  My brother ***won*** *a competition.*
- when we are interested in when the action happened.
  My brother ***won*** *the competition* ***last week****.*

We can also use the **past simple**:

- to talk about experiences which happened over a time in the past.
  When my dad ***lived*** *in France for a month, he* ***didn't learn*** *French.* (= this time is finished. My dad doesn't live in France now.)

Remember, when we ask questions about a time in the past, we use *When …?*
When did *you* ***learn*** *to ride a bike?*
I ***learned*** *to ride a bike* ***when*** *I was five years old.*

1 Complete the table with these time expressions.

already ever for 18 weeks in 2008
~~just~~ last week never recently
since 5th May three days ago
when I was younger ~~yesterday~~ yet

Present perfect	Past simple
just	*yesterday*

2 Complete the sentences with the present perfect or past simple form of the verb in brackets.

1 I ________ (buy) this bag when I was on holiday.
2 I ________ (not be) ill for a long time.
3 My best friend was late for school this morning because she ________ (miss) the bus.
4 We ________ (send) an email to our teacher three days ago, but she ________ (not answer) yet.
5 My mum and dad ________ (know) each other since they were children. They ________ (go) to school together.
6 You ________ (make) a lot of mistakes! Please write this story again.

3 Write complete questions with *How long … ?* and the present perfect. Then, write your own answer with the present perfect.

0 How long / live here?
How long have you lived here?
I've lived here for six years.

1 How long / know your English teacher?
____
____

2 How long / like your favourite band?
____
____

4 Now, write complete questions with *When … ?* Then, write your own answer with the past simple.

0 When / start learning English?
When did you start learning English?
I started learning English four years ago.

1 When / learn to swim?
____
____

2 When / use a computer for the first time?
____
____

UNIT 17 REFLEXIVE PRONOUNS

FOR DETERMINERS AND PRONOUNS, SEE UNIT 6 PAGE 152

I	myself	it	itself
you	yourself	we	ourselves
he	himself	you	yourselves
she	herself	them	themselves

- We use *-self* when the subject and the object of the verb are the same person.
  *I hurt **myself** when I was playing football.* (**not** ~~*I hurt me.*~~)
  *My friends enjoyed **themselves** at my party.* (**not** ~~*My friends enjoyed them.*~~)
- We can use *by* + *myself, yourself,* etc. to mean 'alone' or 'without any help'.
  *I usually walk to school **by myself.*** (= nobody walks with me)
  *They did their homework **by themselves.***(= nobody helped them)

1 **Complete these sentences with *myself*, *yourself*, *herself*, *himself*, *ourselves*, *yourselves*, *themselves*.**

1 My brother hurt ________ while he was climbing a tree.
2 I've just cut ________ with this knife.
3 Is it safe for those children to go swimming by ________?
4 Do you and your friends need help or can you clean the kitchen by ________?
5 If you're hungry, make ________ a sandwich!
6 We really enjoyed ________ at the party.

2 **Read the sentences and complete with *by* if you think you need to. If not, don't write anything.**

0 When Mum broke her ankle, she couldn't drive ________ herself to the station, so Dad took her.
1 I waited for 40 minutes ________ myself.
2 Please help ________ yourself!
3 Alexa didn't have any brothers or sisters, so she was used to being ________ herself.
4 The children are too young to go out ________ themselves.
5 Ben always covers ________ himself in sun cream when he goes out in the sun.
6 I really hope we enjoy ________ ourselves.

3 **Complete the conversation with the correct reflexive pronouns. Add *by* if necessary.**

Lara: Hi, Rosa. What are you doing standing there **(0)** *by yourself*?
Rosa: I can't get into my house. I just came out for a minute and the door closed **(1)** ________!
Lara: Oh, have you knocked on the door?
Rosa: There's nobody in at the moment. I was **(2)** ________.
Lara: Well, come in and wait in our house. We can have a chat and a sandwich and enjoy **(3)** ________! Oh, sorry. I've just remembered. Callum and Ed made **(4)** ________ lots of sandwiches earlier, so there isn't any bread left.
Rosa: Really? They made sandwiches **(5)** ________? They usually ask your mum or dad to do it for them!
Lara: I know. By the way, if you want to ring your mum, there's the phone.
Rosa: Oh, can I? Thanks.
Lara: No problem. Help **(6)** ________!

GRAMMAR REFERENCE AND PRACTICE

UNIT 18 FIRST CONDITIONAL

If + present simple,	*will* / *won't* + infinitive
If you **study** a lot,	you **will pass** the exam.

will / *won't* + infinitive	*if* + present simple
You **will pass** the exam	**if** you **study** a lot.

- We use the first conditional to talk about things that will or won't happen in a situation.
  *If you **talk** about the problem* (situation), *you'**ll feel** better* (result).
  *If he **isn't** careful* (situation), *he'**ll hurt** himself* (result).
- We can use a negative verb in the *if* clause and the *will* clause.
  *If you **don't finish** the book, you **won't know** how the story ends.*
- When the sentence begins with *If* we use a comma. When we use *if* in the middle of the sentence, we don't use a comma.
  *If you **get** to the shop before 10 am, you'**ll get** a free book.*
  *You'**ll get** a free book **if** you **get** to the shop before 10 am.*

1 Choose the correct verb to complete the sentences.

1 If you write to the author, she *send* / *'ll send* a nice reply.
2 You'll be late if you *won't* / *don't* hurry up.
3 Sam *doesn't* / *won't* find out about his surprise party if we don't tell him.
4 If you *won't* / *don't* like the book, we'll give you another one.
5 We won't have a picnic if Leo *doesn't* / *won't* want one.

2 Complete these sentences with the correct form of the verb in brackets.

1 We ________ (go) skiing if it ________ (snow) this weekend.
2 If you ________ (not be) careful, you ________ (fall).
3 He ________ (get) ill if he ________ (not stop) eating fast food.
4 If my friends ________ (not leave) now, they ________ (not catch) the train.
5 We ________ (not stay) at home if the weather ________ (be) nice on Saturday.
6 If Dad ________ (not come) soon, he ________ (miss) dinner.

3 Read the questions and write answers that are true for you.

1 What will your parents say if you're late home today?
If I'm late home, ________
2 What will you wear tomorrow if it's cold?
____
3 How will you feel if you pass all your exams?
____
4 What will you buy if you go shopping on Saturday?
____
5 Will you cook dinner if you get home before your parents tonight?
____
6 Will you watch TV if you finish all your homework?
____

UNIT 19 PRESENT SIMPLE PASSIVE

Present simple *be*	+ past participle
I'**m** (**am**) / '**m** (**am**) **not**	**given** homework every day.
You / We / They '**re** (**are**) / **aren't** (**are not**)	**taken** to school by car.
He / She / It '**s** (**is**) / **isn't** (**is not**)	**taught** by Mrs Kingston.

- We use the passive to talk about what happens to something or someone.
  Cereal ***is*** *often* ***covered*** *in sugar or chocolate.*
  Packets of cereal ***are sold*** *all over the world.*
- We often don't know, or we aren't interested in, who or what does the action.
  The grain ***is taken*** *to the factory.* (We aren't interested in who takes the grain.)
  The cereal ***is eaten*** *for breakfast.* (We aren't interested in who eats the cereal.)
- We can use *by* if we think it is important to say who does the action.
  We are taught maths ***by*** *Mr Green.* (= Mr Green teaches us maths.)
  The grain is mixed ***by*** *a special machine.* (= A special machine mixes the grain.)

» **FOR PAST PARTICIPLES, SEE UNIT 13 PAGE 159 AND THE IRREGULAR VERB LIST PAGE 167**

1 **Choose the correct words to complete the sentences.**

1 Bread *is sold* / *are sold* in that shop.
2 We *is given* / *are given* a lot of homework on Fridays.
3 My bag *isn't made* / *aren't made* of leather.
4 The World Cup *is watched* / *are watched* all over the world.
5 *I'm not paid* / *isn't paid* to help at home.
6 My friends *isn't invited* / *aren't invited* to the party.

2 **Complete the sentences with the present passive form of the verbs in brackets.**

1 My best friend .... (call) Jon. It's short for Jonathan.
2 Thousands of films .... (download) every day.
3 Walking boots .... (not need) for the school trip.
4 I .... (give) money for my birthday by my parents.
5 In my school, uniforms .... (not wear).
6 Cakes .... (bake) in the oven.

3 **Rewrite the sentences in the present passive.**

0 Someone cleans our classroom every day.
Our classroom *is cleaned* every day.
1 People speak English all over the world.
English .... all over the world.
2 We don't use the computers in our classroom.
The computers in our classroom ....
3 They don't cook the food in our school.
The food .... in our school.
4 My friends send me a lot of messages.
A lot of messages .... my friends.
5 They don't grow bananas in England.
Bananas .... in England.
6 Special machines make the food into different shapes.
The food .... special machines.

GRAMMAR REFERENCE AND PRACTICE

UNIT 20 PAST SIMPLE PASSIVE

Past simple *be*	+ past participle
I / He / She / It **was** / **wasn't** (**was not**)	**given** a special award.
You / We / They **were** / **weren't** (**were not**)	**taken** to see a castle.

- We use the past passive to talk about what happened to something or someone.
  *This museum **was built** 150 years ago.*
  *Animals **were kept** in that building.*
  ***Was** St Paul's Cathedral **built** by Christopher Wren?*

FOR THE PRESENT PASSIVE, SEE UNIT 19 PAGE 165

FOR PAST PARTICIPLES, SEE UNIT 13 PAGE 159 AND THE IRREGULAR VERB LIST, SEE PAGE 167

1 Write complete sentences in the past passive. Remember to use *by* if you say who did the action.

0 This castle / build / a prince
This castle was built by a prince.
1 This photo / take / my sister.
....
2 The cakes / eat / my friends.
....
3 The Summer Palace / make / into a public park / in 1924.
....
4 We / not invite / to Megan's party last week.
....
5 We / show / around the library / the tour guide.
....
6 You / not give / a present / your brother.
....

2 Choose the correct words to complete the sentences.

1 Our school *is built* / *was built* in 2005.
2 I *am driven* / *was driven* to school because my dad's a teacher there.
3 My mum's mobile *is stolen* / *was stolen* yesterday.
4 London *is visited* / *was visited* by millions of people every year.
5 These sandwiches *are made* / *were made* last night.
6 That book *is written* / *was written* many years ago.

3 Read the questions and write answers that are true for you.

0 What's your best friend called?
My best friend is called Nick.
1 When were you born?
....
2 What were you given for your last birthday?
....
3 What fruit is grown in your country?
....
4 When was your house built?
....
5 How much homework are you given?
....
6 How old were you when were you were first taught how to read?

LIST OF IRREGULAR VERBS

Infinitive	Past simple	Past participle
be	was were	been
become	became	become
begin	began	begun
break	broke	broken
bring	brought	brought
build	built	built
burn	burnt/burned	burnt/burned
buy	bought	bought
catch	caught	caught
choose	chose	chosen
come	came	come
cost	cost	cost
cut	cut	cut
do	did	done
draw	drew	drawn
dream	dreamed/dreamt	dreamed/dreamt
drink	drank	drunk
drive	drove	driven
eat	ate	eaten
fall	fell	fallen
feel	felt	felt
find	found	found
fly	flew	flown
forget	forgot	forgotten
get	got	got
give	gave	given
go	went	gone/been
grow	grew	grown
have	had	had
hear	heard	heard
hit	hit	hit
hold	held	held
hurt	hurt	hurt
keep	kept	kept
know	knew	known
learn	learned/learnt	learned/learnt
leave	left	left

Infinitive	Past simple	Past participle
lend	lent	lent
lie	lay	lain
lose	lost	lost
make	made	made
mean	meant	meant
meet	met	met
pay	paid	paid
put	put	put
read	read	read
ride	rode	ridden
ring	rang	rung
run	ran	run
say	said	said
see	saw	seen
sell	sold	sold
send	sent	sent
show	showed	shown
shut	shut	shut
sing	sang	sung
sit	sat	sat
sleep	slept	slept
speak	spoke	spoken
spell	spelled/spelt	spelled/spelt
spend	spent	spent
stand	stood	stood
steal	stole	stolen
swim	swam	swum
take	took	taken
teach	taught	taught
tell	told	told
think	thought	thought
throw	threw	thrown
understand	understood	understood
wake	woke	woken
wear	wore	worn
win	won	won
write	wrote	written

Acknowledgements

The authors would like to thank all the editors who worked on the project for their hard work.

The authors and publishers are grateful to the following for reviewing the material during the writing process:

Argentina: Diana Ogando; Italy: Ilaria Longhi; Mexico: Gabriela Navidad; Spain: John Hayward; Turkey: Souad Alsayyed

The authors and publishers acknowledge the following sources of copyright material and are grateful for the permissions granted. While every effort has been made, it has not always been possible to identify the sources of all the material used, or to trace all copyright holders. If any omissions are brought to our notice, we will be happy to include the appropriate acknowledgements on reprinting and in the next update to the digital edition, as applicable.

Key: U = Unit, LS = Life Skills, C = Culture, R = Review, PE = Prepare for the Exam

Text

U16: Susanna Zaraysky for the text about Susanna Zaraysky website, createyourworldbook.com. Copyright © Susanna Zaraysky. Reproduced with kind permission; **C5:** Excerpt from *WONDER* by R. J. Palacio. Copyright © 2012 R. J. Palacio. Used by permission of Alfred A. Knopf, an imprint of Random House Children's Books, a division of Penguin Random House LLC. All rights reserved; Trident Media Group, LLC for the text about R. J. Palacio. Copyright © Trident Media Group, LLC. Reproduced with kind permission; **U20:** Kevin Pearce for the text about Kevin Pearce. Copyright © Kevin Pearce. Reproduced with permission; **PE:** Luke Thill for the text about Luke Thill. Copyright © Luke Thill. Reproduced with kind permission of Greg Thill and Angie Thill.

Photography

The following images are sourced from Getty Images.

U1: monkeybusinessimages/iStock/Getty Images Plus; PeopleImages/DigitalVision; Hero Images; Gabriel Visintin/EyeEm; Hill Street Studios/Blend Images; Neustockimages/E+; **U2:** Antonio Zanghì/Moment; Neil Holmes/VisitBritain; Nico De Pasquale Photography/DigitalVision; Yustinus/RooM; Mauro Ladu; Anna Gorin/Moment; lenzjona/iStock/Getty Images Plus; Diane Cook and Len Jenshel/Stone; Alexander Bennett/EyeEm; mikroman6/Moment; Kiyoshi Hijiki/Moment; VCG/Visual China Group; Cameris/iStock/Getty Images Plus; Kenneth Canning/E+; Visuals Unlimited, Inc./Robert Pickett; AndreAnita/iStock/Getty Images Plus; Rpsych/E+; Daniel Pankoke/EyeEm; guenterguni/iStock/Getty Images Plus; Ger Bosma/Moment; Fotosearch; throughmyviewfinder - Peter C Braddock/Moment Open; Robin Bush/Oxford Scientific; mrtom-uk/iStock/Getty Images Plus; **C1:** Photo by James Keith/Moment Open; Diana Robinson Photography/Moment; Grant Faint/Photolibrary; Allison Achauer/Moment; Chris Robbins/Photodisc; BirdofPrey/E+; JasonDBrown/iStock Editorial/Getty Images Plus; Globe Turner, LLC; WIN-Initiative; **U3:** EduLeite/iStock/Getty Images Plus; Linas Krisiukenas/EyeEm; william87/iStock/Getty Images Plus; Rainer Dittrich; Jason Langley/robertharding; BROOK PIFER/DigitalVision; Holger Leue/Lonely Planet Images; William Manning/Corbis Documentary; rapier/iStock Editorial/Getty Images Plus; FS-Stock/iStock/Getty Images Plus; Tholer/iStock/Getty Images Plus; Francesco Vaninetti Photo/Moment; sborisov/iStock/Getty Images Plus; koromelena/iStock Editorial/Getty Images Plus; Amith Nag Photography/Moment; Lingxiao Xie/Moment Unreleased; Yuri Kadobnov/AFP; **U4:** pamspix/E+; nedomacki/iStock Editorial/Getty Images Plus; Koichi Kamoshida/Getty Images News; Khrizmo/iStock/Getty Images Plus; **LS1:** IMAGEMORE Co, Ltd.; David Young-Wolff/The Image Bank; **U5:** asiseeit/E+; Fuse/Corbis; Westend61; **U6:** ozanuysal/iStock/Getty Images Plus; reportman1985/iStock/Getty Images Plus; hidesy/iStock/Getty Images Plus; Neyya/iStock/Getty Images Plus; De Agostini/G. Dagli Orti/De; Agostini Picture Library; Hugh Threlfall/Photolibrary; s-cphoto/iStock/Getty Images Plus; Radionphoto/iStock/Getty Images Plus; Mandrixta/iStock/Getty Images Plus; kickers/E+; Marc Romanelli/Blend Images; georgeclerk/E+; Tarzhanova/iStock/Getty Images Plus; akiyoko/iStock/Getty Images Plus; Andy Crawford; arkady2013/iStock/Getty Images Plus; Ruth Jenkinson/Dorling Kindersley; Customdesigner/iStock/Getty Images Plus; Pannonia/E+; doomu/iStock/Getty Images Plus; Ableimages/David Harrigan; filo/E+; **C2:** DGLimages/iStock/Getty Images Plus; Hero Images; **U7:** Anthony Lee/OJO Images; Hero Images; Ben Welsh/Corbis; GibsonPictures/E+; ultramarinfoto/iStock/Getty Images Plus; Onne van der Wal/Corbis Documentary; akrp/E+; SolStock/E+; Monikah Wiseman/EyeEm; Geri Lavrov/Photographer's Choice; Adam Burton/robertharding; jonpic/E+; Christine Balderas/Photodisc; TEK IMAGE/Science Photo Library; nikitabuida/ iStock/Getty Images Plus; hudiemm/E+; Grassetto/iStock/Getty Images Plus; Bluemoon Stock/Stockbyte; kiruk/iStock/Getty Images Plus; Believe_In_Me/ iStock/Getty Images Plus; Richard Villalonundefined undefined/iStock/Getty Images Plus; Piotr Polaczyk/ iStock/Getty Images Plus; gopfaster/iStock/Getty Images Plus; Steve Gorton and Andy Crawford/Dorling Kindersley; GomezDavid/iStock/Getty Images Plus; **U8:** Maskot; Daniel Schoenen/LOOK-foto; Holly Hildreth/Moment; Walter Leporati/Scott McPartland/Archive Photos; **LS2:** Andreas Stamm; DGLimages/iStock/Getty Images Plus; **U9:** Hero Images; digitalhallway/E+; Dirk Steuerwald/LOOK; PeopleImages/DigitalVision; oleg66/E+; Jupiterimages/Stockbyte; DragonImages/iStock/Getty Images Plus; Russell Underwood/Corbis/Getty Images Plus; Thomas Barwick/Stone; ultramarinfoto/E+; PeopleImages/E+; Douglas Sacha/Moment; medlar/E+; Erik Isakson; heshphoto/Image Source; Daxus/E+; Daniel Shirey/Getty Images Sport; Kevin C. Cox/Getty Images Sport; VI Images/Getty Images Sport; Kuruneko/iStock/Getty Images Plus; **U10:** Hero Images; Juanmonino/E+; Rob Lewine; princessdlaf/E+; mustafahacalaki/DigitalVision Vectors; Vicky Kasala/Photodi; Nancy Brown/The Image Bank; drbimages/E; Erik Von Weber/Stone; **C3:** Steve Debenport/E+; MacGregor/Topical Press/Hulton Archive; Bongarts; Eric Verhoeven/Soccrates Images/Getty Images Sport; **U11:** Andia/Universal Images Group; altrendo travel/Stockbyte; simonlong/Moment; Travelpix Ltd/Photographer's Choice; James Balston/ArcaidImages; Flory/iStock/Getty Images Plus; View Pictures/Universal Images Group; Chris Mellor/Lonely Planet Images; Yongyuan Dai/The Image Bank; by CaoWei/Moment; Tetra Images; Julian Elliott Photography/Photolibrary; **U12:** Visual China Group; ozgurcankaya/E+; nkbimages/Getty Images; isitsharp/Getty Images; Jamie Grill; **U13:** Eric Audras/ONOKY; Westend61; Jeff Greenough/Blend Images; Pulp Photography/Stockbyte; Afton Almaraz/Taxi; John & Lisa Merrill/Stockbyte; Copyright Zoe Chipperfield/Moment Open; Alfredo But/EyeEm; Ariel Skelley/DigitalVision; kate_sept2004/E+; Victor Chavez/WireImage; Dougal Waters/DigitalVision; guruXOOX/iStock/Getty Images Plus; Maica/iStock/Getty Images Plus; eggeeggjiew/iStock/Getty Images Plus; Manuel Breva Colmeiro/Moment; **U14:** David Miller/EyeEm; labsas/iStock/Getty Images Plus; Jeff Greenberg/Universal Images Group; jacqueline harriet, photographer/Moment; Ken Welsh/Perspectives; Steve Prezant/Corbis; Spaces Images/Blend Images; luanateutzi/iStock/Getty Images Plus; Alexander Palm/EyeEm; Joe_Potato/iStock/Getty Images Plus; Nodar Chernishev/EyeEm Premium; michaelpuche/iStock/Getty Images Plus; JGI/Jamie Grill/Blend Images; pecaphoto77/iStock/Getty Images Plus; nickpo/iStock/Getty Images Plus; Artfully79/iStock/Getty Images Plus; Charlie Drevstam; Susanna Price/Dorling Kindersley; Richard Drury/DigitalVision; Paul Bradbury/OJO Images; **C4:** Cultura RM Exclusive/WALTER ZERLA; Rudi Van Starrex/Photolibrary; Jon Boyes/Canopy; Eurasia Press/Photononstop; TkKurikawa/iStock Editorial/Getty Images Plus; Jason Kempin/FilmMagic; typhoonski/iStock Editorial/Getty Images Plus; **U15:** Chris Ryan/OJO Images; skynesher/E+; Vicky Kasala Productions/Photodisc; leaf/iStock/Getty Images Plus; tirc83/E+; Mordolff/E+; Betsie Van der Meer/Stone; Westend61; LeventKonuk/iStock/Getty Images Plus; Thomas Barwick/Iconica; Sirinarth Mekvorawuth/EyeEm; mrPliskin/E+; Qvasimodo/iStock/Getty Images Plus; calvindexter/DigitalVision Vectors; **LS4:** gawrav/Vetta; Chanayut Sansri/EyeEm; **R4:** Barry Winiker/Photolibrary; Tom Hopkins/Aurora; Jon Boyes/Canopy; Neil Setchfield/Lonely Planet Images; Nikada/E+; Dave